'At last – some inspiring, practical, fresh thinking about how we can hasten Scottish independence.'
**Murray Ritchie, Convener,
Scottish Independence Convention**

'Russell and MacLeod grasp the thistle of change with both hands, something that is essential for us all if Scotland is to have the national debate we now urgently need.'
Professor Neil Kay

Dennis MacLeod is a successful businessman and entrepreneur who has conducted business in the mining industry in a dozen countries. Throughout his career he has maintained his Scottish links as well as a keen interest in Scottish political affairs. He lives on Vancouver Island.

Michael Russell is a well-known Scottish writer and commentator who lives in Argyll. He was a front bench SNP Member of the Scottish Parliament from 1999 to 2003 and has worked in the media and politics for most of his life.

Author's Note by Michael Russell

All the substantive work on this book was undertaken before I was selected to stand for the SNP in the 2007 Scottish Parliamentary Elections. In fact the book was originally scheduled for publication in the winter of 2005 but the amount of research and discussion that we found necessary (both authors were each eventually devoting considerably more than 50% of our time to the project) caused a number of delays. Consequently it should be understood that whilst it appears at a time when I am a candidate nothing in it is claimed as being SNP policy, nothing is being formally proposed as SNP policy and nothing in it is direct, indirect or implied criticism of SNP policy.

Indeed, quite the reverse is true. I have been an SNP member for more than 32 years, have served the party at every level and want more than anything to see the party win power and move Scotland to independence.

The SNP, of course, has already developed a portfolio of policies and an election strategy for 2007 which offer much of importance to the Scottish people. It is essential that its candidates promote that portfolio and that strategy with enthusiasm and energy and win the chance to deliver it. I am not only happy but also proud to do so both as the Prospective Scottish Parliamentary Candidate for Dumfries and as a regional candidate in the South of Scotland, where I served as a MSP from 1999 to 2003.

If there is anything in this book which contradicts any part of that portfolio or strategy I therefore wish to make it clear that the SNP portfolio and strategy will, in my actions and statements as a candidate, take absolute precedence.

GRASPING
the Thistle

**How Scotland must react
to the three key challenges
of the twenty first century**

Dennis MacLeod & Michael Russell

ARGYLL✣PUBLISHING

© Dennis MacLeod & Michael Russell 2006

First published 2006
Argyll Publishing
Glendaruel
Argyll PA22 3AE
Scotland
www.argyllpublishing.com

The authors assert their moral rights.

**British Library Cataloguing-in-Publication Data.
A catalogue record for this book is available from
the British Library.**

ISBN 1902831861

Printing: Bell & Bain Ltd, Glasgow

IN THE SCHOOL of Political Projectors I was but ill entertained, the Professors appearing in my Judgment wholly out of their Senses, which is a Scene that never fails to make me melancholy. These unhappy People were proposing Schemes for persuading Monarchs to chuse Favourites upon the Score of their Wisdom, Capacity, and Virtue; of teaching Ministers to consult the Publick Good; of rewarding Merit, great Abilities, eminent Services; of instructing Princes to know their true Interest by placing it on the same Foundation with that of their People: Of chusing for Employments Persons qualified to exercise them; with many other wild impossible Chimaeras, that never entred before into the heart of Man to conceive, and confirmed in me the old Observation, that there is nothing so extravagant and irrational which some Philosophers have not maintained for Truth.

Jonathan Swift *Gulliver's Travels* Book III

Acknowledgements

Chapters 1.3, 2.2 and 2.3 contain some ideas and proposals first put forward by Dennis Macleod in the 'Donaldson' Lecture at the SNP Annual Conference in 2000.

Chapter 3.2 (Creative Scotland) is an expanded and edited version of an article by Michael Russell that appeared in the July 2005 edition of the *Scottish Review of Books*.

Chapter 3.3 contains some material first used by Michael Russell in columns for the *Herald* and *Holyrood* magazine.

The final chapter includes two paragraphs which were originally included in Michael Russell's column in the March 2006 issue of the *Scots Independent*.

Contents

Introduction
by Michael Russell

The Scotch always had one direction in which they could speak and act with unrestrained liberty. In politics they found their vent. Their mind was free. And this was their salvation.

Henry Buckle *History of Civilisation in England* (1857-62)

Who we are –
and what this book is about

. . .the natural love of your native cuntre suld be inseperblye
rutit in your hartis, considerand that your lyvis, your bodies,
your habitatone, your frendis, your lyvyngis, and sutentain,
your hail, your pace, your refuge, the rest of your eild ande
your sepulture is in it

> From *The Complaynt of Scotland* – an anonymous and
> polemical work published in 1549
> which defended Scottish identity and independence

In late 2004 Dennis MacLeod and I were talking on the phone
about politics. We were both aware that whilst I wished to return
to an active role in the SNP and to membership of the Scottish
Parliament, that was likely to be almost three years away. We
were also acutely conscious of the fact that the SNP leadership
campaign which had concluded some months earlier with the re-
election of Alex Salmond had thrown up lots of new ideas.

In particular we knew that there was once more a developing
sense of curiosity about nationalism and that there was a need
for some fresh thinking with regard to Scotland's national
prospects. I was more than aware of Dennis's own original views
on such matters, having discussed them with him into the wee
small hours on many occasions since we first met in 1996.

However he had, unbeknownst to me, already been working
on ideas for a book about our national future. He now encouraged me to consider doing the same and it was therefore not
surprising that we quickly found ourselves drawn to writing such
a book together. *Grasping the Thistle* is the result.

We knew it would be a major task, requiring much research,

reading and discussion between ourselves and with others. It has taken almost two years from beginning to end and at the outset I want to express my gratitude to Dennis for his strong belief in the project, his substantial investment of time and money in it, his constant good advice and his willingness to share and develop radical new thinking. From the earliest days of our friendship I have heard him talk about the need for more democracy, about the ways in which Scotland should embrace success, and about the threat of too much government. Now these ideas will have a larger audience, as they deserve.

We are both nationalists, in the Scottish sense. We believe that Scotland should be an independent nation, bound only by whatever decisions its people make about their future. We take that stance because of our own experiences, because of the economic, political and cultural logic of the case and because we believe it is better for individuals and nations to take control of their own destiny, rather than have their destiny controlled by others. And we take it because, in the modernised words of that 450 year old defence of Scottish identity, *The Complaynt of Scotland* it is a 'natural' thing to love our country, considering that we ourselves and much we hold dear were nurtured by it and are contained within it.

But not all, of course. Scottish nationalism is not about separating from the world, but about joining it again. Winnie Ewing got it exactly right when she said to the crowds outside the count on the night she won the Hamilton by-election in November 1967 (the first moment of a new era for Scottish politics), 'Stop the world, Scotland wants to get on.'

Scottish nationalism is a positive force for change. It does not found itself on hostility to any other nation, it is not based on race or religious creed and it is not, most definitely not, rooted in feelings of superiority. It is, essentially, a desire for normality – for being as other nations are, neither better nor worse.

Yet paradoxically for nationalists the fundamental choice that now faces a modern nation is how much of its sovereignty it is willing to trade off rather than how much it is able to protect. Even the world's greatest superpower, the United States of America, cannot now insist on absolute sovereignty in everything and has to work with others through bodies such as the United

Nations. Indeed when that superpower does try to impose its absolute sovereignty at the expense of sensible co-operation, disaster usually follows as in Iraq. The lesson is all the stronger as a result.

There must be, of course, some aspects of sovereignty – for every nation – that can never be traded away and that is the problem of Scotland today. We have as a country, to put it simply, traded away far, far too much of our own sovereignty first to the UK and then to the EU. And as a people too much power has drained away from us to the political process and parties.

Until we take back the right to make key decisions, choosing to do so of our own free will, then we cannot (collectively and individually) flourish. Scotland's people need to get back many of the things which have been discarded. They need to be put back in the driving seat, so that they can then decide how they wish their country and their government to be run.

The challenges of democracy, of economics and of the environment are particularly important to Scotland.

How is that to be done?

The short answer is by gaining independence yet independence is not an absolute, but a condition which reflects the times. Twenty first century independence is not the same as nineteenth century independence, and becoming independent is very different now for Scotland than it was, for example, a century ago for Norway or Ireland.

Our primary focus is therefore on the immediate challenges of our times and the nature of our response to them. There are many things that confront this country and indeed all countries, but we believe that three are particularly important to Scotland – the challenges of democracy, of economics and of the environment. If we can find the right way through these difficulties – some of which are very pressing and which are already impinging on our ability to survive even in our present dependent state – then we believe we can emerge all the stronger. If we choose to we can emerge as an independent state.

That concept of choice is vital. Those who do not wish Scotland to become independent are presently in the majority. Yet they also know that the challenges we are considering in this book are very real. Accordingly we prefer solutions that are practically liberating rather than ideologically limiting and those are the solutions we have set out to find. By so doing we hope not only to help our country, but to illustrate the positive nature of nationalist thought.

In this book we shall outline some possible responses to the challenges Scotland now faces. They are not prescriptions, still less the outlines of a manifesto. They are ideas, culled from various sources, developed and debated between ourselves and refined in discussion with others.

They are also not unanimously agreed between us. Our partnership has been harmonious and stimulating but we have not agreed on everything. Indeed that is one of the strengths of this book. We hope we demonstrate the fact that it is possible for those of disparate view to co-operate, collaborate, learn from each other, agree to differ and still produce something of value.

Importantly, however, we have never made a star chamber matter with regard to these differences, some of which are annotated in the text. This book is more than anything about the necessity of Scotland and the Scottish people being opened up to free and full debate and being willing to recognise the value of other people's ideas, without either signing on to them lock stock and barrel or being so divided by them that they become barriers to co-operation and dialogue. It is very much a book that takes to heart the 'unrestrained liberty' which has been the hallmark of politics and political dialectic in Scotland in past generations and which needs to be nourished and protected once again. It celebrates the salvation that comes from a 'free mind', as Buckle puts it in the quote that opens this section, for only through that process will the whole nation progress. The past few years of Labour spin, petty point scoring and negative destruction of any ideas but their own have proved that beyond any doubt. So anyone who attempts to use this book to indulge in the damaging and debasing ritual of polemical political abuse for personal political gain will not be able to do so. Its content has no status within the SNP or any other party, it is about possibilities and prospects not policy intentions and nothing in it can be attributed to one or other of the authors, still less a party, in that way.

When, in July 2006, a full draft of the book had been completed and edited, we took the unusual step of distributing a very limited number of publisher's proofs to a selected group of people in order to gauge reaction and seek comment about content and presentation. Those comments and views have been valuable and we thank everyone who participated, some anonymously. Their input encouraged us to make some further changes in every part of the text and to clarify a number of issues including my own role as an SNP candidate, a definitive note about which appears opposite the title page.

Overall our purpose has been threefold. In putting forward a wide range of ideas, suggestions and possibilities – and never more than that – *Democratically* we seek to find ways to move Scotland from representation to participation, limiting the powers of politicians and enhancing the powers of ordinary citizens. That is the overall topic of our initial section. In order to explain how that might be done, our first chapter outlines how Scots found themselves suffering the present level of democratic disengagement whilst the second chapter looks at the theory and practice of democracy worldwide. In chapter three we put forward some radical and far-ranging options which would alter the nature of our democratic process and lay requirements on ordinary citizens that some will find surprising. Many of these would lead to a profound transfer of power not, as at present, away from people but back to the people.

Our second section deals with present day *Scottish government* which – by common consent – is far too large. Whilst we agree in general terms that the potential of our economy is being dragged down by excessive public expenditure and on the fact that dependency upon others for our national financing is poisoning us we do however occasionally differ on some of the precise details about how that might be changed. We realise that the state cannot and should not do everything and we must learn lessons from other places including from the tiger economies of the east. If they are not learned, then gradual impoverishment will be the result.

The third part looks at *the environment* and encourages a wide debate about national change so that Scotland can move into sustainable prosperity. Once again we bring the individual centre-stage with a series of ideas about personal action as well as some suggestions for national policy. Our view of the environment is, however, a wide one for we wrap up into it all aspects of our multi-faceted culture. In so doing we espouse a more positive and forward-looking approach to our history and our heritage.

Finally we challenge Scots to respond to the ideas we (and others) are bringing forward. As part of that process we propose the establishment of a Citizens' Convention, drawn at random from the electorate (as the British Columbia Citizens' Commission was in Canada) which would be charged with the responsibility of developing a radical new blueprint for our society and our governance.

This being a book about politics, our critics will wish to pigeonhole us and our ideas as being either 'right' or 'left'. We hope to confuse those critics for whilst we will argue that capitalism has succeeded worldwide and that Scotland needs to be much more enthusiastic about enterprise and success, we will also argue that the state should be deeply involved in education and in guaranteeing other basic services. We will also insist on the primacy of the individual voter in national decision making.

A Citizens' Convention, drawn at random from the electorate would be charged with the responsibility of developing a radical new blueprint for our society and our governance.

At the root of our approach is a rejection of divisive labels and even more divisive entrenched positions. Indeed the way in which we ourselves have come to this task is perhaps an illustration of what we believe is first of all needed in Scotland today: a coming together of disparate talents, diverse ideas and even some continuing disagreements, all pooled and overcome in order to seek joint success.

One of us is an entrepreneur, with wide international experience, a dedicated Atlanticist with a profound suspicion of the European Union, nurtured by the philosophy of individual achievement yet deeply rooted in a Highland sense of community and mutual aid. Acutely conscious of the contribution of Scots worldwide and the paradox that such a contribution arose largely from suffering and enforced exile, he has sought to awaken Scotland to that heritage and its force. He is not, and never has been, a full-time politician.

The other comes from a creative background and has spent his entire career in Scotland. A full-time politician for over a decade, and a part-time one for twenty years before that, he is a convinced European. On the liberal wing of Scottish politics he believes in strong public services and has taken time to come to an appreciation of the vital role of business and enterprise in any successful national life. A lowlander, with adopted Highland connections, his cultural and economic nationalism is an expression, for him, of modernity and the need for change.

We are both, and we admit it, to some extent, outsiders. One has spent much of his life living furth of Scotland and still does. He sees Scotland with the keen, affectionate but not uncritical eye of an exile. The other, whilst living at home, has been forced in recent years to take a different perspective on politics and his own country and his seen many things which he failed to notice from the inside.

This book is our contribution to Scotland's continuing story, but it is only one contribution amongst many. It has, of course, been strongly informed by many of those with whom we have worked, whom we have met and listened to and whose observ-ations and ideas we have read. Yet strangely, despite the range of seminars, conversations, conferences, workshops, meetings, dinners and other gatherings at which these things are agonised about, there has been surprisingly little substantial work published on these issues, and still less that comes not from academic observers of the political scene or from transitory journalistic coverage, but from those involved and concerned for another reason – because of their deep affection for their country and its peoples, and their deep frustration that so much that is good is being wasted.

complacency, apathy and dependence are all in evidence today

In discussing the fall of the first democracy, the Athenian republic, the Scottish enlightenment thinker Alexander Fraser Tytler asserted that every civilisation progresses through a recognisable cycle:

> From bondage to spiritual faith. From spiritual faith to great courage. From great courage to liberty. From liberty to abundance. From abundance to complacency. From complacency to apathy. From apathy to dependence. From dependence back into bondage.

It would be tempting fate to try and assess at which point Scotland now finds itself though certainly complacency, apathy and dependence are all in evidence today. But Tytler does not have to be right. It is possible for our society to renew itself and to find again, by dint of some courage, the route to liberty and then to abundance – in other words to reverse the cycle.

We both hope we can contribute to that. We have enjoyed

trying. We hope you enjoy reading about it and then participating in the website associated with the book, which can be found at www.graspingthethistle.com.

August 2006

1. The Challenge of Democracy

'Even good government can never be a substitute for
government by the people themselves.'

Sir Henry Campbell-Bannerman,
Speech in his Stirling Constituency, 1905

1.1 How did we get here?

'There shall be a Scottish Parliament. I like that.'

Donald Dewar, quoting the first words
of the Scotland Act, in his speech
at the Royal Opening of the Parliament, July 1999

IN ORDER to address the problems we believe Scotland
presently faces – and the three central problems we have
identified in particular – it is necessary to start with a brief
description of how we have got into to this position of national
and democratic difficulty.

It seems hardly any time since most Scots were celebrating
the return of their Parliament after three hundred years of its
absence. There are two abiding images from those days during
Spring and early summer of 1999 when Scottish democracy appeared to be getting re-established in the heart of our capital city.

The first is from the initial sitting day, 13th May 1999. It is
that of Tommy Sheridan, the Cathcart Castro, standing in the
Chamber with clenched fist as a protest at having to take an oath
of loyalty to the Queen – a necessity, alas, if he was to draw his
salary and be allowed to speak.

The oath had been a subject of controversy since Labour
ensured that, enshrined in the devolution legislation, was the
standard pledge of loyalty to the Queen and her successors in
law. Not just nationalists argued that this oath was legally wrong,
for a landmark judgment in the Scottish Courts in 1953 had
explicitly recognised the differences between Westminster
sovereignty (the Queen in Parliament and all that mumbo jumbo)
and the Scottish type in which the people were supreme.

But the Blair government and its Scottish henchmen regarded
enough ground as having been given to the Nats, so the standard
Westminster oath was inserted as a prerequisite for all members.
Any fuss about it was simply pointed up as another example of
nationalist intentions to wreck the Parliament.

Consequently when SNP members came to take their oaths,
it had been agreed beforehand that only their leader, Alex

Salmond, would raise any protest and he did so with dignity and brevity. Of course one or two could not stomach having their moment of publicity snatched away, with the inimitable ego of Dorothy Grace Elder pushing so far as to insert extra words, resulting in her having to go through the whole process of oath taking twice.

At the start of the second session of the Parliament, in May 2003, the protests were revived but in more muted form. This time Tommy was upstaged too, and by several of his new comrades including his ultimate successor as leader of the SSP, Colin Fox, who thought it a good idea to sing, even though he can't.

The second image comes from the Royal opening of the Parliament on 1st July at which Sheena Wellington, that magnificent traditional musician, sang the anthem of international solidarity, Burns's poem *A man's a man*. In front of her sat not just the Queen, who at least seemed interested, but also the Duke of Edinburgh who had a look of extreme discomfort on his aristocratic features, which only deepened when the MSPs rose to their feet – completely unrehearsed – to join in the last verse. To those in the hall, as well as the millions watching, this spontaneous performance seemed to signify a new start for the country, based on a new egalitarian democracy. One wonders what Burns would have made of it all, particularly as at least some of those who joined in from the floor of the chamber were soon behaving just like Burns' 'birkies'.

Undoubtedly the singing and – to give him the benefit of the doubt – Tommy's theatricals were moments of belief and passion. They appeared to underline a different approach to power and politics. The Labour MSP Susan Deacon talked of seeing 'everyone smiling' in Edinburgh's High Street during those early days, and the mood was one of a fresh, confident, new start.

Both moments also illustrated that for Scotland, power lay with the people. Yet there is a difference between sovereignty and democracy. The Parliament may have restored a measure – though by no means all – of sovereignty. The practical working out of its democratic role had only just started.

Such a working out has proved to be difficult, for both

politicians and the people. Perhaps that should not be surprising, considering that no Parliament sat in Scotland for over 290 years after the Act of Union.

Since 1707 British governments of any hue have always needed to be dragged kicking and screaming into constitutional reform. When eventually they have been forced into change, they have usually responded with general limited and mollifying proposals no matter the specific and particular strong demands. They have rarely sought, found and implemented the right solutions to clear and well-defined problems. Accordingly British constitutional reform tends to be reactive and designed to see off pressure for greater change, rather than pro-active in terms of securing the most appropriate innovations. It is also rarely based on carefully worked-out democratic principles, still less on any view of how democracy should be developed and deepened.

> Since 1707 British governments of any hue have always needed to be dragged kicking and screaming into constitutional reform.

There is no doubt that a substantial minority – and perhaps even a majority – of Scots opposed the Act of Union of 1707. Modern scholarship has conclusively represented this seminal moment in our history as being something which was bought by bribery, rather than accepted because of logic. We know, for example, that the English writer and pamphleteer Daniel Defoe spent some time in Scotland in the run-up to the final decision applying, behind the scenes, his propaganda skills as a paid agent of the English court and acting as a conduit of information between those who supported the Union on both sides of the border.

Nonetheless actual physical resistance to the Union was limited. Some have sought to present the Jacobite risings of 1715 and 1745, and all intrigue and agitation before and between, as signs of nascent Scottish nationalism, but in fact religion had a great deal more to do with such stirrings, as had the personal ambitions of the Stuart family. They appear to have regarded the restoration of a Scottish Parliament as a necessary evil that would attract some supporters to their cause, rather than a point of principle which should be achieved at all costs.

The lack of a substantive or effective movement against the Union was mirrored on the other side of the argument because there appears to have been no clear idea of how to run the joint country once Union had been achieved. No detailed plans existed

in the minds of those who wished Union and no effective programme emerged thereafter.

The office of the Scottish Secretaryship continued intermitt-
ently after 1707 but fell into final abeyance around 1746. The
administration and management of Scottish business was never
a post-Union priority for the British government and soon
became a minor part of British administration. In British politics
Scotland was a fiefdom for patronage, and a succession of
powerful individuals – the Dundases in particular – controlled
Scottish affairs and Scottish public life as part of a network of
preferment that was designed to secure their power base whilst
propelling them upwards in London circles.

Scotland was a
fiefdom for
patronage, and
a succession of
powerful
individuals
controlled
Scottish affairs
and Scottish
public life as
part of a
network of
preferment.

The worst abuses occasioned by that system were seen towards
the end of the eighteenth century when the pressure for
democratic reform, led by individuals such as Thomas Muir of
Huntershill and fuelled by an emerging prosperous and educated
middle class, collided with the narrow reactionary conservatism
of a controlling elite, panicked by the French revolution. These
times were perhaps the first in which any real understanding of
democracy entered into Scottish political debate, and the brutality
with which such ideas were oppressed gives the period a bleak
aspect and highlights the casual cruelty of the era.

The slow process of democratic reform within Britain in the
early part of the nineteenth century onwards was of course felt in
Scotland, but in a different way and at a different pace. The 1820
Scottish insurrection certainly had more to do with a wish for
the re-establishment of a Scottish political democracy than almost
any public action before, but it was also a product of working
class agitation and a fear of mechanisation. In addition it was
poorly supported, and not just because of the rigorous mechanisms of repression that existed within the country. Sentiment aside,
very few Scots were inspired by that ancient cry – repeated by
the 1820 martyrs – of 'Scotland, free or a desert'.

However by the middle of the nineteenth century the marginal-
isation of Scottish business in London – by both Government
and Parliament – was creating considerable problems for those
who were charged with the responsibility of managing Scottish
governance. Initial Parliamentary reform came two years later
than in England and other legislation was constantly delayed or
deferred.

The process culminated in a debacle over the 1872 Education Act. Despite a strong and very long lasting Scottish groundswell for educational reform this measure was delivered a full two years behind the different, more modest and less keenly desired English model, a fact which prompted the Lord Advocate of the day, James Moncrieff, to pen a bitter attack upon the system that held such changes back. Even so, no serious attempts were made, for example, to echo the Northcote-Treveylan reforms of the Civil Service in England, with patronage and a system of 'boards' still running Scottish affairs whilst merit and professionalisation were making inroads into public administration in England.

The establishment of a distinct department of state would, many believed, institute a process of reform to tackle such problems and, by so doing, improve Scottish governance. Pressure for such a reform had been growing for most of the nineteenth century and the eventual bill of 1886 which established the Office of the Secretary of State for Scotland had been under consideration for more than a decade.

Of course the establishment of the post of Secretary of State for Scotland was not only about a general desire for greater efficiency. It was also a response to a growing, if equally generalised, groundswell of feeling in Scotland that more decisions needed to be taken at home. But although some of that pressure now abated, not all of it did. Public meetings and the formation of societies were the precursor to political acts. Those political acts included agitation, education and legislation.

The earliest political party to adopt the cause was the Labour party, which in its first incarnation, contested (in the person of Keir Hardie) the mid-Lanark by-election in 1883 under the slogan of 'Home Rule for Scotland', though other slogans were also to the fore including ones committing Labour to temperance. The Liberals followed, as did a trickle of legislation. In fact over the next century or so, no less than 35 Home Rule Bills were presented to the House of Commons though none succeeded.

That is, in itself, a very curious thing. For despite at times enormous backing by influential parties and politicians, it never actually happened until the very closing years of the twentieth century. Labour for most of its political history has been in favour: the Liberals were strongly supportive and might have delivered except that they quickly declined from power in the early decades. Even the Conservatives had periods of more than lukewarm commitment to the idea. The problem appears to have been one of timing: the periods of most enthusiasm were usually when a party was in opposition and were usually cut short by other events which rose above party politics, such as world wars; the periods of least enthusiasm were when parties were actually in power, when other priorities beckoned.

It is more than likely that the establishment of Home Rule for Ireland would have led to Home Rule for Scotland had World War I not intervened and had the Irish situation not developed in a way that was regarded with horror by most Scots. When movement for change started building again – and the 1920s saw the establishment of two political parties in Scotland which were centred on home rule, and which merged in the early 1930s to form the present day SNP – it was the depression which held it back for then nationalism was widely seen, in the words of a character in Robin Jenkins' novel, *Fergus Lamont* as 'an irrelevance at this time'.

Nonetheless cultural nationalism still carried on developing apace. Indeed the expression of Scottish identity through the arts both drove and reflected the general progress of the idea of a distinctive Scottish nation for most of the first half of the twentieth century.

World War II and the establishment of the Welfare State were also inimical to any form of constitutional change. Thus it was the 1960s before the political national movement returned in any strength and only with the transformational discovery of oil in the North Sea was that political campaign thrust into the mainstream of Scottish life. Those parties which had put 'Home Rule' on the back burner now had to place it centre stage again and sometimes had to be dragged kicking and screaming to do so – the forced conversion of the Labour Scottish Executive to active support for devolution during the 1970s being a case in point. This forced conversion was of course made all the more urgent by the spectacular success of the SNP in both 1974 elections, particularly with regard to the number of constituency second places taken by the party, providing an incipient threat to Labour seats throughout the country.

Yet once more progress came to a sudden halt, when a referendum failed to produce the necessary vote in favour. Rigged as this 1979 referendum was, with a threshold which was virtually impossible to meet as well as being profoundly undemocratic in its conception, it is also fair to say that the SNP challenge faded as the referendum drew nearer, largely because of the pressure imposed by the UK Government.

Such pressure was unremittingly intense and usually highly unfair (as we now know as the result of significant revelations regarding the improper and indeed illegal use of civil servants by the Wilson government in order to counter political nationalism). Labour recognised that its hegemony in Scotland – on which it depended if it was to remain a principal challenger for UK Government – could be destroyed by the nationalist movement and acted with ruthless and well-financed determination in order to remove such a possibility. Securing its own policy of devolution for Scotland was of much less importance than preserving its own power in London.

It should also not be forgotten that the Tory position at this time was that it would deliver a better devolution settlement than Labour could. But within weeks of Thatcher coming to power in 1979 any idea of constitutional change had been placed firmly in political deep freeze, which was where it was to stay during the next eighteen years of Tory rule.

Had a Parliament been established as a result of the 1979 referendum it would have been substantially weaker than that eventually established twenty years later. Given the circumstances of the time it would also have had to contend with Tory governance south of the border and might have been emasculated or even abolished when the Tories won power. But it might also have had better circumstances in which to find its feet.

The story of devolution during the 1980s and most of the 1990s is a story of growing Scottish unanimity about the need to bridge the 'democratic deficit' – the situation in which governments elected by English voters could rule Scotland without majority.

Although the development of the Constitutional Convention produced a scheme that was endorsed by Labour and the Liberals and by much of civic Scotland (which was in any case largely Labour supporting being the effective establishment of the country) the failure to draw in the SNP (which after the debacle of the first devolution bill had developed a deep suspicion of cooperation with Labour and which believed that its favoured policy of complete independence would be stifled) meant that electoral politics was as divided and divisive as ever and that no overwhelming groundswell of protest could be garnered to produce change. Extravagant statements after each General Election by disgruntled Labour MPs, and new initiatives that started with high hopes of securing long term cross party action, always faded away as a Parliament at Westminster wound to its end, and a fresh electoral contest for British power loomed.

However the fact that there was a consensus in Scotland that something needed to be done – though exactly what was not agreed on – meant that when Labour finally won in 1997 there was a huge pressure on that party to deliver at least that something. As there was in place a scheme agreed by more than one party, it was that scheme which was (by and large, but with some important differences) adopted and the sensible decision of the SNP to support the principle of devolution in a referendum (having received assurances that such a Parliament would not be blocked by statute from moving on to independence) meant that the 1997 referendum produced a strong 'Yes' vote.

Although the opportunity now existed for all the parties – though the Tories only reluctantly abandoned their opposition and most Tory supporters remained hostile to devolution – to come together to devise not just a Parliament, but a process of national reconstruction and progress, this did not happen. Agreement on a range of technical and procedural matters in terms of the institution was not matched by agreement on national priorities, still less on the means to achieve them. Instead Civic Scotland was encouraged to put its hope in vague principles by which the Parliament was meant to be run – openness, transparency, accountability – but no attempt was made to define those principles in terms which would define and guide actual day-to-day governance.

The Constitutional Steering Group – which the Tories did join – undertook its planning in that environment without asking difficult questions about exactly what type of Parliament the proposed proportional electoral system would create, and about how – exactly how – the relationship between Government and Parliament would work. The legislation was similarly short on anticipation of how better government would actually be delivered in practice and what sanctions could be applied to the various players to ensure a more consensual form of politics.

These problems were exacerbated by the circumstances surr-ounding the first election to the Parliament, held in May 1999. The tribalism of the 1970s was re-asserted and Labour, believing it was once more struggling for its long term hegemony, fought the bitterest and most brutal election campaign, determined in the words of the one-time Labour General Secretary, Jack McConnell, to 'smash' the SNP.

The election took place at the same time as controversial military action in Kosovo (which became a Scottish election issue largely because of Alex Salmond's principled, but perhaps impractical, intervention) and the SNP was unable to match, in resources and in press influence, Labour's well-financed and superbly operated (largely from London) machine. An inevitable Labour victory was followed by the creation of a coalition that was able to resort to 'one vote is enough' debate on every subject, confident that it could always win.

To add insult to injury the principle of all newly elected members of the Scottish Parliament being treated equally was abandoned within days, when the Labour / Liberal administr-ation, consisting primarily of first-past-the-post members, forced through a set of allowances and internal rules within the Parliament that disadvantaged regional members, most of whom came from the SNP and Conservative parties. This was designed to further weaken any opposition within the Parliament and the country.

During its first year the Parliament appeared increasingly internally focused, fractious and at times even unthinking and the whole devolution project was further damaged by the untimely death of Donald Dewar, its undoubted key figure. That was followed by the election to the post of First Minister of a politician who however vaguely, did aspire to a change in Westminster ways and to a renewal of Scottish self-confidence, but who was tragically inept in managing his own affairs. Then Henry McLeish's downfall (within a year) allowed the rise of a political clique whose two guiding principles were to hold power, and never to let the nationalists have it. As a result the Scottish Parliament soon became not a sounding board, but a sterile battleground and continues to be one.

If any party should have been able to rise above this type of Westminsterism, it was the SNP. Yet in addition to the pressure it was already under as a result of the ground rules set by the Labour / Liberal coalition, it also suffered a number of accidental – and sometimes self inflicted – injuries which marginalised its contribution and reinforced its tendencies to division and oppositionism.

During its first year the new Scottish Parliament appeared increasingly internally focused, fractious and at times even unthinking.

The relentless bad publicity that the Parliament and its members have attracted has added an additional dimension. As fewer and fewer people vote – in itself not a uniquely Scottish phenomenon – so fewer and fewer people feel drawn to enter politics. That number is further diminished by the sight of parliamentarians dragged through the more lurid newspapers, sometimes on the flimsiest of pretexts. The quality and range of members decline and the power of the party grows. But as the parties gain influence, so they appear to be more and more distant, and the public have less and less confidence in the political process. And so the cycle continues.

It was never meant to be like this. Certainly – and as with the Union, and the re-establishment of the post of Secretary of State for Scotland – the expectations with regard to devolution and what it might achieve were probably always too high. In part that was because it was delivered in response to ill thought-out and very general pressure for something greater. To convince the public it was sold as something as more powerful than it could ever be. That was a mistake.

Constitutional change is also impossible to implement easily. Trying to establish new means of governance is hard, working as it often does against long-established practices and threatening long-vested interests. The civil service, traditionally minded and with theoretical lines of responsibility that still run to London, is one obstacle. Another is Labour's innate fear of moving the argument and the delivery onto nationalist turf.

Even mechanistically however it is obvious that devolution is not working. That view is held across the political spectrum and in terms of analysis of the problem (though not of the solution) it is hard not to agree with, surprisingly, the former Labour Minister Brian Wilson who, writing in *Scotland on Sunday* in April 2006, commented:

> The problem is that, having created devolution, its architects' radicalism stopped there. They were largely content to inherit existing structures – the civil service hierarchies, the self-contained bureaucracies and of course the quangos. . . Much of the scepticism about the workings of devolution stems from the fact that 22 ministers are not seen to be making enough of a difference.

In the late 1990s the hope was that devolution would give Scots, for the first time in a generation, the opportunity to go out into the world not as forced emigrants from a country of inequalities, but as representatives of a dynamic, cooperative and energetically focused nation, successful and confident in its own abilities and potential. Indeed much was made, at the time, of how much potential we had, and how we might now fulfill it for having been one of the first nations to enter – and then suffer from the decline of – the industrial age, we were now ahead of the game as the digital age dawned. No matter one's individual position on further constitutional progress it was devolution that finally seemed to be unlocking the door to the future. But to do so it had to be based on efficient government and a more responsive and relevant politics.

There was a national groundswell of optimism.

Politics is, of course, a minority sport. Yet it was not just those who had political affiliation or enthusiasm who felt that Scotland would change in this way as a result of devolution. There was a national groundswell of optimism.

That optimism has faded, and left behind it a hangover of disappointment. Of course it may be that relentless press and media coverage of the political game has meant that we have all come to over-value matters of governance and in Scotland that condition might have been exaggerated by the long struggle for a new settlement, particularly by the almost twenty years between the failed referendum and the successful one.

Yet even the briefest of considerations will lead people – even the most sceptical – to conclude that government provides the unifying context for national development, co-operatively expresses the national mood and the state of national ambition and has a strong role – though not the only one – to play in ensuring that individuals are enabled and assisted in living full, productive and happy lives. That is why it is important and why the absence of that type of government is important too.

Accordingly institutional stasis and concomitant national dissatisfaction with governance need to be taken seriously and that matter assumes the status of an imperative for any country, such as Scotland, which has so recently made major changes in its systems yet feels that not much has improved.

Some may argue that the present problems in Scotland are merely minor teething issues as new structures bed themselves in but that does not appear to be the national mood. Politicians, who are used to being disliked in general, are often held in personally high regard by individual voters. Today in Scotland that may still be true. Yet there is a feeling of a national malaise and a concomitant feeling that the politicians and the political system are not working to best effect. 'We can do better than this' is the common complaint.

There is no doubt that some of the legislation passed by the Scottish Parliament in its first six years has been of importance and long overdue. But ensuring a flow of legislation better than was possible at Westminster (and a flow that rights some long-standing wrongs) is one thing: making sure that such legislation is not only right for the country now and in the future and which expresses a radically different and radically inspirational vision is quite another. There is no such feeling in Scotland at present. It looks and feels as if it is all make do and mend most of the time, with one *ad hoc* initiative succeeding another.

'Where there is no vision, the people perish,' says the Book of Proverbs. Scotland needs a clear and compelling vision if it is both to enable its people's success and ensure their place in a dynamic, competitive and challenging world. It needs, in business terms, a unique selling point which is understood by all of us at home and abroad. Such a vision would be – and must be – articulated by our politicians, refined by our parliament, approved by our citizens and brought into operation by our government. Yet it is not being articulated in that way, or in any way at all.

It is difficult to dig down to the root of this problem. Its symptoms are clear – lack of public confidence in the new institutions and those who operate them: repeated failures in achieving even the basic targets for improvement, which are then massaged out of existence to avoid public opprobrium: press hostility which has become obsessed with the trivial at the expense of the larger issues: a vacuum in policy particularly in the origination and development of ideas which can be supported across the political and social spectra: disillusionment from previously strong supporters of home rule which has led to a decline in support for further constitutional change.

These perspectives are commonly held. So, within individual sectors of society and the economy, are others: in business and enterprise there is a strong feeling of alienation for it appears as if the Parliament and the Executive have little or any knowledge of, or concern for, economic growth: in the public services, and particular in the crucial health service, both providers and consumers are dissatisfied with continual government interference which, despite massively increased resources, has produced little improvement in delivery and quality: in culture Scotland's artists and creators despair of having any policy agreed and acted upon, as one Minister, commission or task force succeeds another: and in rural Scotland depopulation continues to gather pace as a result of bureaucratic meddling and constant new regulation.

> It appears as if the Parliament and the Executive have little concern for economic growth.

It does not have to be like this. There is plenty of innovative talent in Scotland, although it is not usually to be found in our politics. There are ideas aplenty, but they are not coming from our political parties. There remains a thirst for a better way of doing things, but that thirst has gone underground and is being expressed in community groups and in a plethora of think tanks, as well as in private initiatives all of which arise out of a growing alienation from the democratic process. Indeed there has arisen almost a whole new industry which seeks to ensure personal and national progress either by determined confidence building (in itself no bad thing) or by deliberately diminishing the importance of the state and politics.

Whilst sympathetic to such initiatives they seem to us to beg the question. If the crucible of our national life – our Parliament and our democratic process – was worth so much effort in terms of changing even part of its focus from Westminster to Edinburgh, is it not worth trying to work out why that has not as yet succeeded and then discovering and implementing solutions that would make it do so. In other words should we not go on attempting to rediscover and re-establish our democracy even if we have failed to do so at our first attempt?

Part of the problem, it has to be admitted, is not particularly Scottish. There is a weariness with politics and politicians in many parts of the world, expressed in movements such as that led by the self-labeled 'cultural creatives' in the United States.

Increasing prosperity may also play a part, for such prosperity and the coming of the communications and then digital revolution has not brought with it any similar major changes in the basic process of democratic government. Real participation is still not expected from, or permitted to, most electorates in most countries. For them, four or five years between choosing the national direction is an age, particularly as time has, in a sense, speeded up. The inability of individuals to influence, let alone control, fast-moving decisions that affect their daily lives has become frustrating and has led them to disengage with politics.

> Real participation is still not permitted to, most electorates in most countries.

That situation has been exacerbated by a succession of disappointments and worse. Those disappointments include not just the inability of governments to tackle crucial issues of modern living such as the delivery of good and reliable public services and the maintenance of law and order but also the increasingly obvious gap between the poor world and rich world, which no amount of government hand-ringing or pompous pronouncements seem to overcome.

To add to such alienating factors in many places governments have proved insensitive to public opinion and have often acted in defiance of popular will – and yet they have survived in office. This is particularly galling for those who have watched a succession of illegal and immoral wars entered into against the wishes of most citizens and with justifications which are now revealed as threadbare and often dishonest.

Such issues have fueled, of course, media demands for ever increasing transparency and accountability but these have not only left most politicians flat-footed, they have also seemed to result in a rising level of distaste at the low and high level scandals which emerge when the bright light of public scrutiny is shone on fallible human beings.

The changing nature of expectation may also have something to do with it. If representatives are merely there to provide a convenient means of resolving individual difficulties, their role in legislation and in setting the context for national progress becomes devalued. If governments are simply welfare providers, then they will inevitably interpret their role as being to deny as well as to enable. No one will be responsible for seeing the bigger picture, and ensuring that such a picture becomes real. Much evidence exists that whilst politicians tinker with voting methods in order to increase turnout and interest, the public itself is quite clear that the reason people do not got to the polls is because of the actions of politicians themselves. 'Voting doesn't change anything' is a widespread belief.

The Scottish Executive and the Scottish Parliament, in that context, came into being at a difficult time. Expectations for change, and a desire for change, were high and remain high. Yet our very conventional politicians continued to see their job as being one of fine detail and largely to do with social engineering. The domestically focused powers of the devolution settlement exacerbated such a perspective. Consequently most of what has been done by the Executive and Parliament can be represented as being negative – stopping or banning things, rather than making things happen. The political process as a national enabler, liberating individuals and empowering them, is not much in evidence.

> The political process as a national enabler, liberating individuals and empowering them, is not much in evidence.

However we think we can see a way through all these national and supra-national difficulties. We contend that if Scotland can tackle the pressing issue of renewing and extending democracy, if it then secures a healthy and growing economy and if it can finally face and resolve the problems presented by climate change as well as by the increasing globalisation of culture, then Scotland can and will rediscover and re-energise its public life and with it, its national vision and its national prospects.

It will also radically improve the life of its individual citizens. But to do so it must first of all trust them, and engage them much more fully in national decision making. That means that they must understand what democracy really is, and then play a part in making democracy suitable for them and for the times they live in.

1.2 Democracy on the march!

'John, we'll soon change all this.'
David Kirkwood MP to John Wheatley MP
on arriving at Westminster, one of
the 'Red Clydesiders' in 1922

SOME MAY WISH to tinker here and there with the structure of Parliamentary Committees, or the nature of the Parliamentary day, and many more think that potential democratic progress may lie in changing our voting systems but few Scots question the basic assumptions that underlie our democracy and our shared understanding of how we are ruled.

That understanding of what democracy is – government of the people by the people for the people – underlies the whole Western civilisation in which we live, and although some jingoists constantly claim that the British version is 'the best in the world' the basic tenets have a range of ambassadors. Indeed George Bush wishes to export his version of it worldwide, and although the details vary, his image is little different from ours – a system in which the people choose representatives who then legislate without the obligation to consult again prior to the next election.

This is seen as the fullest flowering of the democratic ideal, and one which cannot be improved. Indeed some think it goes too far, with voices raised from time to time that would seek to limit public involvement, rather than increase it. For example Ken Livingston, the Mayor of London and a former Labour MP, told the City of Edinburgh Council during its ill-fated referendum on road charging that politicians, once in office, should just tell people what to do. Similar sentiments surrounded the various referenda on the European Constitution in 2005.

More democratic voices do prevail however, even if their moderation is always (and merely) directed towards tinkering with the present structures. The two most common attempts at tinkering surround the issues of voting and consultation.

Thus it is that voting systems are constantly under review throughout the developed world. In British Colombia a Citizens' Commission – drawn in a structured but random process from the electorate – recommended a move to proportional representation, which was endorsed in a referendum by 57% of those voting, a decision which is likely to dominate BC politics for some time, given that it only just fell short of the statutory requirement of 60% for automatic implementation. In the USA the way in which people vote has been under scrutiny since the shambles of the 2000 Presidential election. In the UK the results of the 2005 General Election led to considerable discussion of the need for a fairer voting system. Italy is constantly considering whether its method of PR encourages fractured and unstable government (which it certainly may given the very narrow result experienced in the Italian General Election of Spring 2006) and in Scotland the Arbuthnott Commission spent eighteen months looking at the multiplicity of voting systems in use in the country and made suggestions about their simplification.

Certainly any democracy should have a clear and transparent basis, and that means having a voting system that is well-regarded and well-trusted. There is nothing intrinsically wrong in all this concern about how we vote, but we should always remain mindful that the evidence shows – and it was particularly well put by the report of the Jenkins Commission into PR for the UK – that most of the alienation from politics presently being observed comes not as a result of technical barriers, but from individual dislike of politicians. In particular where politicians are regarded as being 'all the same' and where politics is not seen to be providing clear leadership and positive change, voters find it harder and harder to believe that their own participation is meaningful.

But despite this obvious difficulty, politicians still focus on other issues with regard to securing greater participation. Effort is not only applied to voting issues: it is also applied to finding means for more effective 'consultation'. Indeed so prevalent has this move become that, with some irony, Westminster included in the Scotland Act a set of procedures making such 'consultation' mandatory at the pre-legislative stage of Scottish bills. Ever eager to please, the Scottish Executive now consults to death on virtually every proposal it makes, though its list of consultees is often narrow and there is no obligation on ministers, or indeed on the Parliament, to pay any heed to what they hear or read.

Useful as public involvement in legislation would be, the lack of any binding effect or indeed any over-riding influence (particularly in the way it is operated here) is usually its undoing. In Scotland this is starkly illustrated by the way in which the First Minister, and some of his colleagues, regularly pre-empt the outcome of consultations by announcing or hinting at their firm intentions during the process. This was particularly obvious during the early consideration of the anti-smoking bill when Jack McConnell made a well-publicised showboating visit to Dublin to see such rules in action and expressed himself keen to introduce them at home even though the formal consultation period was still running.

Similarly, and just as brazenly, some years earlier the then Junior Minister for Culture was forced to admit in evidence to the Parliament's Education and Culture Committee that her consultation on changes to the national heritage bodies had produced an overwhelming rejection of the plans, yet she and her civil servants had simply ignored those views.

There are many other examples. In addition consultative processes on vital matters – for example the change to Section 2A of the local government act, or the vexed matter of fox hunting – have been subject to a degree of contempt by the Parliament as well as by the Executive. In the case of fox hunting a vote to reject the bill by the Parliamentary Committee considering the legislation was overturned despite the majority weight of evidence presented to the committee being against the bill as drafted.

The issue of Section 2A was even more dramatic, with a private referendum galvanising public opinion and resulting in a very large (though not in any sense properly representative) vote against changing the legislation. Many politicians, and most of the press, poured scorn on the businessman Brian Souter for financing such an exercise and were blatant in their view that this was a misuse of democracy. Yet Souter was quite open in his advocacy of an alternative approach and also open in his view that he had been forced into a public position because the Executive's failure to consult properly and to bring forward proposals that were adequately thought through.

It is interesting to note that the final position the Executive adopted, which included a revised clause, was very similar to that suggested by all parties – for and against repeal – prior to the premature announcement of change that was casually tossed off by an Executive Minister without consultation with anyone.

Both these matters were issues of democracy, first and foremost. No matter what side one took, or still takes, the failures of the democratic process were glaringly obvious. As in its approach to voting issues, Government in Scotland pretended to listen, claimed to be innovative and radical and assured the nation that it would take into account all views. But in reality, by sleight of hand it was always determined to get – and it did get – what it wanted. The public exercise of a contrary view was treated with contempt. The public were not fooled. They sought leadership after listening. They got mute arrogance.

> True democracy is not about consultation, but about participation. In particular it is about ensuring effective participation in the decision making process.

Of course true democracy is not about consultation, but about participation. In particular it is about ensuring effective participation in the decision making process, and in large and complex modern societies this has proved difficult to accommodate. Consequently the power of those elected to rule has grown and the power of those who are ruled has declined.

Size is, admittedly, an important factor. But it is not, and never has been, the only one.

What we call 'democracy' has its origins in the city state of Athens during the sixth century BC. Its best definition comes from the mouth of one of it leaders – the immensely influential Pericles – and is reputed to have been part of a speech he made to a ceremonial funeral in 430 BC. However it is virtually certain that the words themselves came from the pen of Thucydides, who ostensibly is merely their recorder.

Pericles – an effective leader in war and peace who also knew how to listen – defines democracy by the people themselves whilst acknowledging that the system under which Athens ruled itself was unique for its time. He says:

> We alone regard the man who takes no part in public affairs,

not as one who minds his own business, but as good for
nothing. For we Athenians decide public questions for
ourselves or at least endeavour to arrive at a sound
understanding of them, in the belief that it is not debate
which is a hindrance to action, but rather not to be
instructed by debate before the time comes for action.

Greek democracy of course was not based on universal
suffrage. In the city state only something like 30,000 men from
a population of 100,000 free citizens (supplemented by about
150,000 slaves) were fully entitled to participate in the Assembly,
or be represented (or be representatives) in the smaller Council.
In addition Greek democracy's time was already numbered when
Pericles spoke. Its enemies included Plato and Aristotle (who
abhorred the dumbing down of rule by the uneducated), and
when it vanished, it vanished for nearly two thousand years.

When it surfaced again, it took some time to assert itself.
Early examples include the foundation of the United States of
America, whose tradition of 'town meetings' arising from the
state's democratic roots, are still as close to the Athenian model
as one can find. The word 'democracy' itself took longer to be
re-established, emerging from the chaos of the French Revolution.
But since then it is has been an idea of immense potency, and it is
now one that has near universal appeal, particularly in the minds
and hearts of western government leaders for whom it seems at
times almost a panacea for all the ills of the world.

Democracy though is now not just a system of governance.
It is an idea, associated with freedom, shared responsibility and
the establishment of a more equal and just society. And it has
been becoming that for a long time. For example from the
'Federalist Papers' onwards, Americans have shown a keenness
to debate not just what form of government comes into being,
but also the proper methods and levels of such government. They
explore the tension between the primacy of the individual (often
with rights defined once again in terms of property ownership
though no longer as a qualification for citizenship) versus the
power of wider and more distant government. This type of
democracy, whilst based on individual participation, is however
very much a 'representative one' – a point stressed by James
Madison at the outset and still stressed today.

The fact that this remains a lively issue within the world's largest democracy is a sign of some hope as is the fact that American citizens can and do make use of procedures that can call the governing classes to account. The recall of the Governor of California in 2003 was a case in point and several American states have mechanisms to allow public initiation of legislation and the proposal, by members of the public, of schemes of taxation, criminal justice and civil law which, if passed, become statutes.

The American system also encourages accountability, with public hearings on the suitability for office of all Cabinet rank posts, at both federal and state level. These posts, whilst still in the gift of the Chief Executive, are in the most part filled by people from outwith the formal political structures and parties who may be better qualified to serve in a particular role.

Nonetheless public endorsement of politicians at elections remains as low in America as it does in many European countries. Between a quarter and third of American citizens never vote, and the system of registration (as well as the system of casting ballots) is often defective. There is no indication of strong enthusiasm for politics as we understand them, though there is a stronger enthusiasm for identifying with the written constitution and the rights and responsibilities it brings.

Other democracies tackle the same issues in different ways. Some of the most centralised hold power firmly in the hands of the political elite, and severely limit the opportunity for others to enter the power structures, let alone interfere in them. France is well recognised as one such centralist democracy, whilst the perpetuation of a closed circle of politicians and their cronies has bedeviled Italy for most of its democratic history. The power of representatives in these circumstances is even stronger than in our model, sometimes carrying immunity even from the laws of the land.

Of course, chauvinistic as ever, English commentators like to point to the UK representative system as being not only the oldest and best rooted but also the one which produces the most stable type of society. Often the blatantly unfair 'first past the post' system of election – which in 2005 allowed a majority Labour government to be formed though it received positive assent from less than 25% of the total electorate – is seen as a key to such stability though there is no evidence whatsoever to attest to such a belief.

In any case the stability of the UK system of government, with a winner-takes-all bias and a surrounding mess of unwritten tradition seems to many like the stability of a democratic grave-yard. Lacking a written constitution, with the increasing erosion of civil liberties, with considerable decision making taking place in Brussels, with more interventionist courts and with a highly sceptical media the process of government in Britain appears more and more distant and more and more separate from the actual will of the people, and more and more unable to be influenced by it. Of equal concern is the narrow spectrum from which British politicians are drawn, and the infrequency in which they are forced to consider the views of their electorates. Prime Minister Blair made much of being a listening Premier after his bruising during the 2005 election, but spin soon over-rode substance and the gap between his rhetoric and the reality as experienced by the people went on growing.

In order to understand democracy as practised in Scotland today, and to envisage its development, we must delve back into its past. At the outset of that task we make the perhaps controversial point that Scotland is no more inherently democratic, nor more likely to be so, than any other part of the UK, or other part of the world.

Much is sometimes made of the Declaration of Arbroath as a founding charter of democratic accountability. But that declar-ation, even though it implies a negotiated kingship, takes a very narrow view of participation. In essence a group of powerful men is giving a warning that the leadership of that group has to be agreed with them. As ever in such matters, the key element is property: those who have wealth and position do not want their privileges to be taken away or eroded. The conditions by which they will consent to be lead are defined in order to protect such rights. It owes little or nothing to the Athenian model of true participation.

Similarly the last pre-Union Scottish Parliament was no more democratic than its English equivalent. Power lay firmly in the hands of the wealthy and propertied few, and if there was more concern about the attitudes and reactions of the un-enfranchised public, it was because of a fear – born out of experience – of the damage that manipulating this public could do to either side of the debate, and to the individuals involved.

Because progress towards our present level of democracy has mostly taken place since the Union, the story of Scottish democracy also has to be understood by looking through the prism of UK-wide developments and the religious fervour of the English Civil War is an important issue to consider even though only the Crowns were united at that time.

The prospect of property being controlled by the views and voices of those without property was terrifying.

The Putney debates of the Cromwellian Army Council – debates that first crystallised the issue of a universal franchise as being the lynchpin of real democracy – brought forward ideas that were also current in Presbyterian thinking in Scotland. Rainsborough's famous proposition – 'I think that the poorest he that is in England hath a life to live as the greatest he and therefore truly, Sir, I think it is clear that every man that is to live under a government ought first by his own consent to put himself under that government' – seems quite unexceptional today, but was revolutionary in its time for it challenged the hegemony on power held by the propertied classes, which included Cromwell himself. The prospect of property being controlled by the views and voices of those without property was terrifying and no less terrifying to the Scottish ruling class than that South of the Border. It was not allowed to happen.

Certainly the rise of the democratic intellect and the egalitarian nature of the various types of Presbyterianism that Scotland had either created or imported, gave Scots a belief that the worst aspects of unrepresentative government were at least tempered in their country. Yet the repressions of post-Restoration Scotland, the rapid rise of industrialisation, with as much exploitation and social carnage as in England, and the arrogant cruelties of the Clearances suggest that such a view was and remains somewhat self-deluding.

It would be another century and a half before British agitation for electoral reform produced any results even if the activities of the Friends of the People, and the United Irishmen did galvanise society in the last decade of the eighteenth century, and give evidence to both the widespread desire for political change and the ability of the emerging modern state to resist such pressure.

The story of the 1832 Reform Act is a long one, but the gradual nineteenth century extension of the franchise through various levels of property ownership until a universal male franchise was finally achieved in 1918 – along with the first limited voting rights for women – involved many Scots in both countries.

Yet what was being established bit by bit, was not, even in the view of those establishing it, a full democracy. Benjamin Disraeli said exactly as much in the debate on the second reading of the 1867 Reform Act, of which he himself was the sponsor. The bill brought into the franchise very few new voters, a matter which Disraeli confirmed by saying proudly – 'We do not live – and I trust it will never be the fate of this country to live – under a democracy'. Disraeli believed that the Platonic view of the horrors of 'true democracy' – and in particular the way in which it prevented the living of a 'good life' because it promoted the tyranny of the less educated – was the correct one. What we might call a 'modified' or 'limited' democracy was his aim, not a 'complete' or 'participatory' one.

Thus the understanding both of what a democracy was, and what it should be varied from individual to individual and continues to do so. The root determinant in our society is now that of universal suffrage but for the early Labour movement, for example, such franchise reform was not nearly as important as the democratisation of the economic and social structures of power. The movement for women's suffrage was asked at times to choose between its sex and its class, as demands for votes for women, if those women were merely middle class, was seen as much less desirable than using the existing settlement to eliminate capitalism.

That of course, was the original aim of the Labour movement – to eliminate the capitalist system and replace it with a socialist system. Marx actively supported the extension of the franchise in England in order to secure the overthrow of the capitalist system, and whilst Engels was far from sure that this would be the result (pointing amongst other examples to France where universal suffrage was introduced during the middle of the nineteenth century and to America which was based upon the principle) most socialist thinkers were only concerned with democracy in so far as it would give socialists the chance to make the rules and change society for ever. Even Ramsey MacDonald, in his 1919 book *Parliament and Revolution* is explicit in his criticism arguing that the 'actual working of the territorial system of constituencies does lend itself to the dominance of rich men'. He anticipated a Labour government establishing a new approach to democracy, and others such as Stafford Cripps went much further, talking of means by which 'people's government' could be made perpetual.

That matter was thrown into sharp relief by the failure of the first Labour Governments and then by the debacle of the National Government, which MacDonald chose to lead and which split his own party. RH Tawney was only one of the writers who saw in the failure of Labour to make necessary progress, the failure of the democratic system itself. English democracy as it then existed was and would always be 'unstable as a political system'.

Tawney – who was lauded by many senior postwar Labour figures – wanted a different form of democracy to do two things: eliminate 'all forms of special privilege which favour some groups and depress others' and convert 'economic power into a servant of society'.

That other influential socialist thinker Harold Laski went further:

> The history of political democracy in the period since the French Revolution is the history of its acceptance as long as the masses do not seek to extend it to the planes of economic and social life.

The eventual achievement of a universal franchise took the contentious issue of who should vote out of the equation. It was now accepted that everyone above a certain age had rights within a representative democracy. After that the task of developing society so that everyone also had a financial share (albeit still an unequal one) in the wealth of that society became the objective and whilst originally a socialist ideal, the broad postwar consensus on social and economic policy eventually led to this being a common aim across the political spectrum, although the means to achieve it often varied widely and had vastly differing degrees of success.

For example the core socialist vision of taking into public ownership the means of production was by and large a failure. We can now see that delivery of core public services by government works only when limited in its scope and focused on a few key issues. It does not work in the long term – despite its initial benefits for those working in them – in most areas of supply and demand.

What does work to the benefit of all, however, is the gradual enrichment of the vast bulk of the population, with increased living standards, and an increased share in national wealth. Although the differentials between the richest and poorest have not declined – indeed they have grown – the overall enrichment of each part of society has produced an upward effect on those most disadvantaged.

This has usually been achieved by strategies which encourage enterprise and reward success, operating within what Tawney called 'clearly defined limits and accountable to a public authority' – in other words with a clear safety net in place, and clear responsibilities laid on government in terms of both compassion and enterprise. Those policies only became possible with the establishment of the type of democracy we have today.

Tawney's wish to make economic power the servant of society was one of the factors which shaped our present form of capitalism, that in which checks and balances attempt to prevent excess. It did not lead to socialism in the form that he would have reognised, nor did it lead to the abolition of 'all forms of special privilege'. Instead it leveled up, rather than leveling down, increasing the privileges of virtually all citizens. Absolute poverty, of the type that was not uncommon even seventy years ago, has been all but eliminated even if real poverty still exists in some places and most notably in the housing estates of Central Scotland where decades of Labour dominance have failed to tackle its existence and effects.

There are those in Scotland – and not just in the Scottish Socialist Party – who continue to argue that true democracy means the control of all the levers of the economy by the state. They continue to believe that the establishment of so-called 'full socialism' must be the goal.

This position is often a comfort blanket for those who cannot accept that the mixed economy in which we now live has partially succeeded. It is also a happy haven for sentimentalists of the past and those who attempt to gain power by imitating (several generations too late) those who used to wield it.

That is not to say that our society cannot improve. Nor is it to avoid the most interesting question of all. If democracy as a matter not just of votes but of social and economic empowerment has succeeded so well, should it not be taken further? Could we not envisage an ever improving set of democratic structures? And if we could, what are they, and how should they be brought into being?

We all know that the society in which we presently live needs to be more mindful of its poorest and most disadvantaged members at home and abroad. The events surrounding the G8 summit at Gleneagles, for example, emphasised the point, as did the revelations early in 2006 that life expectancy in the poorest parts of Scotland remained at Third World levels.

To avoid the twin evils of apathy and demagoguery we urgently need to open up politics and issues to those who presently reject them.

But the 'Make Poverty History' campaign also emphasised another point. If democratic structures lack legitimacy – if we don't believe in their authority – then we stand the risk of allowing other structures to supplant them, whose legitimacy is even more open to question. When Bono at the Murrayfield Live 8 concert claimed a mandate to tell the leaders to 'spend your money' he did so in the name of 37 million people who, according to him, had either texted or signed up to his petition. He – and the audience – regarded this as proof of his argument. But it is no such thing. It is not even as scientific or objective as opinion polling. Real proof of support would have lain, and could only lie, in a democratic process in which each and every individual had been consulted and had had an opportunity to respond.

Consequently to avoid the twin evils of apathy and demagoguery we urgently need to open up politics and issues to those who presently reject them, but we cannot do it as individuals, or even as pop stars. We must do it as a society, and to do it we must find a way of overcoming not just indifference, but also relative prosperity.

Most of our fellow citizens enjoy material circumstances, which would have been unimaginable even two generations ago. In addition very few people in Scotland believe that they are oppressed or 'not free'. Various constructs to prove the opposite to voters have been tried, and have failed. There may be a vague desire for more (though of what is not often specified), and many complaints about individual issues and circumstances, but Scotland at present is not either in a pre-revolutionary or even potentially revolutionary situation.

That is largely because the establishment of universal suffrage as the basic building block for the establishment of that wider understanding of what a democracy is, actually worked. It did lead to a fairer society and to one which has much greater potential, for individuals as well as for us all collectively. But we contend it did not go far enough. There is more to do.

We think that a further development of democracy will produce equally important results providing it is done properly. If it is, we expect it to be the engine that can begin to move Scotland ahead once more, and towards achieving that basic goal of politics: greater human happiness.

Our argument therefore is for further democratic progress, and by means of that progress achieving the better, fairer, more pleasant and more productive state which all democratic activists – the Levellers, the Chartists, the Suffragettes and the original socialists – saw as their goal. One in which the people really rule.

> Our argument therefore is for further democratic progress, and by means of that progress achieving the better, fairer, more pleasant and more productive state which all democratic activists saw as their goal.

Having achieved the present level of democracy, people think that politics is no longer of much use to them. They do not trust their representatives (usually collectively rather than individually) and they are resentful that their priorities do not seem to be shared by those they elect.

Here, in particular, they are, as we have seen, increasingly doubtful as to whether the new Scottish Parliament has made much difference. They may not wish to get rid of it, but they show few tangible signs of wanting it to move on or even to make more effective use of it and the opportunities it might offer.

At the heart of this problem is the fact that we still see democracy as being about representation, not about participation. That is what is holding democracy back.

As Hannah Pitkin has pointed out representation means 'as the words entymological origins indicate, *re-presentation*, a making present again'. The classic models of a representative democracy – what McLean calls the 'microcosmic' and the 'principal-agent' models – present two clear ways of so doing: that which replicates society as a whole, making the formal system a microcosm of society, and that which – as Professor James Mitchell puts it – 'does not require that Parliament reflects the socio-demographics of a community, but that it acts in its interests.'

The debate about which type of model should be established in Scotland as a result of devolution was confusing. Whilst many wished to see a 'microcosmic' approach – primarily in terms of gender balance, and sometimes to the exclusion of other issues in terms of representation such as ethnicity – the Westminster model which is much more that of the 'principal-agent' was strongly influential. Accordingly although the new Parliament often talks in terms of a 'microcosmic' role, it usually acts very much as the 'principal-agent'. That not only causes confusion for academic study, it also sends mixed messages to the electorate: messages that indicate an openness to be as the population is in its views and actions, but which are not fulfilled as the Parliament often behaves in a semi-dictatorial style.

The 'principal-agent' model might be defined in part as 'having democracy done to you' and it is no surprise that Scotland remains in that mode given its history. Another of the abiding images of Scottish democracy comes from 1922 and is the departure of the Red Clydesiders for London. Hoisted aloft at St Enoch's station, they proclaimed their intention of bringing home not only social justice, but also a measure of devolution. But the picture says it all – they were being sent away to participate in democracy, and sent as the autonomous representatives of the larger population. Democracy was something done by others, on your behalf, in a distant place, not done by yourself in your own home and amongst your own people.

Even so there was a huge optimism that such democracy would, and in short order according to figures in the movement such as David Kirkwood quoted at the top of this chapter, change society for ever. But although progress was made, the type of real democracy and transformed society in which full participation is the norm still eludes us. Worse, the enthusiasm for creating that type of society has waned as well.

There was a moment when that enthusiasm returned. But the long delayed advent of devolution, whilst it restored legitimacy to politics in Scotland has not yet returned any greater satisfaction

The 'principal-agent' model might be defined in part as 'having democracy done to you' and it is no surprise that Scotland remains in that mode given its history.

with the outcomes of politics. That alone should give the citizens of Scotland some pause for thought. They know that democracy in Scotland – despite those great hopes of the late 1990s – has returned pretty quickly to a static and somewhat depressed state. It does not seem to operate effectively and if there is presently no widespread agitation to change that, it may be because changing it does not seem like a priority. It would only encourage politicians, whose behaviour is confusing and inconsistent and whose distance from the public can seem vast.

We believe that we need to renew Scotland's democracy in order to move Scotland forward. We want to see a participatory democracy, not a confused representative one and we think that this is the next major democratic change that needs to be enacted.

> We want to see a participatory democracy, not a confused representative one.

The nineteenth century Chartist movement envisaged, amongst the essential democratic reforms it championed, the annual election of Parliaments. This was seen as essential in terms of ensuring a closeness of view between the electors and the elected – in other words as essential in producing a real democracy. The early framers of the American constitution were also keen on annual elections, and incorporated them into the governance of several founding states.

It is however, the only Chartist demand that was not eventually met. Instead a Prime Minister retains the right to call elections at will, with a maximum period of five years between allowing a choice of government. Even in Scotland, which has fixed parliaments, the period is four years and there are few mechanisms that can truncate that time.

That missing demand is of great significance. Annual Parliaments, as expressed in 1848 and thereafter, were not about more frequent elections, or at least not about more frequent elections alone. What they were really about was participatory democracy – a democracy in which the voters did much more than simply give their occasional assent to the choice of representatives. They were envisaged as a means by which the political debate, and the final decisions in that debate, would be taken by the people themselves. This was not even microcosm, but true participation. The pace of politics at that time meant that almost every issue would have become an election issue, and would have been ventilated in public meetings and on the hustings on a regular basis. That was seen as real democracy and it still should be.

Some view occasional referenda as a possible modern substitute for such democracy but useful as they are, they would not go far enough.

Referenda were unknown in the UK until the European Union Referendum of 1975, and are still rarely held: there has not been a further UK-wide referendum, and only two more in Scotland – both of which were on the subject of devolution. Governments have also resisted and continue to resist being bound by the results of referenda, Parliament being sovereign, a fact which was borne out by the refusal of the Callaghan government to implement Scottish devolution in 1979 despite a majority in favour. Even in the Scottish Parliament, where closeness to the people is claimed as a constant concern, there has been no movement in support of more frequent referenda and indeed the only current discussion of the topic is again one which would deal with the constitutional issue. The fact is that professional politicians find referenda threatening to their hold on power and an interruption to their enjoyment of the right to decide. If they were to introduce more regular referenda, it would be to avoid accountability and participation, not encourage it.

However the history of referenda gives a clue to the thirst that does exist for true participation and in that context there have been at least two further referenda in Scotland which are worth noting.

We have already mentioned the privately funded ballot on Section 2A. That showed that the public would respond to a call for their opinion, even when politicians derided such a call.

Another non-state referendum of importance was that held by Strathclyde Region on the issue of water privatisation. This referendum had no national backing and was indeed directed against the government of the day. But once more it received strong public support and produced a very clear result. No one claimed, with any legitimacy, that the issue was too complex for voters to understand, or that the right to decide had already been abrogated to politicians.

Certainly it was used to back a political stance, yet it did more than simply lend veracity to an existing position. The people were invited to speak, and they spoke. The Conservative Government, while dismissing the result, nonetheless made no moves either to surcharge the Strathclyde Councillors for holding the referendum, or to defy it with the introduction of a contrary national policy on water.

The Scottish Parliament does not even, according to the legislation, have a clear right to hold referenda as it sees fit although, as with the Strathclyde Water Referendum, in practice it is unlikely that it could be stopped from so doing. Yet there is no mechanism either in existence or proposed that would make any such referendum at any level of governance binding on the politicians themselves. Behind the bright new façade of improved democracy and improved accountability that Scotland is meant to present, there lies the ghostly edifice of our 'Sovereign Parliament' dominated past.

> Behind the bright new façade of improved democracy and improved accountability that Scotland is meant to present, there lies the ghostly edifice of our 'Sovereign Parliament' dominated past.

This is a sign of a stasis in democracy. The infrequent election of parliaments which rarely listen to the public and which are increasingly distant from them along with the complete absence of any move to increase direct and decisive participation suggests to us that democracy needs to become more dynamic. Democracy did not achieve its full and final flowering either in 1918 or in 1999 even though we presently behave as it if did. It is not at is finest and complete development anywhere in our world, nor ever will be. Like all human constructs it is a work in progress, which can be bettered.

We believe that the information age has changed the context for democracy worldwide, and we want to apply that change to Scotland. The information age is one of individual empowerment: it places in the hands of each citizen the means to gain knowledge of, scrutinise and decide on the widest range of issues. By this we mean not just the growing influence of the internet and of personal computing: it is an age of mass media, or constant exposure to views and opinions, and of strong participation in public discussion of political issues, even if those discussions are presently in the pub and in the workplace and do not spill over into the Parliamentary chamber.

One of the greatest contrasts of the information age is indeed that between a high level of public concern about a whole range of topics, and a decline in participation in formal politics. As we have indicated all studies of that phenomenon place the blame firmly on politicians themselves, whose behaviour and actions are clearly a major factor in distancing members of the public from their structures. Politics – particularly party politics – is seen as a game played by irresponsible and depressingly similar individuals, whom no one in their sane mind would wish to imitate. As an exercise in ego it has little parallel – as something which can improve lives and create new opportunities it is largely ignored.

Democracy, as we presently practise it, seems to offer little chance of real change and little opportunity for the people's priorities to become the politicians' passions. Even the social and economic benefits it has brought are taken for granted. Those people who still vote are far from sure that they are choosing real alternatives, as a study for the Electoral Commission prior to the 2005 General Election clearly showed. To bring about change, democracy must itself change from being passive to active.

> The information age gives an unrivaled opportunity to create a democratic revolution.

The information age gives an unrivaled opportunity to create a democratic revolution. In fact it provides, for the first time in history, such an opportunity. Representative democracy as we know it is largely a product of size – and that is best illustrated in the chaos of the French Revolution.

Two of that revolution's keenest thinkers – the Abbe Seiyes, whose pamphlet *What are the Third Estate* lit the fuse of violent change, and the extraordinary and deeply cruel Robspierre who apart from being responsible for 'The Terror' also had some profound thoughts on equality and participation – recognised very clearly that whilst the ideal democracy was that in which all had an equal part and all made decisions, it was size that made such a democracy impossible.

'Democracy,' wrote Robspierre, 'is a state in which the sovereign people, guided by laws which are its own work, does by itself what it can do well and by delegates all that it can not'; whilst Sieyes believed that 'representatives are not democrats . . . since real democracy is impossible amongst such a large population, it is foolish to presume it'.

But two centuries later it is no longer foolish to presume that real democracy is impossible. Technology and expectation have changed that. The sovereign people can do all things well by itself, or at least participate in deciding on all things. We have the means to guarantee that, to quote Seiyes again, the 'Third Estate' – the people – are 'Everything', as they should be in terms of democratic choice.

We are going to propose just such a revolution, starting with a completely new structure for the Scottish Parliament and for its Executive. We will seek to actively engage the public of Scotland in decision making, and restrict the potential for elected politicians to decide without such public engagement. And we will indicate the ways in which political parties will have to change to accommodate such a revolution.

We are conscious however, that at present the route to such change is far from clear. All the parties in Scotland embrace the existing democratic structures. Very little work has been done on developing new ideas about democracy itself and replacing the present democratic structures with merely their independent equivalents would do comparatively little to genuinely empower ordinary Scots. In fact a form of independence which only enhanced the power of Scottish politicians would not be much of a step forward at all, for it would not release the power and potential of the Scottish people. Similarly, when the Liberals talk in a more limited way about 'more powers' for the Parliament all the powers envisaged seem to be those which would keep control firmly within the hands of the politicians. There would be little enablement of the people.

> A form of independence which only enhanced the power of Scottish politicians would not be much of a step forward at all, for it would not release the power and potential of the Scottish people.

When politicians have been willing, or have been forced, onto the ground of democratic reform, the proposals that have come forward have been largely empty measures, full of window dressing and gimmicks. We would have expected to have seen, if there is a genuine concern about democracy in our country a much deeper engagement with the reality of Scotland's needs, and with the demands and expectations of ordinary people.

We are also aware that whilst our focus is Scotland, these ideas are being discussed in many different places worldwide. One of the problems, however, is that they are regularly straitjacketed into conventional ideologies of right and left and not allowed to breathe as ideas which may unify rather than divide. Scotland needs some unifying vision at present, and we are keen on a major democratic revolution as part of the process of enlisting all Scots in the task of rebuilding their country and re-asserting progress towards fulfilling our joint and several potentials.

In order to create the conditions by which that unifying vision can be brought forward and implemented we need major change. It is our intention to review, to a greater or lesser degree, the role and function of all the parts of the political process in Scotland – the citizens, the MSPs, MPs and MEPs as well as Councillors, the Executive, the Political Parties, the media, trades unions, corporate organisations, business and communities as well as that amorphous entity called 'Civic Scotland'. In so doing we hope to illuminate some dark corners as well as set a challenge for all of Scotland.

1.3 A People's Democracy

'Democracy means many things. How do you define
democracy? As a Chinese journalist, you may have your
own definition of democracy which corresponds to your
history and your way of seeing the world. I may have
another definition. Someone else may have their own
definitions. Democracy means a lot of different things.'

Philip Bennett, Managing Editor of *The Washington Post*
interviewed in Hong Kong
by Yong Tang of *The People's Daily* March 2005

MR BENNETT is no doubt correct, though he was much
criticised by his fellow Americans when he made the
remark. His purpose in responding in this way does indeed seem
craven but it is true that democracy, as we have seen, does mean
different things to different people though whether the definition
can be stretched so far as to imply that a totalitarian society is
actually fulfilling even the bare minimum in terms of delivering
rights to its citizens may need some close examination.

Of course one of the problems in discussing democracy is
just that: the word itself has been so abused, and so spun by
various individuals and regimes to justify their own actions and
their attitudes to power, that achieving a clear understanding of
what democracy is, or should be, is very difficult. In fact more
than difficult because democracy in the modern world is also
about self image and projected image, and many of those who
claim it understand it only as a fig leaf for something else.

Only in the eighteenth century did the description 'democrat' begin to lose a host of negative connotations – 'leveler', 'fanatic', 'revolutionary' – and take on more positive ones. Before that those who wrote and argued for a democratic structure of governance – such as the philosopher Spinoza – were seen as marginal and usually dangerous. Sometimes – also like Spinoza – they admitted that democracy itself was intrinsically dangerous too.

In looking at some of the history of democracy in our previous chapter we have stressed the representative nature of democracy as it became established as the norm for western societies. We have also argued that modern technology now allows a transition from such 'representation' to active participation. That is what we seek to achieve

We seek to achieve it for a clear reason. We contend that Scotland now faces a democratic crisis. Low voter turnout, lack of interest in governance and lack of faith in delivery of government services is creating a situation which is weakening our potential as a nation to progress, and weakening the life chances and opportunities of everyone who lives here. Life expectancy in the poorest parts of Glasgow is the lowest in the UK, but to treat that as simply a matter of health, or even of economics, is to provide at the very best only a partial solution. All of us have to take responsibility for that situation, and find a way to change it. We can only do so by means of our democratic institutions, but if they are not working then we have no tool to hand.

Scotland has tried to find the right tool by means of devolution, but that has, if anything, made the situation more stark, because it has shown us that we are not yet very good at governing ourselves. The old problem, which we illustrated in our first chapter, has come back to haunt us, for expectation was high and public demand for change very great. Yet the type of change needed was not thought through well and was in any case grudgingly conceded by the UK, not willingly offered and tailored to actual circumstances.

Certainly part of the solution is to have in our hands the complete set of tools of government, but whilst those are needed, at present Scotland might have difficulty in using them effectively if we remain thirled to the democratic system as we know it. We need to change the democratic system itself to engage all Scots in our decision making process in order to invigorate governance and begin to provide long-lasting solutions to the long-lasting problems of our nation.

In short Scotland needs to show that it understands the necessity of good government, and that it has a population capable of securing such good government, first of all by doing it itself.

Within Scotland today it is possible to define at least what type of democracy we have, and what its shortcomings are. Our democracy is based on universal suffrage, delivers not just the right to vote but also certain economic and social conditions and is representative in function and operation. But it seems clear that representative democracy no longer serves us well, and indeed given the pace of today's society, the expectations of its citizens and the ability of those citizens to access information and act upon it promptly, representative democracy as presently practised is having the effect of driving citizens away from political involvement. It is simply no longer responsive enough.

However, revolutions once begun, even democratic revolutions such as we propose, have a habit of accelerating beyond initial expectations; with the old order, once seen as invincible, suddenly crumbling in disarray as its inadequacies and failings become apparent to all. It may well be that the much needed transfer of power from the political classes to the citizens will follow this route.

We hear the word 'enlightenment' being used a lot by our politicians of today although there is little sign of new thinking in politics. There is an obvious disconnect between politicians and people for as politicians march down the road blowing their trumpets and waving their flags the parade behind them has thinned to a trickle as the people march more and more to the beat of their own drum and in a different direction. The information age is the age of individual empowerment and it is indeed leading to a second age of enlightenment except that enlightenment is one in which knowledge and original thought are being opened up to all, and are no longer the preserve of the few, and particularly no longer the preserve of the democratic gatekeepers.

It is time for our politicians to join the people's parade and to begin to think beyond the content of today's soundbite and tomorrow's election. They must be encouraged to apply their undoubted talents and intellect to the problems of our shared

Scotland needs to show that it understands the necessity of good government, and that it has a population capable of securing such good government, first of all by doing it itself.

world and to move into an era which has put in the past the divisive aspects of slavish party politics.

In fact all politicians know this but they find radical solutions difficult to accept and frightening in their implications. Some, like Labour minister Geoff Hoon in a lecture in July 2005, suggest drastic action to try to shore up the present model, including compulsory voting. Others, as we have shown, believe in endless tinkering with systems. We argue however that there is a clear way to change it, but that requires changing democracy itself.

Our present understanding of democracy is one in which the rights of the individual citizen are lauded, but in practice there are considerable checks and balances placed as barriers to allowing those rights to be exercised in the determining and operation of national policy. Democratic systems that operate in that way were, and are, legion.

The Roman commentator Polybius in his *Histories* commends the Roman system in which, although there was election by citizens, power was held by the aristocrats and by monarchs, who constrained the decision making process and made sure that it followed their wishes. Such modified democracies – in which no matter the lip service paid to the rights of the citizens the real power was retained or modified by other elements – are ones with which we all remain familiar, not least because we ourselves live within one. In our society politicians can act almost at will, within certain constraints. They defend that situation by regularly and publicly doubting the wisdom of attempting to deepen the involvement of ordinary people in complex decision making. We are sure that such voices will grow more strident the more they are challenged.

There are good arguments for saying that in previous ages such modified democracies were in fact practical solutions for there was an undoubted difficulty in regularly consulting the people. They were often less well informed and less well educated than those who ruled and it would have been difficult if not impossible to seek their views in any reasonably efficient way given the low level of technology and infrastructure.

But we live in a different age. Information is everywhere and educational standards are higher than ever. In addition technological progress has provided easy means for mass consultation and mass participation. We therefore believe that the time has come – in Scotland at least, because that is where the centre of our concerns are – to imagine and then over time bring into being a new form of democracy in which the people are at the centre. We can, by means of technology, re-create the Athenian ideal and in this chapter we unashamedly lay out what we think that ideal might look like here, today.

However before we outline some ideas for that new system, let us enter some caveats. Our ideas are just that – ideas. We have been, and continue to be, informed by debate that takes place worldwide, and involves groups as diverse as extreme socialists and extreme conservatives. We do not believe that we have all the answers, but we do think it is time that there was discussion in Scotland about alternatives to the present structure of governance. It seems that even post devolution we take the Westminster model, and the Westminster approach, too readily for granted. There are other options, and some of these need serious consideration.

> We therefore believe that the time has come to imagine and then over time bring into being a new form of democracy in which the people are at the centre.

We acknowledge, also, that establishing any new structure would take time. A party in Scotland expressing interest in these ideas – including the diminution of its own power and that of other parties – would require to enter government and then to bring about major constitutional change in terms of the Union before they could set about implementing the most radical of such proposals. We are accordingly talking about generational change rather than instant alteration not least because getting any party to take these ideas seriously will require major effort.

Yet that is a positive thing, rather than a negative one. Any and all discussion and debate on these topics – and on the overall topic of democracy in Scotland – would be a positive step forward, even if that step was more drawn out than we would wish.

Even then the process would not be easy. Many vested interests are threatened by such changes, not least those of the existing representatives. The public themselves may be reluctant to engage at first, given their present disengagement. We are sure that many reasons can be found – such as those enunciated almost two millennia ago by Polybius – for the continued retention of real power by those who should first and foremost be the servants of the people. But to accept those reasons as a justification for doing nothing would be to continue to hold back not just necessary progress, but also to hold back Scotland itself.

However, as we will suggest later there is a method by which the inevitable opposition and stonewalling by the political classes could be truncated – the formation of a Citizens' Commission to solicit ideas and make recommendations to a people's referendum on how our political process should be improved. A popular campaign for such a Commission would take time but might in the end prevail. If not, then perhaps a private referendum – such as the one on Section 2A financed by Brian Souter – could test the will of the people in terms of moving democracy onwards by means of a Commission. A revolution by ballot would certainly be an innovation for democracy but it would be a welcome one.

> Every citizen has a right, and a responsibility, to be a fully participating member of a democratic society.

The foundation of society is the individual citizen. It is the rights and responsibilities of individual citizens – and the way in which they are exercised – which should form the bedrock of a democracy. We believe that every citizen has a right, and a responsibility, to be a fully participating member of a democratic society. They should not just be the electors of the politicians but also the decision makers for the politics. They should have the right to propose legislation, to be consulted on legislation and to vote on such legislation. In other words to participate as completely as they wish, not just having to accept that they are represented by those who seek their mandate from time to time and ignore them between times.

The people of Scotland are, essentially, the Scottish Parliament. If the people are indeed sovereign then that conclusion is inescapable. Accordingly they must be entitled to act in the way that a Parliament should, or at least have the opportunity to do so should they so wish. For that reason we will call them the 'First Chamber' of a new Scottish democracy.

Citizens should have clearly understood, and quite fundamental, rights and responsibilities. This holds true in any democracy.

Firstly they should have the responsibility and the right to choose their elected representatives. Secondly we believe they have the right to directly choose – given the power of leadership in our society – the key individuals who will lead the nation. Thirdly they have the right to be consulted and listened to by their representatives on an ongoing basis and a responsibility to take part in that process. Fourthly they have the right to propose legislation and to make decisions on aspects of all legislation. This is also a responsibility. Fifthly they have the right to recall their representatives at any time and to recall the leaders whom they have elected and consequently they have a responsibility to maintain contact with, and involvement in, the process of democracy.

These five rights and responsibilities should underpin our democratic society. Presently the Scottish people only posses the first of them.

In such a democracy – in a really new Scottish democracy – the MSPs elected by the people become the 'Second Chamber'. They are placed there by the people to do certain things: to listen to them, to pay heed to their views, to debate the details of legislation, to propose legislation for approval by the people, but above all they are there to ensure that the people's decision is always final.

> Five rights and responsibilities should underpin our democratic society. Presently the Scottish people only posses the first of them.

In such a democracy MSPs become what they should be – the instruments of the people. This means that they must cease to behave as if their first loyalty is not to the people, but to the parties to which they belong. MSPs – in such a democracy – must take their primary advice and instructions only from those who elect them.

A strong implication of this change is that citizens would be asked at the ballot box to choose individuals rather than mere political party cardboard cut-outs. Democracy is the exercise of the power of the people, but in recent generations this power has been usurped by political parties and is now held too closely within them. It is now time to give power back to those who should possess it by right.

Of course the borrowing of power is nothing new. An individual monarch or tribal chieftain abrogated it to himself (or rarely her) in primitive society. That power was envied by others, who devised structures to share it, diminish it, or take it away. Oligarchies of one sort or another were the next stage, and beyond that the uncomfortable sharing of powers with wider groups. Athens in the sixth century BC was a unique exception, for before and after the real debate was between those whose principal qualification was the strength to challenge for power and – if it was won – to keep it.

The gradual broadening of such groups is the story of the development of modern society but although it now appears as if power is spread amongst all, we have illustrated that this is not the case. Accordingly the next big democratic revolution should be the formalisation of real power sharing amongst all, enabled at last by our rapid recent technological progress.

Political parties are now the biggest barrier to that set of changes. Their power is strong and growing and the best analogy that occurs to us is that of trades unions in the 1960s and 70s.

Political parties are now the biggest barrier to that set of changes.

Despite the wish by some on the fringes to roll back to that time, the reduction of that power (which had reached unreasonable proportions, for example in the insistence on 'closed shops' which negated individual rights and individual views) was a necessary part of making economic headway at the start of the process of globalisation. Now a necessary part of making democratic headway is to constrain political parties which should be a useful and indeed vital part of our structure, but which are in danger of becoming more of a danger to true democracy. Just as the advent of the information age has empowered the people to cut out the middleman and make decisions on their own behalf in a multitude of areas, so we believe it is time for the middlemen of politics – the political parties and their narrow control mechanism – to succumb to the march of time and to be cut down to an appropriate size.

How that should be done is a difficult question. The first reaction from the parties themselves will be to cry foul, and to do so very loudly. But the power of parties, as presently operated, acts against the interests of the Scottish people. Ruthless whipping in the Scottish Parliament makes most votes foregone conclusions despite the issues or the merits of the case. Expenditure by parties (already curbed by New Labour, but in a way that plays entirely to their own advantage as we have seen in the shameful 'loans for peerages' scandal, so well exposed by the SNP's Angus Breandan MacNeil) often determines the outcome of elections, rather than the process of considered debate. Parties can suspend and expel members in a way that works against the freedom of expression and parties can force through decisions at local and national level against the clear will of communities and those they choose to speak for them.

We must stress – for the opposite will be said – that we are far from being against political parties *per se*. Both of us have been members of a party, one of us still is, and we appreciate the benefits of solidarity, of communal working and of shared responsibility. The holding to account of parties for a platform of proposals offered and endorsed at election time is an important part of our democratic process. Parties are also able to encourage and initiate creative thinking about policies and to find ways of implementing necessary change despite initial opposition.

However the balance has slipped too far in favour of the parties against the interest of the citizen. Many of our proposals are designed to overcome that situation, and need to be considered at the outset.

> This tight (party) control has also led to the death of the politics of ideas.

Political parties are special interest groups who advocate a particular set of opinions about how our society should be governed. Their membership is relatively small consisting in total in Scotland today something well under one percent of the population. Despite their constant rhetoric about democracy parties are actually very undemocratic institutions and most of them are controlled, in effect no matter the appearance, by a handful of senior figures.

This concentration of power becomes even more intense should a party be elected to office. At such a time the leader of the party becomes a virtual dictator by virtue of his/her ability to hire and fire ministers and their deputies at will and by substantial command over the MSPs through the whipping system. By such means the wishes of all of the electorate of the nation are – to a great extent if not totally – subjected to those of a single individual or in the case of coalition Scotland two individuals. This is not healthy for any democracy and has not been healthy for ours.

This tight control has also led to the death of the politics of ideas. Policies which were once driven by a desire to innovate and think new thought have given way to a blandness and sameness which reached absurdity when New Labour, having replaced the Tories at Westminster promised that they would adhere to the proposed Tory budgets in their first term. Political parties have become like their modern football equivalents, simply teams of players seeking to win power and to reign supreme for as long as possible. It is the ability to win and hold onto power by manipulation and spin, a euphemism for lying, and not the ability to govern or change the national direction which is the driving force in today's politics.

Of particular importance – in fact of absolute necessity if our political process is to have integrity and an appeal for all citizens – is the need for parties in Scotland to have a broad and unifying vision. This differentiates them from all the other narrowly focused special interest organisations that abound. Politics falls into disrepute when parties fail to realise and act on that difference and instead become completely or even partially in hock to one or more group and act as a mouthpiece for only one set of opinions.

> Of particular importance is the need for parties in Scotland to have a broad and unifying vision.

The most obvious such situation was that which arose out of the relationship between the Labour party and the trade union movement – at least until the advent of New Labour. Born of necessity and initially producing much needed social and economic reform, in time this unwritten pact became highly damaging to both the labour movement and the Labour party. In parts of Scotland it still is, and by extension it is damaging in those places to the community at large and to democracy.

In those places the movement – now a minority in the working population – frequently compromises the real interests of its members in order to receive special privileges for its leaders. The party, on the other hand, finds it harder and harder to take an objective view of the needs of citizens because of the influence of those who pay the party's bills.

New Labour was meant to abandon that relationship, or at least those parts of it that compromised rational and impartial governance. However, whilst it distanced itself, it has retained its financial dependency whilst at the same time moving onto the equally disreputable and equally harmful Tory territory of relying on wealthy individuals and businesses who wish to buy favours. Both approaches are morally wrong, politically damaging and democratically destructive.

Even the Liberal Party has begun to operate in the same way, for the decisive corrupting influence is the requirement to raise the ludicrously large sums of money needed by modern day election campaigns. Major reform of campaign finance including the setting of rigorous national campaign financial limits and the capping of donations is now urgently needed.

Parties, as we presently know them, are very much a product of the industrial age. Their present means of operation is, like representative democracy (as opposed to participatory democracy) past its sell-by date. In our rapidly changing digital world the issues requiring political solutions are more complex than ever before. Thus we expect that movements – driven by modern comm-unications and responding to individual issues – will spring up, and indeed we can see those springing up in many places already. They are often very attractive to those who cannot sign on to the glad bag of vague and easily changed policies of many of today's political parties, which appear indistinguishable, one from another.

> Major reform of campaign finance including the setting of rigorous national campaign financial limits and the capping of donations is now urgently needed.

We would want to encourage the emergence of such move-ments and particularly political movements which might well become associated not just with ideas but with candidates for political office. But the association would be that way round, not the present situation in which the party (and its ideas) is always seen as more important than the candidates. We think most Scots now wish a chance to choose the person, not the party, and such changes would help that process.

We can envisage this development going further. Political parties may need to be subject to reforming legislation which reduces the role they can play in the election and activities of MSPs. A party (or any other type of movement) might retain the right to endorse a candidate for election and offer very limited support but not to be in any other way involved in the electoral campaign of any candidate. Membership of a political party should not permit that party to dictate the manifesto of a political candidate or the voting choices or activities within the Parliament of any individual MSP, and thus the ruthless whipping system which presently distorts the Parliament and our national life would be outlawed.

MSPs would then be elected on their own merits and it might soon become apparent to many seeking such office that devoted membership of a political party might not be the best way to achieve political position. Indeed logic would dictate that it is essential to legislate that all MSPs should resign from all organisations of a political nature on election, thus confirming that their allegiance is to only their constituents, just as, at present, the Presiding Officer of the Parliament has to resign from his or her political party when elected. [1]

Such a profound change in our historical political practice may well be best implemented by increments over time. However, just as parties begin to lose their undesirable aspects, we have a means of offering them something more constructive. We do see an important ongoing role for political parties in the campaigns for direct election by the people of the Prime Minister and Deputy Prime Minister who along with their cabinet will form the executive government of Scotland, our third and last chamber, of which we will have more to say later.

It is essential to legislate that all MSPs should resign from all organisations of a political nature on election.

In order to avoid the corruption of the type of paid politics from which we presently suffer, we believe that the political campaigns of political parties (and what we have called 'political movements') for the election of the Prime Minister and Deputy should be funded by donations from the electorate only, subject to a maximum of say £5,000 per elector per annum, with matching funds provided by the state. These would be the only funds the state would provide to political parties or movements as opposed to individual candidates and members of Parliament.

To further moderate financial influence it may well be desirable to impose a ceiling on the expenditure of each such candidates campaign as is the case at present with regard to the election of MPs and MSPs. Such a ceiling would likely be, for Scotland, of the order of a million pounds to ensure a measure of financial neutrality amongst at least the major candidates. We see one of the main activities of political parties between elections as the evaluation, selection and promotion of future candidates for Prime Minister and Deputy Prime Minister and fundraising for future campaigns.

Campaigns for the election of MSPs would be subject to existing funding ceilings. Again funding would be from electors

---

[1] Whilst understanding the logic of Dennis MacLeod's position on this matter, Michael Russell does not believe that such resignations from parties would be automatically required.

only, subject to a maximum of say £1,000 per elector per annum with matching funds provided by the state and with political parties entitled to endorse candidates but not to control them.

The idea of candidates for MSP having to be, in their primary definition, representatives of their constituents and not their political parties will have some clear consequences. The short, intense campaigns that surround current elections will need to change so that there is time and opportunity for individuals to stand, and for voters to familiarise themselves with these individuals. There will be a stronger role for a new Scottish Electoral Commission, which will have an information as well as regulatory role. Candidates would be required to maintain internet sites listing their electoral platform, nominees, endorsements by political movements/parties, and formal exploratory questions submitted by the media or prospective constituents, along with the candidate's response.

In addition the candidate would be required to archive all matters relating to previous campaigns and in the case of those who had been MSPs the contents of their historical web sites, including their voting records. All of the above would apply equally to the campaigns for Prime Minister and Deputy Prime Minister. Thus there would be complete transparency with regard to a candidate's current and past positions. Short memories amongst the public and the press is a constant factor in Scottish politics and needs to be guarded against!

Those who are elected to the 'Second Chamber' of course must themselves have rights and responsibilities. The rights of the Second Chamber are to propose legislation, to make interim decisions pending final decisions by the First Chamber (the people) and to scrutinise and debate on behalf of the people the detail of all proposals and legislation and the actions and conduct of government. Because these rights are also duties, it is important that this Chamber is dedicated for all of its time to that task. Accordingly we do not believe that members of the Second Chamber should form the government of Scotland.

We see the primary task of MSPs as being threefold – to represent (subject to the power of citizens to participate which would be much greater under our plans), to legislate and to hold the government to account. Undertaking those tasks whilst seeking to be further promoted to be in government seems to us to be inconsistent at best, and likely to be corrupting at worst. Accordingly we believe that the high offices to which MSPs should aspire are either direct election to the Prime Minister's post or office within the Parliament – that is as Presiding Officer or the Chair of a Parliamentary Committee.

The role of the Presiding Officer would obviously change. His importance on the political landscape would be on a par with the Prime Minister. He would be responsible for planning, organising and controlling the business of the Second Chamber in consultation with the members who would be much more autonomous than now and who would – unlike as at present – have control of the timetable. He would do so in liaison with the members of the government (our Third Chamber of which more later) and with the leaders of the Second Chamber's committees. The committees of the Second Chamber would mirror the departments of government with chairs and deputy chairs being equivalent to ministers and their deputies. MSPs would be elected to all offices by their fellow MSPs by secret ballot after a short election process at the beginning of each period of government. They would be subject to removal from such office at the will of the chamber at anytime.

The remaining MSPs would seek and be elected to the various committees, again by secret ballot. MSPs would be seated in the chamber alphabetically thus avoiding definition by rigid identifiable groups, except for committee chairs and deputies who would sit in the front benches. Nevertheless MSPs would be free to associate into informal groups for and against the issues that come before the chamber on an issue by issue basis, according to their perception of the best interests of their constituents. Caucus rooms and support staff would be available to allow such groups to research and articulate their positions. Thus clear and concise position papers would be produced outlining both the pros and cons of each issue which would in due course be made available to the electorate prior to the confirmatory vote by the First Chamber.

The Second Chamber needs the ability to develop a sustained programme of work, but it also needs to be closer to the people in terms of election. We therefore suggest that the term of office of a member of an elected Second Chamber remain four years, but that one half of the chamber be subject to election every two years on a rolling electoral cycle.

One of the more profound weaknesses of the British parliamentary system is the expectation that those who are elected by the narrow political system which we presently have will somehow automatically gain the experience and skills to run departments of government equivalent in size to our largest corporations. This is clearly a fallacy. The qualities required to get elected and the qualities required to govern have little in common.

The consequences of this problem were well illustrated in the closing months of 2005 with the publication of Sir Christopher Meyer's book, *DC Confidential*. He highlights the issue by referring to some of the UK's most senior ministers as 'political pygmies' when compared to their unelected but carefully chosen and approved USA equivalents. Of course the matter is a hangover from the old public school ethos of a world of 'players' being ruled by an elite of amateur 'gentlemen'. Even if that were useful at some stage, its utility has long since past.

This situation reaches the farcical in a small parliament such as Holyrood. Out of the 129 MSPs elected in 2003, 62 were ineligible for office as they did not belong to the ruling coalition. This left 67 persons – 67 persons out of the whole population of Scotland, totaling in excess of five million – who were eligible to run our national affairs in 22 well-rewarded and very responsible offices.

Of course the chances of finding one suitable candidate by such a process, far less finding all 22 is next to zero and that becomes clearer every day as we watch the present crop of ministers and their deputies flounder from crisis to crisis and from gaffe to gaffe. Yet the opposition seems to have learnt little from observing those difficulties, with the SNP going so far as to appoint all of its members to shadow office. But it is, we should stress, not the fault of the individuals caught in this impossible fix – the fault lies in the system which attempts to put square pegs into round holes just because the UK has always done it that way.

The real strength of effective present day politicians lies in their rapport with those they represent, even if that rapport is built upon a less than perfect system. We should build on that strength and allow them to play to it and we believe that our later proposals for the Second Chamber do just that. In fact should an MSP be chosen as a Minister through the procedure given below we believe that he or she should be required to stand down and be replaced by someone whose first duty is to work for their constituents.

We wish to liberate – in the true sense of that word – the real and considerable talent that exists in Scotland to serve our nation. Serious damage is being done to our country, and to the confidence of our country in terms of developing our ability to govern ourselves, by the continuing impression our ministers give of not being, frankly, up to the tasks given them. A cynic might be persuaded to believe that this is all part of the unionists' answer to nationalism – an attempt to demonstrate that the Scots, uniquely in the world, are incapable of managing their own affairs. In order to overcome that we have to apply new solutions and think new thoughts. Building our government from all the best talents our nation has produced and separating it from the amateurish Westminster system is one way to do so.

This government would be our 'Third Chamber'. The Prime Minister and Deputy Prime Minister will be directly elected by the people (elected every four years on a combined platform), probably by Single Transferable Vote, and not selected in the backrooms of political parties as at present. Political parties would be allowed to nominate candidates for these offices and to finance and promote the campaigns of such candidates.

However, the platform on which an election would be fought – and the decisive choice to be made – would be between the offerings from the candidates themselves for the office of Prime Minister and Deputy Prime Minister and not those of the political parties. Parties would match their policies to those emerging from candidates, not *vice versa*.

We believe that political parties will eventually be transformed from being ideological political platforms to becoming supporters of the sharp-edged visionary ideas of their more enlightened leaders and perhaps involvement in a direct election of a national leader will help that process. However it is also our hope that, in time, nominations for these posts would come not just from the political classes but also from all segments of society, for those that are to manage our government must be of the highest calibre and we must encourage the most entrepreneurial and visionary to participate in our national institutions.

In addition we envisage new political movements arising which would encourage, draft and promote leaders from all walks of life to seek our highest political office. The greatest advances in all areas of human endeavour have come about from the brilliance and leadership of individuals. Often those individuals have come from outside narrow specialisms. For the past three hundred years Scots have excelled all over the world and in most areas of activity – and always way beyond what might be expected from a small nation on the edge of Europe. Yet in the field of domestic politics we have not yet produced the visionary leader who can successfully inspire and command the support of our people as we search to recover our nationhood. Loosening the restraints of conformity which are imposed by party politics might well allow such a leader to emerge.

Regardless of what background they come from, however, the successful candidates would be answerable to the Second **and** First Chambers. They would have a duty to present each year a detailed plan for government, covering not only the year ahead but also their ideas for the next four years – a rolling programme complete with financial detail and clear objectives.

Their programme would be open to formal Second Chamber scrutiny and to First Chamber questioning. The citizens would have the means and the right to directly question those seeking or holding our highest office of governance, most probably by web question and answer.

The first duty of the Prime Minister and his Deputy will be to select their cabinet of ministers and deputy ministers. The selection of the cabinet would be at their discretion. They would be required to select persons with suitable experience and ability for the posts although not necessarily experience in a particular field. Although they may approach possible candidates directly they would also be obliged to advertise for candidates. We believe that such appointments would be viewed by many talented Scots, and their employers, as an opportunity to serve their country, even if for a limited period of time. Consequently, we would have such appointments legislated as sabbaticals with their original positions being available to the appointees at the end of their term of office. All such appointments would be subject to scrutiny and final approval by the Second Chamber by means of formal hearings. The present role of the Monarch in formally approving such appointments would be abolished.

The 'Third Chamber' of the Government would have the right and duty to govern during its term of office, subject only to recall and dismissal of the whole government or any of its members by the Second or First Chamber in a clear process such as exists in a number of countries. The Third Chamber would have the right and duty to propose legislation and to take administrative action, in keeping with the prospectus on which the Prime Minister and his Deputy were elected and in accordance with other requirements which may arise from time to time. It is the Third Chamber that will provide leadership to the country and will determine the macro political and economic programme of the government during its term of office. But it also has a duty to regularly consult and report to the First and Second Chambers, who are its masters. Nevertheless, given the scrutiny to which the Prime Minister's programme for government would be subjected to by the electorate it would be expected that the Second Chamber would only object to government actions in exceptional circumstances. In such instances the Third Chamber would have the right to appeal directly to the First Chamber whose decision would be final. They would also have the right, on what should be rare occasions, to table their objections to legislation submitted by the Second Chamber to the First for approval.

> The First Chamber – many will already believe that the people are the supreme and sovereign authority in Scotland.

Having outlined the basic structure of a new Scottish democracy, let us now look at how it will work in more detail.

Let us start with the First Chamber. Many will already believe that the people are the supreme and sovereign authority in Scotland, but in fact they do not get much of a look-in when both the principle and the detail of policy or legislation is being considered. A political party, in putting forward its manifesto for election, generally now avoids anything but the sketchiest headlines in terms of legislative intentions. In addition elections are fought within such narrow confines, which are designed to avoid gaffes rather than give information, and in tune to such orchestrated and headline orientated media coverage that voters find it difficult to make informed choices between policies and parties, especially in complex matters and to any great degree of depth. That is one of the reasons why many do not vote.

At the same time however the ever-increasing complexity of our world demands that, if democracy is to mean anything, it must mean that individuals are enabled to understand the choices facing them and empowered to make them.

That does not happen at present. The proliferation of Government departments and quangos and the vast burgeoning of schemes and structures makes democracy ever more opaque and the central issues ever more difficult to grasp. This enables politicians to distance themselves from accountability and avoid circumstances where genuine participation and public decision making are to the fore. Politicians become not the instruments of the people, but the people's rulers and such a situation negates democracy, treating – as it does – the idea of a sovereign people with such circumspection as to amount to contempt.

> The Second Chamber will have as their first task the constant ascertaining of public opinion within their electoral areas and will be legally bound to represent such opinion.

In our model of democracy members of the Second Chamber will have as their first task the constant ascertaining of public opinion within their electoral areas and will be legally bound to represent such opinion.

Clearly some citizens will be, and always are, pro-active in approaching their representatives and making their views known. But without a means by which the totality of those views become the deciding factor, contact of that nature can quickly become meaningless and tokenistic.

What we are seeking is the opposite. We need a mechanism by which public opinion on important current matters – matters on which politicians presently decide – can be sought and obtained. We need a direct approach to democracy. That approach will secure firm information, give clear results and have statutory force. Fortunately technology has one available.

Our preferred approach is for a rolling, well-structured and clearly understood consultation with each and every voter, taking place every three or four months. The consultation for a constituency will be prepared by the MSP and his/her staff and will contain questions requested by the Government and Second

Chamber committees in addition to those posed by the MSP. The consultation will be conducted by an organisation experienced in such matters under firm contract to the Second Chamber and supervised by the Scottish Electoral Commission. It will use both new technology, face-to-face interview, telephone interview and traditional methods. The results of the consultation will be published on a constituency by constituency basis as quickly as possible after the consultation period.

Each MSP will maintain a website on which the consultation results will be published. The website will also contain the MSP's profile, updated prospectus, voting and attendance records in parliament in addition to the MSP's review of the consultation and details of his/her activities for the period. Electors will be able to post questions and receive answers from the MSP on the website on an ongoing basis. Such questions and answers will be archived for future perusal by electors.

> Each MSP will maintain a website on which the consultation results will be published.

The consultation will have three parts:

The first part will seek voters' views on a range of subjects, clearly outlined and with an opportunity to agree or disagree with a stated position. These subjects will be current, of importance and will be issues on which the Second Chamber is likely to discuss or decide in the coming three or four month period. They will include matters such as the general principle of bills coming to the Second Chamber, issues on which the First or Second Chambers have issued detailed consultative documents, and some issues of policy as well as Government intention. The views in this part will be binding on the elected representative, subject only to a minimum threshold of response and the caveats we make later in the chapter.

The second part will seek voters' ideas and opinions on proposed new legislation and will give voters a 'write in' opportunity to bring forward legislative change and express their views on matters not otherwise covered. It may well be that national movements for write-in legislation will arise in order to build this part of the process. This part will be binding on the authorities in the Parliament, who will be required to have bills drafted and introduced if a certain level of support is shown nationwide.

The third part will be a direct voting section, offering each citizen the opportunity to assent to, or reject certain bills that have already passed their full Parliamentary process. The people will therefore not only be able to propose, but to dispose. Bills that failed to receive public assent in this way, subject to a minimum voting threshold of say 30%, would fall.

Presently Bills approved by the Parliament go for Royal Assent, a mysterious process by which the monarch agrees to what elected politicians have already decided is to be done. This forms no useful or even understandable function. But public assent is another matter, for public assent would signify not only public agreement to legislative change, but also would form a channel for public understanding of legislation, something that is usually completely lacking.

Obviously not every issue raised in the chamber, nor each small amendment to a bill or every detailed Standing Order, would be subject to this process. A sensible approach would define the major issues on which the electorate's views – and sometimes their formal assent – have to be gained before a final parliamentary vote, or before assent is given and the bill passes into law.

These areas need to be the subject of discussion, but they should include significant financial decisions, raising and lowering of taxation (both individual and business), issues of constitutional significance, matters of personal and sexual morality, matters which severely restrict or ban actions that are presently legal and other issues which will materially alter the society in which we live. Other principles to be applied might be to ensure that matters which mark a significant departure from existing legislation or deal with issues never before legislated on should be included. If doubts were to exist as to which matters should be included then the decision should err on the side of inclusion subject to a 'double check' mechanism outline in the statute that sets up this system.[2]

Some procedures for emergency action by the Second Chamber between periods of public voting would be needed, as

---

[2] Some statutory definition would be required. The mechanism by which an issue became one on which public participation was essential could mirror that which presently takes place when a bill is certified as being within the legislative competence of the Scottish Parliament. That is done by the Presiding Officer, working to clear legal guidelines.

would a threshold for triggering assent or rejection of new legislation. If a majority of constituencies within a majority of geographical regions refused assent, although in a numerical minority overall, then that situation might also require a reconsideration by the Second Chamber prior to final decision. Such a mechanism would guard against domination by particular regions favoured by the population distribution.

These means of securing a participative democracy may seem complex, but although they are wide-ranging they are in essence no more complex than methods applied in some of the consultations presently being undertaken by the MSPs and the Executive – consultations moreover that have no binding element, and have no statutory force. Given the speed of technology – and the present slow process of legislation – they are not likely to unduly delay any legislation or decision making. But they would, taken together, immensely strengthen the position of the citizen and immensely aid the work of representatives. If MSPs are taking proper notice of the wishes of their constituents then it is unlikely that there will be many instances where the First Chamber will overturn legislation. It will be the right to use the stick and not the stick itself which will command attention and ensure the proper operation of the system.

Nonetheless we fully expect most professional politicians to throw up their hands in horror at such proposals. They will point to the impossibility of ascertaining the true feeling of the country, outside the regular electoral process. They will claim that such a structure would be regressive, socially conservative and bound to inhibit all positive change, let alone radical change (very much in the manner that Plato and Disraeli opposed what they understood as democracy, and in the way that all major democratic change has initially been resisted by the governing classes).

Some may, in illustration, point to some of the policy propositions put into law by the Californian electorate as a result of initiative referenda, and will predict chaos, confusion and carnage if the public is involved in this way. They will call in evidence issues of sexual morality, such as the repeal of Section 2A.

We would beg to differ. Let us look at another referendum for illustration – that held by the City of Edinburgh Council on congestion charging. Certainly most voters believed, and still

1 The Challenge of Democracy – A people's democracy

believe, that having good public transport is better than allowing completely unfettered private use of cars in city centres. They also believe that congestion charging is one useful way of limiting private usage.

However opinion surveys appear to indicate that the Edinburgh public wished to see transport improvements before accepting restrictions on their personal freedom. They were also sceptical about the City of Edinburgh Council's ability to bring about such improvements, even when they were promised (many had, after all, direct experience of the traffic chaos caused by the present city fathers in their endless meddling with the city's roads) and they had severe reservations about the detail of the scheme being proposed. Their rejection, if properly handled, should have been able to bring about a better scheme, introduced more sensitively and leading to more rapid results. The public's involvement was not a barrier to change – it was an indication of how such change should be handled. And the customer – the tax-paying voter – has, when he or she is forced to shell out such large sums in local charges not only the duty to pay the piper, but the right to call the tune.

The Section 2A issue is also instructive once again. Instead of a grand gesture by an under-pressure minister, the issue of repeal should have been sensitively discussed, first of all in committee. There should have been a real national debate and the proposal from Stonewall, the gay charity – which at the outset argued that an alternative replacement clause needed to be drafted to re-assure public opinion – should have been listened to. If, in the end, such a clause had been included in any public consultation, it would have been likely to have won support, possibly even from the Churches. Instead the whole atmosphere for consideration of social change was poisoned, and poisoned (as we have learnt from subsequent debates on sex education for example) in the long term.

A further – and to most politicians decisive – objection lies in the usual objection to referenda. Politicians will argue that there is no such thing as a simple yes or no, particularly when major issues are being decided. This argument, is however, profoundly anti-democratic for it is a simple Yes/No answer that voters are, in essence, required to give at election time. Yes for one party, and No to all the others. Yet the issues at stake at an election, are by the politicians' own admission, very complex and very wide-ranging. So if the people can be trusted to choose governments then they can be trusted to choose in much more simple referenda and binding consultations. If however politicians believe that the people cannot be trusted to decide on complex issues as part of a participatory democracy, then perhaps the politicians are also close to arguing that elections themselves should no longer be held?

There are, of course, already regulations in place – drawn up and supervised by the Electoral Commission – to cover public consultation by referenda and we envisage that these regulations would be extended to cover our much more radical process of public consultation and decision making and finally promulgated by an autonomous and independent Scottish Electoral Commission which would assume responsibility for their implementation. They would need to include provisions which ensure that both sides of any argument are presented fairly, are communicated to the people, and are – by statute – required to be given equal coverage in the broadcast media or at least in the publicly owned broadcast media. Newspapers, under private ownership, will remain free to take sides but a new press law would insist that a semblance of balance is presented even when accompanied by a clear editorial stance taking one side or the other.

What we propose for the Scottish Parliament has implications for Councils, as well as for Westminster and the European Parliament.

Another and more weighty objection is that of voter fatigue. Some, like John Thurso, the Lib Dem MP for Caithness, have already rightly drawn attention to this problem, with elections now being held almost every year.

But voter fatigue is also a product of voter disillusionment, and more probably arises from it than the other way round. Greater participation and understanding is likely to overcome such fatigue.

In any case whilst our ideas may lead to elections every two years for half of the Second Chamber these need to be, and would be, dovetailed with elections for the Prime Minister and the Deputy Prime Minister(once every four years).

Of course what we propose for the Scottish Parliament has implications for Councils, as well as for Westminster and the European Parliament. It is inconceivable that a revolution in democracy of this nature could be confined simply to one tier of governance, and one level of legislation. We would commend a closer link between the electors and their representatives, and a more active role for citizens, in every supposedly democratic body. We would not wish Scottish legislation to be subject to citizen's assent without also wishing that to be the norm for all legislation that affects individuals' lives and opportunities, so there are issues here for our continuing membership both of the UK as it is, and for our membership of an unreformed and very undemocratic Europe.

We have already stated, and will go on to argue in economic and cultural terms, that Scotland should be independent and therefore no longer part of the UK. Consequently a new democratic structure need not be an issue in terms of our participation in an incorporating union which no longer serves the best interests of the Scottish people. As for Europe, whilst we are strongly in favour of a trading Europe, we find the idea of an 'ever closer union' in terms of legislation to be deeply unattractive, and that seems the majority view of Scots. Even if the European Parliament and European legislation was to continue to play its present role in the lives of Scots, we would wish to insist that it is subject to the same democratic level of approval by Scots voters as domestic legislation, and if that were not possible then the dictates of a true democracy of the type we envisage would demand the establishment of a different relationship.

In any case, as nationalists as well as democrats we believe that once we have firmly established, and at last given life to, the principle of a sovereign Scottish people, which forms the foundation stone for all other democratic structures, this will automatically give rise to a renewed consideration of what structures are actually needed and how they relate to each other. There is no doubt that we are over-governed. Every voter, for instance, after May 2007 will be represented by no less than three or four councillors (elected under the new STV system), eight MSPs (one constituency and seven list), one MP and seven MEPs (from the national list). Such a plethora of elected representatives is simply unnecessary. We need a simplification of governance as well as – as we shall argue – smaller government.

That has strong implications for local democracy. We believe that our present Councils are too large, too bureaucratic and too inflexible. They are also uncertain of their role, jealously guarding some rights and responsibilities that would better sit with national government, whilst preventing more local groupings from exercising power.

We believe that smaller bodies should take responsibility for much local decision making, operating also under the firm principles of public participation. Towns and cities need their own councils, running local services and having their decisions made by local people. In rural areas it is more difficult to create reasonably sized bodies, but a devolution of power to larger community councils, with the same functions as cities may be best. Planning issues in particular need to be decided by local people particularly in rural areas. These councils should of course share back office functions and co-operate together to run major services such as police and fire. But the basic democratic building block should be smaller, really local authorities, which are close to voters. 'Back to the burghs' might be a slogan, but it also represents an aspiration although one that needs to be thoroughly updated. Local councillors should be much more local.

A radical change in democracy will perforce lead to a radical change in how all elected representatives do their jobs. Presently MSPs are jacks (and jills) of all trades, with the necessary corollary applying to many of them. They are required to be glorified social workers, taking up endless complaints which, whilst often serious and indicative of the neglect of individuals which is the present consequence of distant government, often do not belong within either their area of responsibility or competence and are sometimes negated by ideological pressure from political parties.

They are also called on to be legislators, examining the fine print of bills in areas which they lack knowledge or experience and on which they decide most often at the instruction of their party whips. Some go on to hold government office, or opposition briefs, chosen on the basis of their acceptability to their party leader and the weight of support they have within their party structures. They may – in fact nearly always do – know nothing about the subject area on which they must now become instant experts and, in the case of ministers, prime decision makers.

There are other roles as well. They must assume political leadership in their own areas, sometimes take on party responsibilities, and many either continue to undertake elements of their previous jobs, or assume new paying part-time ones.

It would be hard enough for highly skilled and highly intelligent individuals, strongly motivated by a desire to serve the public, to manage even some of these various tasks. To manage most of them would require superhuman effort, and a level of ability which could not exist in most of those who seek election. In addition there is no training offered or taken up for most of these roles, although politicians are always keen to see that others are well trained and to create minimum acceptable levels of qualifications for virtually all other posts.

Some simplification of MSPs' responsibilities is urgently required along with the opportunity to take detailed training. Out of that will come not just better performance by those presently elected, but also the opportunity to attract others who would presently shun any suggestion of standing for election. The erection of the supposed power of the people into a formal structure begins to suggest how that should happen.

First and foremost MSPs must be chosen for their ability to respond to the opinion of their electorate and to act upon it. That does not mean that they must be ciphers but it does mean that they must keep much closer to their electorate than they do now. The present regional list system produces far too distant a relationship and needs substantial modification. Proposals to change the system and introduce open lists which would give voters a more meaningful role in choosing regional members have recently been made by the Arbuthnott Commission and should be implemented and bedded in. If they do not work, then the move to a pattern of multi-member seats elected under a system of Single Transferable Vote might be the best option. We would envisage an increase in the number of MSPs to allow this to happen without creating constituencies that are unmanageable. Cutting out the Westminster tier would compensate for that slight increase. Single member seats for the islands might still be required but as all electoral systems are a balance between proportionality and closeness to the voter, such anomalies will have to be accepted given our geography.

Members should be well-staffed and resourced within their Holyrood office and local areas, able to open local offices and hold regular meetings. The monies which are presently given to political parties should be directly allocated to MSPs and we accept that more may be required. None of our democratic proposals are designed to save money but to ensure that by spending monies in a better way we can achieve a better basis for our society.

A considerable technological and perhaps psychological up-skilling of elected representatives will be needed in order that MSPs in particular can focus on their two key responsibilities – those of representing their constituents (by listening to them and acting on their concerns) and of debating, modifying and voting on legislation in a new multi-stage process, which will conclude in many cases with an assenting (or otherwise) vote in the First Chamber: the chamber of the people.

As we have suggested MSPs should not therefore be the pool from which ministerial talent is drawn. However we do believe that the Prime Minister and his Deputy should, *ex officio*, be voting members of the Second Chamber – though they should not be MSPs with their local responsibilities – and other Ministers (chosen by the First Minister and the Deputy First Minister from outwith the Second Chamber as we have seen) should have the right to attend the Chamber, speak and take part, though not to vote.

We have no wish to emasculate those who are elected to the Second Chamber. Indeed we wish to create circumstances in which a far wider pool of people come forward to be elected. One of the reasons that so few people enter professional politics is because they are themselves disillusioned by it and concerned that those who become MSPs or MPs or MEPs quickly become distant from the voters who choose them and creatures in thrall to the control of political parties.

Our proposals close that gap and that perception, and close it in a way that provides a living and continuing link between citizens and Members. For example Members who had previously taken guidance and instruction from political parties would now do so from those who elect them and we believe that that change alone would attract many more people into this type of public service and, moreover, people better qualified for the tasks involved.

MSPs, as we have said, should not however see themselves as ciphers or mere mouthpieces. The change from a representative democracy to a participatory one will alter the nature of the representatives role, but it need not diminish it. We are prepared to accept, for example, that from time to time an MSP's stance on issues may be completely incompatible with that which he or she is discovering amongst the electorate. Conscience, experience or even prejudice may dictate that fact.

We suggest two mechanisms for dealing with such difficulties. The first is a formal explanation of vote, much as is employed in the European Parliament. MSPs who cannot follow the instruction of their constituents should be required to explain why, both in the chamber itself and in the regular survey.

The second is more radical. We expect that members who take repeated individualistic stances would wish to have confirmed to them the continuing support of their electorate. Consequently we favour a recall mechanism, which would allow a petition for recall of a sitting member to result in a fresh election for that member alone, on a content/not content basis. Clearly such a mechanism would require a threshold of demand that would prevent frivolous or vexatious actions: perhaps ten percent of the registered electorate in any multi member constituency would have to sign a recall petition before a vote was triggered.

We also believe that a recall mechanism for the Prime Minister and his Deputy should exist. Once again the threshold would require to be high enough to deter daft attempts: perhaps ten percent of the whole voting population would be the right trigger for this very rare, but still democratically desirable, procedure. The Second Chamber should also be able to recall these officials and the other members of the government, perhaps by a two-thirds majority vote.

We are aware of the radical nature of everything we have suggested in this chapter. But we believe that our democracy presently does not work, and that new thinking is required. Our ideas are not a menu for action, but a series of possibilities which need to be discussed, and moreover discussed not just amongst the politicians (whose reaction is not likely to be favourable) but amongst the people.

We mentioned earlier the Citizens' Commission in British Columbia, in Canada. We are attracted to the idea of a Scottish Citizens' Commission which could consider these proposals and others, within the overall context of creating a better, more robust and more participative democracy. Such a Commission – chosen by a process which starts with the random selection of a pool of voters as possible members and refines that by meetings and seeking volunteers from the pool with the final commission chosen by lot from those volunteers – would be empowered to consider and recommend change, and in so doing would be enabled to appoint advisors and call witnesses in order to solicit a variety of views. The usual type of Commission – no matter how hard working or inspired – tends to be an acceptable gathering of the great and the good. That is, in itself, undemocratic, and we would want something different to start this whole process off. We consider this matter further in our final chapter.

A Scottish Citizens' Commission could consider these proposals and others, within the overall context of creating a better, more robust and more participative democracy.

In laying out the possibility of radical change we take encouragement from the fact that much of what we recognise today as being essential parts of our democratic structures were seen as wildly utopian in previous ages. Universal suffrage, votes for women, the abolition of property qualifications, the payment of MPs and, at one time, the notion of any Parliament having the right to exercise its will in opposition to a monarch were all issues which were hotly contested (sometimes with blood) and which were denounced as impossible or destructive.

Democracy does evolve. Looking around us in Scotland, we think that a further evolution of democracy is long overdue and moreover we consider that much of the distance from politics that is seen in the population is because that evolution is not even being discussed. We do not expect that it can be achieved in a short period of time. But we do expect that pressure for democratic change will build again in Scotland and we do seek to contribute to that process.

But we go further. We think that renewing our democracy by letting the people in is only a first step in finding the right way to release Scotland's potential.

As nationalists we also believe that other changes are necessary, not least independence. We could not envisage a Scotland that was worthy of independence were it not to be a much more democratic Scotland than that in which we presently live. But equally we could not envisage a more democratic Scotland without it being one which aspired to a greater level of powers for its people than they presently possess: powers that would allow the people to decide on taxation, defence, foreign affairs, overseas aid and a whole host of other issues.

Yet before that happens, our nation must – to put it bluntly – be able to afford such a democracy. Low economic growth, a constant increase in the size of government and a palpable failure to secure full value for public sector investment (particularly in terms of better service delivery) are all issues that need to be addressed in order to create the foundation for both a participatory democracy and the new state of independence. Consequently, as we commend our proposals in this chapter as means to begin the process of democratic development, we must also start to turn our attention to equally crucial economic issues.

These issues also require radical reform, and moreover reform that needs more determination than that which has so far been shown by the Scottish Executive. To bring it about Scotland will need inspired leadership, a focused agenda and competent government: all matters with which our new democracy is concerned, which are central to any third chamber and which can only improve under a new, participatory democracy.

2. The Challenge of Economics

Science is the greatest antidote to the poison of enthusiasm and superstition.

Adam Smith *The Wealth of Nations* (1776)

2.1 Seizing the Tools

Forecasters are predicting that, by the middle of the century, what Business Week calls 'Chin-India' will account for as much as 45% of global GDP with Europe taking a large slice of the pain as its share of world output more than halves. In the west no debate about future prospects is now complete without heavy heart-searching about what the emergence of Chin-India means for the future material well-being of the rest of us.

Alf Young *The Herald* 16th August 2005

ALF YOUNG – one of Scotland's most perceptive commentators – is right. But of course the problem is not just Europe's: it is Scotland's. We are citizens of the world, for good or ill, and therefore each of us in Scotland too stands today at the dawn of a new era. What we make of it, how we survive it, and if we prosper during it are the questions facing us. And such questions, as Adam Smith rightly pointed out, need to be decided upon by using facts and applying rigorous method, rather than by relying on belief or – as happens too often in Scotland – on optimism.

All of humanity is presently experiencing the greatest improvement in their collective welfare that the planet has ever witnessed. The impact of those changes is most profound where traditionally people have had least. In the east, which is finally embracing the market and the benefits of capitalism, fifty percent of the world's population will see their lives transformed as they emerge from the paddy fields and herdsmen's pastures of a largely agricultural society into a modern, almost post-industrial world. That which took the rural workers of Europe several hundred years to achieve will take their eastern counterparts a tenth of the time or less. Such is the pace of global economic progress.

The 'five percent plus club' – those countries with recent annual growth rates in excess of 5% GDP for extended periods – includes such diverse countries as Russia, India, Pakistan, the Philippines and mainland China and has admitted those with underpinning philosophies as varied as Islam, Hinduism, Christianity and Buddhism, to say nothing of that secular religion, hard-line Communism. Add to these the pioneer capitalist states of the east – South Korea, Singapore, Taiwan and Hong Kong and the tiger copycats of Malaysia, Indonesia and Thailand – and the geographic range and cultural breadth of current change is awesome.

All these countries have achieved or are achieving their new-found status by rejecting – even in the case of those who say they have not – the economic constraints of doctrinaire socialism. Despite the rhetoric that still comes from governments, the reality is that they have, lock stock and barrel, adopted that which was in many cases anathema – capitalism.

Equally, and perhaps more importantly, the brand of capitalism that they have adopted is not the watered down version that still appeals to many in Scotland: capitalism hedged about with so many caveats and restraints that it sometimes looks as if is merely tolerated by our governing classes. Their capitalism is the variety in its purest form which sees, for example, China's government resource company bidding to takeover Noranda, Canada's largest mining company, while it also negotiates to become a major player in the development of the Alberta tar sands, the largest hydrocarbon deposits in the world (larger than those of Saudi Arabia). The sheer complexity and interaction of global capitalism is starkly illustrated in the extraordinary fight between the state oil companies of India and China for control of Petrokazakstan Inc., a $4 billion Canadian company with oil and gas assets in Kazakstan, with Russia's Lukoil company sniping on the sidelines in order to get a piece of the action.

China may still be the partner of choice for would-be socialist governments such as that presently in power in Venezuela (itself buoyed up by capitalist oil receipts which are booming) but its leaders are chasing bigger opportunities. Recently they launched a form of economic warfare in the heartland of capitalism – the USA – with a bid for Unocal, a living symbol of America's past economic glories with assets spread around the globe. The fact that this bid was brought to a halt by terrified opposition within the US Congress suggests strongly that the eagle is now in fear of the dragon, for the dragon is more than capable of fighting on the eagle's own perch.

In fact, instead of embracing competition from China and

the east and using it to its advantage – the correct technique in a world economy – the US has begun to show the signs of an empire whose trajectory of power is past its zenith and to whom protectionism is seen as the most attractive option, despite its long term destructive effects. Such negative interference in the business world is sadly echoed in Scotland, most recently by a suggestion that the government should interfere to stop what was merely a rumoured takeover bid for Scottish Power – a suggestion which if invoked would soon see capital flee Scotland's shores and severely inhibit if not completely derail, for example, the Royal Bank of Scotland's attempts to buy part of a Chinese bank as well as many other Scottish-led incursions into companies furth of our shores.

Today wherever you find iron ore, copper, nickel, lead, zinc, coal, uranium and a multitude of other basic commodities you will find not just the entrepreneurs and businessmen of the east, but also their entrepreneurial governments, seeking not just to buy the commodities but also the very companies that produce them. They do this to secure their lines of supply for these materials are essential if they are to continue to build economies that not only satisfy growing demand at home but also – and vitally – fill the shelves of the west with an astounding array of consumer goods of outstanding quality and at prices with which western companies have no hope of competing. In some respects instead of the west becoming, as was only recently anticipated, the providers of intellectual goods and services to the cheaper manufacturing economies of the east, the world is being turned upside down. Indeed the roles are gradually being reversed with the less effective western economies becoming, to put it bluntly, the hewers of wood and drawers of water whilst the east becomes the hi-tech innovative powerhouse of the world.

Consequently it is not just manufacturing in the west that, having been under long term threat, is now faced with terminal decline. Our service economies, long looked upon as invincible to competition, are being chipped away by India's educated and English-speaking workforce. Customer support, sales and servicing are already flooding to that country but so are back office functions. America's large corporations, faced with burgeoning legal, accounting and book-keeping requirements to meet the demands of ever increasing regulation are already finding it cheaper and more efficient to outsource these activities to India. So do American's physicians and surgeons, who can have their medical correspondence transcribed overnight by secretaries in Bangalore, and their X-Ray results interpreted in twenty minutes by technicians in Mumbai.

As India changes – dismantling a restrictive socialist and at times marxist economy and freeing entrepreneurial spirit – former paper-bound and very reactive bureaucrats are becoming the proactive founders and managers of enterprises employing Indian accountants, call centre workers and a growing educated population who are being trained in every conceivable discipline.

It will not be long before Scotland's accountants are faced with a challenge.

Scotland's call centre workers are already feeling the effect of such competition. It will not be long before Scotland's accountants, bookkeepers, administrators, medical scientists and even Scotland's lawyers are also faced with these challenges. What is being seen is a re-invention, but this time in the East, of bold and brash competitive capitalism: the competitive capitalism of Carnegie, Ford, Rockefeller and other entrepreneurs of a past era, an era in which the they ruled the world's economy as firmly as their countries ruled over the world's lands and seas.

These new buccaneers from the east come armed not just with the weapons of capitalism but also with the most potent of wealth creators – small government. Government size in their countries averages less than 20% of GDP. In the west that average is well over 40%.

Moreover, their economics are steered by a responsive tiller – their own currencies – and this gives a recipe for almost unparalleled economic growth and success. 'Almost unparalleled' because the recipe is exactly the one which catapulted our own economies in the west, despite two world wars, from the poverty at the dawn of the industrial age to the prosperity experienced today. As recently as the 1960s the OECD countries were averaging a growth rate of 5.5% of GDP with an average government size of 27% of GDP. Today the comparable figures are 1.9% growth and a staggering 48% government size.

In this book we advocate political freedom for our citizens, in which they take control of decision making in their own societies. We believe that Scotland should start on that process. But we also need to take, hand in hand with political control, economic control as well. Our citizens need economic freedom as well as democratic liberty. We believe that only when Scotland wakes up to the need for political and economic independence will they be ready to take and benefit from national and international independence.

To achieve the circumstances which will produce economic freedom – growth, prosperity and a national cake which can be more fairly shared – we need to reduce the size of government in our country and restore our own currency.

Everything in this book is predicated on the need to reduce government to a size and scope which is affordable, sustainable and which no longer constricts citizens in their daily lives whilst limiting their potential. We shall deal with the role of government in the next chapter but it is salutary to note that a significant proportion of every pound which we contribute in taxation is not being consumed in delivering government services but merely in administrating them.

> To achieve the circumstances which will produce economic freedom, we need to reduce the size of government in our country and restore our own currency.

Consequently considerably less of the taxes we pay are going into society in a way which could lead to well-being and prosperity. 'Could lead' of course is an important qualification, because even that amount which is spent often goes on things which are neither essential nor desirable. Government is poor at making decisions which produce greater happiness and greater satisfaction: people themselves make better decisions on those matters. They also – inevitably and usually overwhelmingly – generate more wealth within their society when they are free to make their own decisions about their own resources. It is therefore not only right, but essential, that individual citizens retain more of their own earnings and choose how to allow them to be utilised for the greater good of both themselves and their fellow human beings.

In order to move forward to that situation, we need first of all to go back in time and read again the work of a Scot who has arguably been this country' greatest gift to the welfare of mankind. *The Wealth of Nations* by Adam Smith has done more to advance the living standards and well-being of our fellow human beings than any other book save perhaps, in some people's view, the Bible. Adam Smith was the father of modern capitalism and it is high time that his own people rediscovered his genius, particularly as, in his own land, that genius is currently tarnished by the half-baked economic models espoused by most of our political parties.

Smith believed in a truly free, open and competitive market in which not just the private sector but also government is exposed to the reality of competition. The force of competition – fair, open competition – is one that exposes weaknesses, assists in rectifying them and provides the best opportunities for all. Government needs to be open to those forces for protectionism and special pleading leads to inefficient, badly devised and badly delivered public services. All government budgets, wherever possible (and it is possible for almost all such budgets) should be spent in a competitive environment and that inevitably means a complete re-assessment of government as subsidiser, government as hander-out and government as sole sponsor. That should apply across the board. [1]

By now many conventional politicians, whose careers have been built on offers of pork barrel support and the nurturing of special interests, will be having a fit of the vapours. But in fact making government efficient and responsive – by making it spend each penny wisely and with a clear focus and intent – is exactly what socialism as well as capitalism is about.

The precedents for doing so are good. It was by such means, together with currency reforms and drastically reduced government size, that in the 1980s New Zealand's newly elected Labour government turned a stagnating economy into one of the world's most dynamic and high growth economies. By 2002 New Zealand had a growth rate of 4.2% GDP and a total entrepreneurial activity index (TEA) of 14 compared to 4 for Scotland. Today, New Zealand's highly efficient, innovative and subsidy-free agricultural industry (to take just one of the content-ious areas) is the envy of the world and employs as many in farming as it did prior to the reforms. If New Zealand, a small country on the edge of the world, can throw away its subsidies and face up to world competition then why can Scotland not be enabled and encouraged to follow suit? Help will be required, but the benefits are obvious.

---

[1] Michael Russell would argue that it will be necessary to set the clearest parameters for, and limits to, the development of competition within the public services and that accordingly no blanket prescription about these matters can be made.

We seek to rediscover the Scotland of careful fiscal reputation, sadly not practised in modern times. It was on the sound common sense of the common man that Adam Smith built his ideas: although the language may be archaic, and some of the social structures outdated, the ideas are still entirely relevant:

> It is the maxim of every prudent master of a family,
> never to attempt to make at home what it will cost him
> more to make than to buy. . . If a foreign country can
> supply us with a commodity cheaper than we ourselves
> can make it, better buy it of them with some part of the
> produce of our own industry, employed in a way in
> which we have some advantage.

Smith knew that in applying the same principles to government as were applied to trade within a nation, a government would be more than likely to achieve the same results: a growing prosperity that had individual benefit. He wished to ensure that his so-called 'invisible hand' – the achievement of maximum economic efficiency through the mechanism of free and fair trade, competition and enterprise – was allowed to operate without constraint. So do we, but with one caveat. We believe that in the modern world the invisible hand needs to be supported by what we might call a 'guiding hand'.

In the modern world the invisible hand (of free and fair trade) needs to be supported by what we might call a 'guiding hand' wielded by government.

This 'guiding hand' must, given the complexity of our society, be wielded by government and should have two roles. Firstly, by light regulation allied to firm penalty it would ensure that trade and enterprise is not just free but also fair and that the excesses to which unbridled capitalism are prone are held in check (and we accept such excesses do exist and wish, perhaps more than the present government, to make sure they are always stamped out). Labour abuse and monopoly are not – as has often been alleged – natural consequences of capitalism but abuses of capitalism: abuses of free enterprise. They were rightly fought and defeated by trades unions, amongst others, and we should not forget that.

The second role of the guiding hand must be to anticipate and forecast the future, to plan the economic path of the nation, to manage the macro economic levers of capitalism such as taxation, government size and currency and to ensure that we at all times have the national potential to maximise our position in the economic tables of the world. In the ever-changing world of today

– and for the future – the above powers are essential if we are to have the flexibility and fleetness of foot to compete and survive.

If historical political allegiances with the UK and Europe stand in the way of Scotland gaining and using such powers then it is time to review and revise such relationships. It is a profound absurdity that Scotland, whose people purport to be a nation, allows its largest trading partner England, in the guise of the UK, to control all of these matters with regard to the Scottish economy – it is akin to a boxer allowing his opponent to set the rules and be the referee. Whilst we permit such a thing it is no wonder that we continuously lag behind England in every economic measurement!

While we may advocate capitalism and small government let us be clear that we do not believe in *laissez faire* capitalism or government. Given the accelerating pace of the modern world such a policy would be disastrous. On the contrary, we believe that it is a prime duty of government to provide the leadership that will unite us and produce the plans with which we may face the challenges ahead. We see national planning and the production of rolling five, ten and fifteen year National Development Plans as a primary function of government. Such plans would seek to forecast international, national and regional economic trends, set goals and make recommendations to government and the private sector. To this end government must form a National Planning Council comprised of the best brains from all levels of government, academia, private enterprise and organised labour, to oversee the ongoing compilation of such plans.

> It is a prime duty of government to provide the leadership that will unite us and produce the plans with which we may face the challenges ahead – we see National Development Plans as a primary function of government.

This is not state socialism as was practised in the former Communist countries. These plans are aids and supports, not diktats. They will be flexible, responsive and above all they will be advisory in so far as they affect private enterprise. But they will allow a better management of resources, services, infrastructure, education, research and development. Their existence will help bring together a unified purpose for the nation and provide guidance to all sectors on trends and opportunities. Business decisions on how to utilise them will be made by business, but on the basis of clear national and international information.

A good precursor for this is the Scottish Parliament Futures Project, instigated by George Reid, the Presiding Officer, and which has engaged the support and attention of the Scottish Executive. This deserves commendation and we hope that it will not simply fade from view once its PR value has been exhausted by Ministers.

To a certain extent the activity of national planning could be carried out even by a devolved government in Scotland. But a devolved government will always operate with one of its hands tied behind its back. On that hand there are several vital digits, the most important of which is that of currency.

Control of its own currency is a country's most potent economic weapon. It allows government to control the money supply, interest rates and exchange rates, all of which can have a profound and relatively rapid impact on our economic growth and international competitiveness. There are simply no other methods by which the economy can be finely tuned and geared to meet the ever-changing and accelerating challenges of the information age. A country without its own currency is a country not only without a steering wheel, but also without brakes and an accelerator.

> Control of its own currency is a country's most potent economic weapon.

Countries, according to their judgment of their best interests, may let their currencies float in the market place or, be they small like Singapore or large like China, they can fix their exchange rate to a major currency, such as the pound, dollar or euro or even a basket of currencies if it is perceived to be in their best interest. By such means they have the flexibility to deal with economic adversity and to seek economic advantage as circumstances may demand. They are always capable of changing decisions and policy if circumstances demand such a change.

When the vanguard of the east, the tiger economies, over-heated and imploded in the late 1990s they turned to money supply, interest rate control and currency devaluation to recover from the doldrums and within a few years were once again members of the 5% club. Without such independence their economies and futures would have been totally in the hands of a currency controller outwith their shores whose interests might well have been inimical to theirs, and whose prime loyalty would inevitably have lain elsewhere. In recent times the primary weapon in curing the economic crisis in Russia, Brazil and Argentina was the devaluation of their currencies.

Of course we have a strong example of the advantages of having your own currency within our own shores. When the UK as a member of the ERM, the 'currency basket' that was the euro's predecessor, found its economy out of alignment with its fellow members and with no means of correction it was forced to withdraw from the ERM and devalue its currency. This action of devaluation laid the base for the UK's economic recovery and a period of sustained economic growth. The ERM debacle also saved the UK from the economic morass that subsequently overtook the euro members.

Euroland has become a sort of economic Disneyland in which the biggest fairground ride is that of currency fantasy.

The idea that one currency fits all economies is nonsense when faced with the diversity in size, economic structure, culture and language between the European nations. Today as Ireland needs higher interest rates to dampen inflation, Italy requires lower interest rates to stimulate growth. While the frugal Dutch adhere strictly to government debt controls, the Germans (until recently) and French (currently) are spending like drunken sailors. Euroland has become a sort of economic Disneyland in which the biggest fairground ride is that of currency fantasy.

The rejection by the French and Dutch of the European Constitution may in part have been occasioned by public dislike of the single currency. However, it has had two important effects for the UK. One is that the issue of further European political integration is largely dead, at least for the foreseeable future, yet it has been made glaringly obvious to every citizen that the demise of that mistaken political ideal has not damaged one iota the existing trade co-operation between the nations of the EU. It is therefore quite clear across the political spectrum that the best way forward for our involvement with Europe should be in the trading sphere and not through further political institutions.

The second result has been the death of the euro as a putative UK currency. No UK party can or will renew that policy without damage to its own prospects. In Scotland the SNP has been in the vanguard of the argument for the Euro, but even there it seems that enthusiasm is much diminished. This new stance is a very sensible position to hold given that the SNP at every opportunity points out the profound differences in the economies of England and Scotland and the unsuitability of the prevailing UK monetary policy and currency to deal with the problems of the Scottish economy.

That fact, taken alongside the death of the euro in terms of Scottish involvement, should make it clear to everyone that the only correct step on independence would be the establishment of a Scottish currency. In the past nationalists have been afraid of espousing that solution, in view of the ridicule that was sometimes heaped on them from south of the border. Now, given the way that the world is changing, that solution will increasingly be seen as the right one.

Economists, as is ever their wont, are of course divided as to whether or not a small country such as Scotland should have its own floating currency or adopt the currency of that of a large trading partner such as the pound or the euro. We contend that there is a third route commonly used around the world, which preserves for Scotland all of the options offered by the afore-mentioned choices, plus a few more. This alternative is to have our own currency, say the Scottish pound, which would have an exchange rate fixed to sterling. We could initially set the Scottish pound at a nominal devaluation[2] to the pound, thus from day one giving the Scottish export economy a distinct advantage over its largest trading partner. However, as we note later it may well be more beneficial to reduce our trade with England in order to diversify our trade internationally, as occurred in the case of Ireland.

Should at any time in the future the fiscal policies governing the pound prove unsuitable for the Scottish economy or should England or Scotland or both experience an economic crisis requiring drastic corrective action then Scotland having preserved its options could: revalue or devalue the currency against the pound; or adopt linkage with another currency; or adopt linkage with a basket of currencies; or if by such time it has demonstrated its fiscal prudence and competence allow the currency to float against the currencies of the world.

We would submit that the preservation of such a wide range of options is infinitely superior to the stark choice of dependency

---

[2] Michael Russell accepts that a theoretical discussion of currency levels after independence is valuable and acknowledges the considerable original research undertaken by Dennis MacLeod on these matters, particularly as he has delved more deeply into them than any previous writer. However as an SNP candidate he asserts the SNP view that no devaluation would be required in such circumstances.

on a currency over which we exercise little or no control. It should also be noted that small countries (by virtue of their small economic impact) can and do often establish linkages with larger currencies, which are skewed in their favour. Indeed in recent times countries as large as China have exploited such relationships, in its case *vis a vis* the US dollar.

In a recent paper for the Policy Institute Macdonald and Hallwood have, in a development of their previous position which was set out in work for the Fraser of Allander Institute, advocated 'fiscal autonomy' for Scotland in the field of taxation, a situation in which Holyrood would be responsible for raising by taxation the monies it spends. We welcome their paper and commend them on taking such an initiative. We are in agreement with this position assuming that it also includes monies due to Westminster for non-devolved services.

However, in the matter of currency, having considered only a floating Scottish currency or retention of the pound (or euro) as the available options, Macdonald and Hallwood advocate the latter as being in Scotland's best interest. They cite transaction costs, currency risk and lack of pricing opacity as being detrimental to trade in the case of a floating currency and go so far as to suggest that Scotland's financial industry would move to London should Scotland adopt a floating currency. The latter comment begs the question as to why a small country like Switzerland with its own floating currency has been so successful in the world of international finance. It also ignores the fact that, in these days of little or no exchange controls, international financial institutes operate in the currencies of the world as dictated by the needs of their clients with little or no impact from their local currency other than on their costs and fees. A fixed exchange rate with a nominal devaluation coupled with the reduction or elimination of corporate taxation – as we advocate later, and which is also possible under Macdonald and Hallwood's taxation recommendations – would have not just London's financial institutions but many of England's corporations beating a path to Edinburgh, Stirling, Glasgow, Dundee, Inverness or Aberdeen. Further, the vast majority of the countries of the world, other than the euro block and a few minor countries, have their own currency – are they all wrong? Many of these countries have linkage to the currency of a major trading country.

Although we advocate linkage to the pound as a prudent first step in the introduction of the currency we have no doubt that in due course an economically strong Scotland will opt for a floating currency and full fiscal control of its economy. We do so despite a further criticism which is sometimes leveled against a small nation, as opposed to a large currency block, which chooses to have a floating currency, namely a fear that higher borrowing costs will result. We contend that these need not be material and that any disadvantages of size could well be offset or bettered by demonstrable sound management of the economy. Further, as we will expand on later, we envisage a Scotland that will become debt free, in terms of national policy and will, because of legislative provision, remain so. Accordingly we would encourage them to give consideration to the obvious additional options with regard to Scotland's currency choices.

But the need for a currency is not just a post-independence need. A currency of our own could be a very useful precursor to independence. In fact, given the urgent need to improve Scotland's economic performance and the pressing imperative of maximising Scotland's economic potential, there is an argument for a devolved Scotland having its own currency.

We would argue that if the full powers of taxation were to be repatriated (as many even outside the SNP such as Macdonald and Hallwood argue) then along with them should be returned all the other powers of economic management. Full economic management, as we have shown, needs full control of currency and this argument needs to be put into the equation. Unionists may baulk at it, for the pound is so clearly a symbol of political union, but that is precisely the error that the euro fell into; the view that currencies were in some way merely symbols of something else, and in particular symbols of political agreement.

They are not – they have a unique function which is of importance in its own right, and in fact of central importance in its own right. It is therefore to be hoped that even those from outside the nationalist movement who agree with the gaining of tax and other economic powers for the Scottish Parliament will now actively consider arguing for a Scottish currency as well, even if some institutions remained shared between the nations. The need is certainly urgent.

Of course we contend that, particularly in modern times, the United Kingdom has not worked for Scotland. By every important economic measure Scotland is severely economically disadvantaged relative to its English neighbour. This is starkly illustrated by the steady decline in Scotland's population: a decline that is taking place whilst England's population rises. Even the new figures from the Registrar General for Scotland, which are not quite as gloomy as those published some years ago, still show that disparity.

There can be no greater harbinger of impending economic disaster than a declining population – it is a death knell which if not reversed will see a nation wither and die. Yet our leaders do not seem to have grasped the enormity of the fate with which we are faced – or more likely they are unwilling to face up to the failure of their policies.

Population decline is not just about excess mortality, though that exists here too and most shamefully in terms of the effect of fuel poverty. Population migration within a monetary union is a direct consequence of economic disparity. Consequently our citizens are obviously voting with their feet on the Scottish economy and on what they believe are its prospects day and daily. So, intriguingly, do many of our politicians who seek Westminster seats in the south. A drastically low birth rate often tells the same story – a reluctance to trust the future.

For our young, ambitious, economically (and reproductively) active citizens higher unemployment and lower wages are the key determinants of a decision to stay or go. The problems their departure causes, however, are exacerbated by traffic that takes place the other way. Retirees – from where it does not matter – who are reproductively inactive and who are also relatively economically inactive in many remote communities, add a further difficulty. Their presence exacerbates the imbalance between the economically active and the economically inactive, which is another key issue which we will have to confront in the future and in which, once more, the prospects for Scotland are worse than for those in England.

All these concerns have their roots in long term economic imbalance. Some attempt to overcome them has been made by encouraging inward immigration from other EU countries and from further afield, but the nation's long term economic weakness is likely to work against that solution. Immigrants – nearly always ambitious and determined – are no fools. Why should they seek the lower wages and job uncertainty of Scotland when faced with the stronger economy of England? Even if they come here for education, they are likely to migrate south as soon as that becomes practicable or desirable.

The numbers tell the tale – Scotland's share of UK immigrants for the period 1992-2001 was only 4.7% as opposed to an expected 8.5%. Only when Scotland's economic performance unequivocally surpasses that of her immediate neighbours and her direct competitors will our young stay and those that left, return. We only need look across the Irish Sea to see such a future and understand such a turnaround in fortunes. It must surely be clear that unionism with its inherent Anglo-centric economic bias will never allow or even contemplate such an eventuality.

We clearly need an agenda which will address all these problems. Those countries with a focus on the problems ahead, with clear-cut national strategies, the flexibility to adapt to change and a united and dedicated populace, will succeed and prosper. Some indeed revel in the challenges presented to them. We must be one of those countries, but to become one we will have to rediscover our old ingenuity and gain control of all our national assets, for they will be needed for the task.

Yet survival, or even reveling in the challenge, may not be enough. What should our ambition be?

We, strangely enough, agree on that with the First Minister. But we should aim to be number one in every international measure of success, not for reasons of hubris (we have no desire to call ourselves the best small country in the world) but for reasons of performance and ambition, for only when we have goals in front of us can we hope to achieve our full potential.

But unfortunately we presently lack the ambition, the focus, the strategies and the political will to win the battles ahead even if, economically speaking we are actually at war; a war already being fought out all over the world not in blood, but in money, ingenuity, productivity and innovation.

Even to start out on our attempt we are going to have to put away the politics of division, and make some clear decisions about what type of society we want to create. We will need renewed powers of analysis, reason and cooperation and we will have to build upon the many strengths with which our people and our country are blessed. But if we can put in place a firm commitment to a dynamic, capitalist economy and a stable and nationally controlled currency (and do that whilst renewing our democracy) then we have a strong foundation to work on.

In parallel, however we must turn to another very pressing matter – that of securing small and responsive government. Until we establish such government, growth and excellence will remain mere pipe dreams.

2.2 Government *v.* Growth

If a Government is big enough to give you everything you
want, it is big enough to take away everything you have.
                                    President Gerald R Ford (1960)

O NE OF THE GREAT puzzles in recent Scottish life has
been that presented by public spending in the health service.
The amount of money devoted to this has increased greatly – in
fact by 2009 it will have doubled over a decade. Yet even the
Executive's Health Minister, Andy Kerr, had to admit in the
autumn of 2005 that the public had not seen anything like a
doubling of service and personal benefit. The statistics, he
conceded, had indeed gone the wrong way in certain key areas.

There are several reasons for this anomaly. Much of the
increased spending has gone in wages and in the ever-rising cost
of drugs and medical equipment. Even if the much reported wage
inflation amongst GPs is in part a media exaggeration, there is
no doubt that at every level of the health service personal income
has increased for those who work in it, and (as usual) for those
in the upper echelons the increases have been the most significant.

Money has also been spent on spending the money – increasing massively, as a result, the amount of bureaucracy and the size
of health service administration. Constant tinkering with the
delivery mechanisms – the health boards – and micro management
by government of these boards and their delivery has also led to
sizeable cost increases.

But there is another factor, which, it can be safely assumed,
Mr Kerr has not even considered. It is no disrespect to Mr Kerr
to say that out of the five million or so Scottish citizens he may
not be the absolutely top choice for running such a complex and
large-scale operation. Indeed that is axiomatic for Mr Kerr has
no previous experience in the health service, nor in the management of huge organisations. His work within the bureaucracy of
Glasgow City Council was no doubt important, but it was not
an obvious career path to running the largest employing organisation in the country.

Of course in this lack of experience or training for his post,

Mr Kerr is far from unique. The same disadvantage applies equally to the civil servants who advise him and it applies across the board to all other ministers and their civil servants, with virtually no exceptions in present day Scotland.

By ensuring that such vitally important jobs are opened up to a much wider selection of candidates – one of our proposals for governance in an earlier chapter – we may be able to improve the situation. But in so doing we might also stop to consider another point – is it really the job of government to deliver in such minute detail this very complex and vitally important set of life or death services? Certainly government needs to ensure that each and every citizen can access health care free at the point of need. But that does not mean that government has to provide every aspect of such health care itself, for it seems manifestly obvious that government as we know it does not have the skills, or the ability – and perhaps it does not even have the resources – to do so.

> If we are prepared to change our views as to what government should directly provide – without losing any of the guarantees of essential service which are the hallmarks of a modern and civilised society – then we could free up our nation.

What citizens expect from their government will be a key issue for Scotland in the twenty first century. If we expect – as Gerald Ford so succinctly indicated – everything we want, then we will have to tolerate a size of government that is a constant drain on our personal resources and which constantly interferes in every aspect of our lives. We will also have to tolerate continuing low economic growth, as all the evidence worldwide shows that big government depresses economic opportunity. To add insult to injury we will also have to tolerate increasingly poor services which are delivered in an increasingly poor manner.

However if we are prepared to change our views as to what government should directly provide – without, as we shall later argue, losing any of the guarantees of essential service which are the hallmarks of a modern and civilised society – then we could free up our nation so that it can meet the challenges of the new age.

The relationship between a citizen and their government is one of the fundamental relationships of life. It ranks in importance alongside family relationships in terms of its impact on our personal fortunes and happiness. We have already outlined our suggested changes in how we elect a government, and how we participate in our democracy which are designed so that all of us may take a bigger stake in decision making about our national journey. Now we want to explore further why we think the size of government is also a crucial issue. We will make it clear that we regard our government as far too big. We shall then consider how to reduce its size by considering what it should deliver, and how it should deliver it.

For people, as for governments, money can work wonders. But when a system becomes clogged with spending, in government as in business and indeed in personal life, then problems arise. The Scottish health service, like many of Scotland's public services, is having its arteries clogged with more and more misdirected and un-directed spending. If however, the only solution either applied or discussed is simply more of the same – more and more money – then far from effecting a cure either the dosage will eventually prove fatal or the system will be running so badly that no improvement can ever be made. Either way the effect will be the opposite of what citizens want and what government expects.

The problems of Scotland's health service are but one symptom of a much wider disease – the disease of over-sized government.

The truth is that public spending, which was once the oil that lubricated Scottish governance, has steadily become more viscous with every increasing dose until it has taken on the characteristics of a glue, which has slowed our nation's development to a virtual standstill. That may sound strange, but we believe it is true for the problems of Scotland's health service are but one symptom of a much wider disease – the disease of over-sized government. Bad government, making bad decisions, based only on trying to keep the nation alive, rather than returning it to health. Reform of our public services is not only required because it makes better economic sense and gives better value for money: it is also essential because the ever increasing size of government is actually killing us. It is changing us from a potentially wealthy and growing nation into one which has embedded within it inefficiency, lack of flexibility and steady decline.

The fault in all this lies not in any individual, or even in any succession of mistakes even though those are often manifest. The fault lies in a relationship that has gone wrong, although very few people are prepared to talk about it. That relationship is the one between Government size, economic growth and national well-being.

Government size (GS) is usually measured as total government expenditure expressed as a percentage of the country's GDP. According to Scottish Executive statistics for 2002-2003 [1] total government expenditure in Scotland (including Westminster spending on Scotland's behalf) is about £40.9 billion per annum or a staggering 50% of Scotland's GDP (which stands at around £82 billion). Some estimates put it even higher, at around 54%. These figures exclude the GDP contribution from Scotland's share of North Sea oil, an omission based on politics and not on correct economic protocol or even common sense for if such oil revenues are not attributable to the Scottish economy then to whose economy should they adhere?

Government size is still far bigger than it should be in terms of economic well-being.

If we add Scotland's oil to its GDP then we reach a GDP of about £104 billion per annum or £20,600 per capita, equal to 116% of the UK average as opposed to the 91% derived from Scottish Executive statistics. This is in itself significant, because the figures clearly show that Scotland is far from being the poor neighbour in our inter-island relationship. We are much more like a rich uncle!

But of course if the overall value of our GDP rises, then the percentage that is Government size falls. Our present GS may therefore not be as high as 50% though it is undoubtedly much higher than the 35% that Ireland achieves. However, as we shall explain later, there is a question mark over the extent to which the inclusion of oil and gas output is entirely meaningful within the calculation of Scotland's GDP and hence GS, particularly when government size is as fixed as it appears in Scotland and whereas oil and gas are wasting assets whose management and resultant economic benefit is skewed towards priorities that exist to the south of our border.

Consequently whilst we do accept that GS is not quite as big as some commentators claim, it is still far bigger than it should be in terms of the potential for economic well-being. It should

[1] Throughout this book, unless otherwise stated, we use 2002/3 as the year of fiscal reference. During that year the oil price averaged around $25 a barrel. While we write this the official 2003/4 fiscal statistics have been published. These figures show an ongoing decline in the physcal well-being of Scotland with government size escalating out of control to the extent that the government is in panic mode as it scrambles to spend every last penny.

be noted that the quality of information available on the Scottish economy is lamentable (a deliberate slight to the nation from the UK Government, not least because it makes the whole business of our financial situation opaque and therefore hard to understand which benefits the continuation of an unfair and unproductive union). But even accepting such a difficulty there is no getting round the fact that Scotland has, at present, a considerable problem and it needs to find a way through it.

That problem can be seen by putting these figures into a historical perspective. The GS for today's developed nations has steadily increased throughout the industrial age from 11% in 1870 to 18% (1920), 22% (1937), 28% (1960) and eventually to 43% (1980) leveling off at about 45% in the 1990s. There is substantial variation between industrialised countries ranging, in the year 1996, from 33.3% and 34.7% for USA and New Zealand to 54.5% and 64.7% for France and Sweden.

The rapid increase in GS in the 1960s and 1970s led economists to examine the impact this might be having on economic growth. Professor Gerald Scully of the University of Texas produced an economic model known as the Scully curve which plotted the relationship. An example of this relationship is illustrated overleaf, and gives a graphic presentation of growth data for the OECD countries in the period 1960-1996, grouped according to Government Size, expressed as a percentage of GDP. The graph shows that initially increasing government expenditure produces steadily increasing economic growth until there is reached what is called the 'point of optimum return' between 15% and 20% GS. Thereafter, if government expenditure goes on increasing, the curve drops rapidly indicating a negative effect on the growth rate.

In our speculation of what occurs between 0% GS and 18% GS (dotted line) we have chosen to assume zero growth for zero government and to maximise the average annual growth at about 8% per annum. However, as we well know in some emerging countries, and particularly China, average annual growth rates as high as 10% have been achieved. Certainly the range from 30% GS to 10% GS is one of rapid change and spectacular growth and is worthy of closer scrutiny by the world's economists.

This relationship is very similar to that illustrated by the better

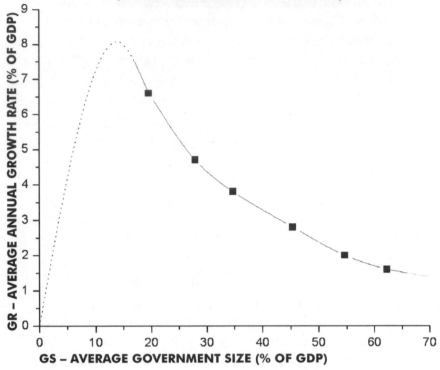

**GRAPHICAL PRESENTATION OF DATA FROM
US JOINT ECONOMIC COMMITTEE STUDY APRIL 1998
(OECD COUNTRIES 1960–1996)**

known 'Laffer curve' of which much has been made by the SNP. That charts the link between government revenue and taxation rates and shows that after the point of optimum return, increased taxation produces lower revenue growth. It has been used as an argument for reducing business taxation in particular. However, a focus on optimising corporate tax returns using Laffer as a guide may have been a distraction which evaded a more obvious question – why have corporate taxes at all? We shall return to that question later.

Scully went on to apply his model to historical USA economic data for the period 1949 to 1989 concluding that the GS which maximised growth was about 22%. Later he carried out a similar study on data for New Zealand concluding that the optimum GS in that country was about 20%.

Of course the optimum GS will vary from country to country depending on the different nature of their economies but subsequent work by Scully, looking at over 100 nations, has demonstrated that the average optimum GS is 19.3%. Others doing similar work in a range of different places have reached similar conclusions, and all those conclusion show that GS levels significantly lower than the prevailing norm are required to maximise economic potential.

Another comparative study by Tanzi and Schuknecht compared the annual GDP growth of countries with big government (>50%GS), medium government (40% to 50% GS), small government (<40% GS) and newly industrialised countries (approx. 19% GS) finding average growth rates of 2.0%, 2.6%, 2.5% and 6.2% respectively. They went on to suggest a GS of 30% as a useful benchmark target for industrialised countries whilst Folster and Henrekson conclude that a 10% increase in GS is associated with a decrease in the economic growth rate of between 0.7 and 0.8 percentage points per annum.

A 10% increase in Governemnt Size is associated with a decrease in the economic growth rate of between 0.7 and 0.8 percentage points.

In 1998 the Joint Economic Committee of the USA Senate and House of Congress commissioned three of the country's leading economists to conduct a study of GS entitled *The Size and Functions of Government and Economic Growth*. The following excerpts from their conclusions fully support the positions of Scully *et al.*

> Government provision of both (a) a legal and physical infrastructure for the operation of a market economy and (b) a limited set of public goods can provide a framework conductive for economic growth. However, as governments move beyond these core functions, they will adversely affect economic growth because of (a) the disincentive effects of higher taxes, (b) diminishing returns as governments undertake activities for which they are ill-suited, and (c) an interference with the wealth creation process, because governments are not as good as markets at adjusting to changing circumstances and finding innovative new ways of increasing the value of resources.

It goes on:

> An empirical analysis of the data from 23 OECD countries shows a strong negative relationship between both (a) the size of government and GDP growth and (b) increases in government expenditures and GDP growth. A 10 percentage point increase in government expenditures as a

share of GDP is associated with approximately a one percentage point decline in the growth rate of real GDP. An analysis of a larger set of 60 countries reinforces the conclusions reached by analyzing OECD countries. After adjustment for cross-country differences in the security of property rights, inflation, education, and investment, higher levels of government spending as a percentage of GDP exert a strong negative impact on GDP growth.

And it concludes:

The five fastest-growing economies in the world from 1980 to 1995 had total government expenditures as a percentage of GDP averaging 20.1 percent, which is less than half the average of OECD countries.

Reducing government size also lowers the unemployment rate.

This evidence is solid and wide-ranging. It should serve as a wake up call to Scotland.

One of the wonders of the information age is the ease with which huge and diverse sources of information can be processed and analysed to arrive at conclusions which even a generation ago would have been beyond our reach. In our own area of present study never a month goes by but that this process of modern enlightenment brings to the fore new thinking on the factors that both help and hinder the economic well-being of nations. Unfortunately the vast majority of politicians seem unaware of this revolution and consequently remain stuck in industrial age analysis and ideologies. In this vein and as an addition to the work of Scully *et al* we would like to briefly mention the work of Abrams and others.

Reducing government size does not just boost the growth rate; it also lowers the unemployment rate which is of course a matter of immediate concern to most of our fellow citizens. In 1997 Professor Burton Abrams of the University of Delaware after studying data for the G7 and then a larger group of twenty OECD countries established a direct relationship between GS and unemployment rate with a 1 percentage point decrease in GS accounting for about a 0.33 percentage point decrease in the unemployment rate. This relationship has become known as the Abrams curve.

Dimitris Christopoulos *et al* from Panteion University, Athens carried out a similar study on data from EU countries and agreed with Abrams' findings, concluding that:

> . . . if government spending as a percentage of GDP
> increases by 5% then the unemployment rises, *ceteris paribus*,
> by 2.45%.

Horst Feldmann from the University of Bath studied data from nineteen individual countries and expanded the exercise to include specific employment groups and particular functions and actions of government. His conclusions are, given the teachings of Adam Smith, not surprising but nonetheless startling if viewed through the prism of modern Scottish political dialogue. He states that:

> • Our results indicate that as the size of government
> grows the unemployment rate increases among the total
> labour force *and particularly* among women and among
> the low skilled. Long term unemployment is likely to
> increase as well.

> • The more important the role of the state-owned
> enterprises in the economy and the larger the share of
> government investments in total investment – the higher is
> unemployment among the total labour force as well as
> among women and the low skilled and the larger is the
> share of long term unemployed among the unemployed.

> • The higher the top marginal income rate and the lower
> the minimum threshold level at which it applies, the higher
> is unemployment among the overall labour force as well as
> among women and the low skilled.

These findings directly and obviously contradict many of the accepted economic practices and policies in Scotland today. They are of particularly crucial relevance to the issues presented by long term unemployment amongst the low skilled and amongst women and young people and consequently they are of vital importance in Labour's own heartlands. Yet no Scottish politician seems even to have discovered this information, far less acted upon it.

Our growth rate averaged 1.6% for the period 1973 to 2001, one of the lowest in the western world suggesting an average GS of over 60% during this time. GS is highly unlikely to have decreased since 2001 – in fact it almost certainly has risen. However, as we have already suggested, and as we will outline in more detail later not all of Scotland's growth rate woes may be due to its GS and its GS, although high, may not be as high as at first appears.

Nonetheless, no matter the other difficulties and issues, including Westminster neglect and historic inequalities, it is more than likely that Scotland's lower GDP and lower economic growth is *primarily* a product of the fact that our government is too large and has been getting larger – most recently thanks to the Barnett formula – at a quicker rate than that south of the border. And because that process is sustained and indeed accelerated by the Barnett formula, it is likely that Barnett, far from starving Scotland to death as is often asserted, is actually fattening us to the point of dangerous obesity. Bizarre as the thought may be, could the UK actually be killing us by kindness?

Another example can be found in Ireland. Ireland's GS has fallen from 51% in 1986, through 41% in 1990 to a current level of less than 35%. At the same time Ireland's economic growth rate has steadily picked up, and now vastly outpaces ours. This, in our analysis, would seem to be an entirely predictable result for the Celtic Tiger has been fueled not by EU handouts (the popular and very dismissive British reaction to Irish economic success) nor by the sensible lowering of corporation tax and increased expenditure on education. In fact economic success has largely come from government restraint and by sensible development of natural resources. Lower government size has led to higher growth, which in turn has helped to produce a virtuous circle of growing economic prosperity.

There is nothing mystical about all this and there is no reason at all why an independent Scotland could not emulate such an example. We can do so by developing a simple plan of action which substitutes earnings from our own oil and gas revenues for the poison of the Barnett formula, whilst cutting government size, reducing taxation and developing our own natural talents and resources. But if we do go down that route we must throw away the comfort blanket of expecting everything to be delivered by the state. We must also learn once more to apply the prudence in fiscal matters for which we have a worldwide reputation, but which we seem to have neglected to cultivate at home in recent years.

The very considerable increase in the size of government in the industrialised world between 1960 and 1980 was due to the rapid increase in areas of government expenditure such as social welfare and income subsidisation. This was justified on the basis that it would result in significant improvements in the well-being of the population and hence would indirectly benefit the GDP. No population would wish to give up those things if it meant a fall in the standard of living and one of the perpetual arguments against limiting government size (indeed an argument that is used to keep on increasing GS) is that any attempt at reduction will hit individual citizens and in particularly the needy, very hard.

> We must learn to apply the prudence in fiscal matters for which we have a worldwide reputation.

It is vital to say at the outset, and to go on saying, that this assertion is simply not true and that the evidence shows it not to be true. Tanzi and Schuknecht also studied this relationship and concluded:

> . . . countries with small governments generally do not show worse indicators of social and economic well-being than countries with big government – and often they achieve an even better standard.

Scully also came to the conclusion that there was little or no difference in social outcomes among countries with GSs of less than 40% and those with GSs greater than 50%.

In fact Adam Smith may have, as ever in matters of economics and their effect on individuals and populations, got to this conclusion before anyone else. For he observed more than two centuries ago:

> . . . in the progressive state, while the society is advancing to the further acquisition, rather than when it has acquired its full complement of riches, that the conditions of the great body of the people seems to be the happiest and the most comfortable. It is hard in the stationary, and miserable in the declining state.

Scotland today is definitely in the stationary, and perhaps is already in the declining state and consequently is discontented and, indeed, at times 'miserable'. Only by encouraging new growth can we re-discover new goals and new ambitions.

Moreover if government size can be reduced without damaging in any way the social indicators which we use to signify our level of development and our concern for our fellow human beings, then we owe it to a world of scarce resources that we make such reductions. In short we should do it to stop wasting money for we may well have been paying a much higher price to deliver to those in real need than we had to, or should have been. That in time should lead to more resources for the needy, not less.

If government size can be reduced without damaging in any way the social indicators . . . then we owe it to a world of scarce resources that we make such reductions.

This is not magic or sophistry. One of the inevitable outcomes of lowering GS is that the resulting acceleration in growth rate *in itself* leads to a much larger GDP. A smaller slice of the pie taken by government results over time, given natural growth which is then accelerated by a reduction in GS, in a much bigger pie. So even if the government keeps its percentage share the same year on year – in fact even if it decreases it – it is more than possible that actual numerical size of that percentage continues to grow. Paradoxically less government and a low GS leads, in fairly short order, to more resources for any government wise enough to follow this route.

Let us, however, enter a word of caution about the Scottish situation. We are convinced that reducing GS is the most significant step we can take to create a Scottish economy capable of succeeding in the modern world and there is no doubt that a downward trend in GS will result in increasing GDP growth rates. However, what is equally clear is the likelihood that the increase in GDP growth rate may not be the same for all countries at a given GS value, particularly if there is a significant deviation from the average economic mix. In the Scottish context with oil and gas, a wasting asset, apparently forming 21% of the GDP, we must be particularly careful not to be complacent even if we were to achieve, with some ease, lower GS values.

So let us look again at our current GS – 50% without the oil and gas statistics or around 39% with them included. Given recent Scottish percentage economic growth in the region of less than two points rather than an expected three it would appear that our GS *must be* significantly higher than 39%. This would tend to indicate that the spin-off effects of oil and gas to the Scottish economy are in fact not overly significant and that perhaps the oil and gas component of our GDP should be partly discounted, as we indicated earlier.[2] We have accordingly determined that a discount of about 29% of the industry's total production income is probably appropriate, although this is clearly an area requiring further study particularly as it raises the question of whether or not Scotland is receiving its fair share of the industry's activities. Applying our 29% discount to the 2002-2003 data with an expenditure of £40.9 billion and a GDP of £99.1 billion, comprising £82 billion from the conventional economy and £17.1 billion from the oil and gas economy, we compute a GS for Scotland of 41.3%, about average for the western world. We must admit to being surprised by this conclusion for like many others we had assumed that Scotland's low growth rate was due in the greatest part to exceptional government obesity. In reality we appear to be unfit, and need some intensive training, but we are not as yet in a terminal state – although we are moving that way and perhaps rapidly given the excessive increases in government expenditure over the past four years.

---

[2] The figure of 90% is commonly used by the SNP to quantify the geographic portion of North Sea oil production that would be applicable to an independent Scotland – a figure which is underpinned by domestic and international law and with which we agree. However it is vitally important to realise that geographic boundaries (which govern taxation and legal issues) and economic impact are not necessarily the same, particularly as control of the industry has been exercised from Westminster and therefore its impact on the economy has been skewed in favour of the south. This is borne out by an examination of UK oil industry publications which show that only 71% of direct industry jobs are actually located in Scotland and that only 71% of direct GVA occurs in Scotland versus the 90% of production within Scottish boundaries. It is clear that this gap of 19% must be accounted for by a disproportionate amount of direct production administrative and support services being performed outwith Scotland. This contention is supported by the fact that only 40% of the industry's UK headquarters are located in Scotland. In addition statistics also indicate that the indirect and induced economic impact of North Sea Oil (figures already presumably included in Scottish GDP) is also only a shocking 40%. Thus it is apparent that the direct economic impact of the industry on Scotland's GDP is not 90% as used by the SNP but **at most** 71% of the industry's total production income. Of course if this is so, then it is, *inter alia,* a very poor reflection on how our politicians have looked after our interests over the last 30 years. However, in fairness to the SNP it is more than likely that an independent Scotland would be in a strong position to take actions which would decrease the 19% disparity in economic activity.

Before we go any further we should consider the future of oil and gas revenues, as they will have a strong impact on our plans for Scotland and overcoming the three challenges that face us. Major oil field production traditionally follows a classical bell curve of ascending production rates for a period of twenty to thirty years followed by declining production rates for a similar period. Recent production data from the North Sea shows that production peaked about 1999 and that we are starting on the downward leg of the bell curve as illustrated in the following diagram. Since 1999 production has been declining at about 5% per annum to a production rate of about 3.5 million barrels (equivalent) per day. The industry expects to reduce this decline rate to about 2.5% per annum to a production rate of 3.0 million barrels per day by 2010 after which it will probably decline rapidly to a production rate of about 1.7 million barrels per day by 2015, including expected further discoveries.

The economic strength of our oil and gas industry is not just a function of production rates. It is also very much affected by variations in the commodity prices. This has been apparent in recent years where rising energy prices have resulted in rising total incomes and tax revenues despite lower production rates and unfavorable exchange rates. In other words we are still on the ascending leg of the tax revenue bell curve though on the downward leg of the production one. The question for Scotland is how much time do we have before we start on the downward road to eventual oil and gas tax revenue oblivion.[3]

We would also want, of course, to be protected as far as possible from the volatility of the oil price and currency markets. In so far as any country is able to take such steps we should have

---

[3] There are three areas in which we may obtain temporary relief. The first and within our control is oil and gas taxation rates. As oil fields decline so does capital and exploration expenditure as companies struggle to maintain profit. Never far away is the grim reaper, the Chancellor of the Exchequer, who inevitably raises taxes to get his last pound of flesh from the dying corpse. Our approach would be different for we would treat the oil and gas industry as our partners, as they surely are, and we would maintain a close relationship with regard to their current and future plans. At present times with higher oil prices politicians are strongly tempted to increase taxation rates on the companies so called windfall profits. Ever conscious of where we are on the bell curve and if appropriate at the time we would take the opposite position and offer them a taxation rebate for increased

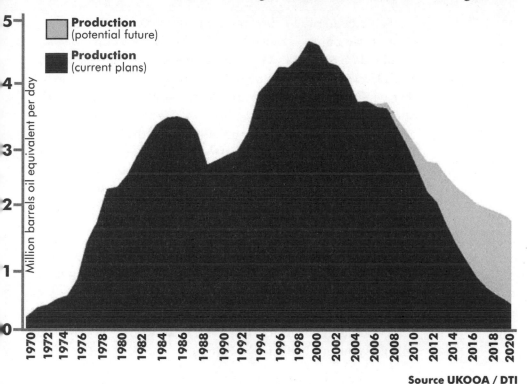

Source UKOOA / DTI

in place a policy which would require oil companies to sell a significant portion of their production forward on long term contracts and hedge against currency variations, thus smoothing the tax revenues over time. We would also insist that, all things being equal, and having satisfied Scotland's requirements, our oil and gas production should first and foremost be sold to our friends in the south. Both those initiatives have never featured in nationalist rhetoric about oil, and they should, particularly as oil is becoming a key political issue in Scotland again.

---

exploration expenditure. The second area of relief may continue to be increasing commodity prices. There is an increasing body of opinion which holds that we are at the zenith of the bell curve for worldwide oil and gas production and that the recent rises in prices are the beginning of a long-term trend as world supplies slowly decline. That this should coincide with the likely top of the North Sea production bell curve would be fortuitous for Scotland. A third means by which the industry could significantly boost our economy would be by the return of outsourced oil and gas activities from south of the border. There is in fact a fourth factor which could transform our offshore energy production – the use of our redundant oil and gas facilities and pipelines to gasify and recover our vast offshore coal reserves. We will have more to say on this topic later in this book.

So accepting the issues with oil and with our dependence upon it, we can then move forward and ask precisely how we could reduce Scotland's GS from somewhere about 41% to say 33%. However, before doing we have to digress for it is apparent that while such a reduction in GS would increase our growth rate (GR) by about 1%, more has to be done. Scotland, for its government size, consistently underperforms the OECD GR by from 1% to 1.5%. Thus, we have to find an improvement in our GR of at least 1% from other sources, in addition to the 1% from GS reduction, if we are to join Ireland with a GR of 4% or better.

It is clear that there are major structural weaknesses in Scotland's economy which are contributing to our poor perform-ance and exacerbating the difficulties created by a high GS. It is our belief that the two areas which account for this weakness are our membership of the UK (the Union Factor) and old fashioned 'state socialism' which remains central to Scottish governance (the Government Inefficiency Factor).

Let us consider these matters in more detail and in particular their actual effect. While Scotland's GR is 1% (or more) lower than it should be given its government size it also consistently underperforms the UK's GR by at least 0.5% – the Union factor. The remaining 0.5% or more we attribute to the effect of 'state socialism' on the functions of government, a matter we will deal with shortly. So why is the Union detrimental to Scotland's growth rate?

First and foremost all of the macro economic levers of power, currency exchange rates, interest rates, money supply, corporate tax rates and personal tax rates (we don't consider the 3% variance allowed to Holyrood to be materially significant) are controlled and set by Westminster. Undoubtedly, and quite rightly, these levers of economic power are used to enhance the growth rate of the UK for the greater good and for the area of greatest population and economic activity – England and particularly the south of England. It is highly unlikely that parameters so set will optimise a minor, peripheral and markedly different economy such as that of Scotland. Even if the deviation from the optimum is only marginal it will over time have a collective significance. England is Scotland's largest trading partner and it is inevitable that in such trade the macro economic parameters which will maximise

England's performance are unlikely to maximise that of Scotland.

Earlier we suggested that Scotland should have its own currency, initially tied to the pound with perhaps a nominal devaluation to redress some of the aforementioned imbalances and help our export trade with England. Any such move would require considerable forethought and no degree of devaluation could be arbitrarily chosen. Of course one option would be to maintain par value with the pound. But we also accept that this will leave interest rates and money supply still under Union control – a matter which should be rectified in due course, when Scotland has established a strong and demonstrably well-managed economy, by floating the Scottish unit of currency.

The Union factor affects all aspects of Scotland's national life. Scotland's largest industry, the oil and gas industry, which accounts for about 20% of Scotland's GDP is directly controlled by Westminster. The high consumpion of oil and gas by the larger England means that North Sea production is rapidly reaching a point where it is no longer able to meet their needs. Therefore, policies aimed at boosting short term production to the detriment of the longer term are prevalent as are tax gouging policies which reduce the ability of the industry to invest in long term exploration and development. On the other hand, Scotland, because of its small consumption level but greater reliance on the industry for its economic well-being and taxation revenue (as we will propose) will inevitably require very different policies to meet its needs – for example policies such as forward selling to alleviate price fluctuations and tax incentives to favour long term exploration and development. In other areas of energy we would also deviate from UK policies and prioritise the development of our massive tidal power potential and huge offshore coal reserves as discussed later.

The Union factor is dominant in our relationship with the EU, which is controlled by Westminster. In this area Scotland would have undoubtedly taken very different positions in areas such as fisheries and agriculture. We would have most certainly not given up control of our fishing grounds which were effectively sold off in exchange for lower UK contributions to the EU.

In the area of defence there is an economic impact from the Union factor as well, for here we find that Scotland is required by its membership of the UK to spend 2.7% of its GDP on defence – an exceptionally high level for a nation of Scotland's size. It is a legacy of the empire and the UK's desire to maintain a level of importance in the world which is quite frankly beyond its means. The Scots have repeatedly shown that they are opposed to the costly nuclear deterrent and it is extremely unlikely that given a choice they would spend 2.7% of their GDP on defence – it is more likely that they would emulate Ireland (0.7%) or New Zealand (1.1%). We believe that Scotland should be able to control the cost of its defence force even within the Union by putting Scotland's military forces under Holyrood's cost control but for military purposes under a joint UK military command.

The consequences of the Union contribute to a negative effect on Scotland's growth rate.

These and many other consequences of the Union, mentioned elsewhere in this book, contribute to a negative effect on Scotland's GR versus that of the UK. These are inherent but now quite obvious structural effects which result in the Scottish GR being persistently and consistently at least 0.5% lower than that of the UK – a loss of £500 million every year to the wealth of Scots.

The economic truth is that the Union, which once served Scotland's trade so well, is now a millstone round our necks. The advantages of Empire are long gone. We are, in a sense, the last colony, with our assets being openly pillaged in true colonial fashion. But we have only ourselves to blame for we are too afraid to seek the autonomy which other countries demanded, struggled for and won. In fairness to Westminster, though, all we would have to do is to decide and then negotiate.

However we seem to wish to cling to the notion that some-how, in some mysterious way, there are some undefinable advantages in being a member of this now less than glorious Union though in reality the only advantages are for those of our exported politicians who seek to parade on a larger stage. The price which we pay for their delusions of grandeur is a heavy one and it is surely time for our people to call them home, for it is our people who are paying the bill.

An argument consistently put forward in favour of the Union, indeed the only argument of serious economic consequence, is the contention that independence would threaten Scotland's export trade with England, reportedly 50% of our total trade, and that such an occurrence would somehow be to Scotland's detriment. In this regard it is worth observing that in the 1950s 90% of Ireland's export trade was with the UK but by the end of the 1990s, and its transformation into an economic powerhouse, its export trade with the UK had shrunk to about 20%. In fact Ireland has gone from having a large trade surplus with the UK to a large trade deficit yet it has prospered beyond belief and has left the UK trailing in its economic wake.

Consequently we would suggest that it is not trade *per se* that is important but rather the profitability of such trade. The problem with long established trade such as that between Scotland and England is that over time profit margins tend to get squeezed and then accepted in the interests of trade continuity. Continuity becomes dependency which begets risk aversion which precludes the search for alternative and more lucrative trade destinations. What Ireland has achieved by such a huge diversification of its export trade could also be achieved by Scotland, should Scotland desire to do so, regardless of whether or not it seeks to increase its profit margin *vis a vis* England by adjusting its currency as we suggested earlier. In Scotland's case such a move would involve seeking to expand our export and import trade horizons to encompass all of the world and particularly the far east.

The solution to the Union factor is, quite obviously, independence for Scotland. However, we are very much aware that some further time may be needed before the majority of our fellow Scots are fully ready to take that step. What we may need, therefore, is Devolution Stage Two, a necessary staging post on the way to the future.

Some might call such a staging post a New Union; a constitutional watering station which allows Scots to continue to move forward, works as a means of persuading those who are still reluctant and opens up new opportunities by removing the economic disadvantages of the 'Old Union'. It would also be a dynamic place where Scotland could continue to prepare itself for full independence and start to regain its international voice.

Devolution Stage Two, or the New Union, is of course not an essential step but for many Scots, who have a preference for careful change and a predilection for cautious adaptation, it may be a desirable way to proceed. And given our strong desire for independence, it seems us that if we have to move forward in this way, it would be better to do so and to take our more timid fellow Scots with us, rather than to fail to move at all, a point that was made by the Convener of the Independence Convention, Murray Ritchie, in an article in the *Scotsman* in July 2006. We are sure that were such a New Union to come about, it would not hinder, but underpin and strengthen, Scotland's continued constitutional journey.

In such a New Union all of the matters reserved to Westminster would be devolved to Holyrood apart from foreign affairs (though, as with Flanders and to an even greater extent, the Faroe Islands, certain parts of the foreign affairs realm, including trade matters would be in Scottish control) and military command. We would also assume responsibility for our share of the UK debt and other liabilities and we would take over all of the UK assets located within our onshore and offshore geographic boundaries. These matters and the monarchy would be what constitutes our shared responsibilities and these alone. Temporarily at least our Westminster MPs would be incorporated into the Scottish Parliament based fully on a system of proportional representation as we start to put in place a new participatory democracy.

A 'New Union' would not hinder but strengthen Scotland's continued constitutional journey.

We accept that tensions with regard to the remaining matters of foreign affairs and defence could be problematic, particularly given the strong Scottish revulsion at the invasion of Iraq in 2003 and Scottish outrage at the use of Prestwick airport for shipping American munitions to Israel during the Lebanon conflict of July 2006. But a suitable power of veto, the protection of our rights by the use of financial control and constructive participation in the administrative and command functions of diplomacy and military deployment should provide necessary safeguards. Most importantly our economic powers would be absolute and we would then be able to move forward to the first stage of full independent economic life by launching our currency tied to the pound with an appropriate level of devaluation if that was deemed necessary. We would also be able to begin to adjust our relationships, including that with the EU. In that regard we should, as a priority, seek to recover control of our fisheries and to negotiate the appropriate parameters for our involvement with the EU, again dictated by the people.

We contend that all such changes and development would be beneficial, and are possible – if we agree to make them our goals. But nothing will happen if we have no goals!

Let us now consider that third factor which stands in the way of our economic growth, the Government Inefficiency Factor. In the days before Margaret Thatcher we would have been considering a fourth detraction to economic growth in the form of militant trade unionism and a fifth factor in the form of nationalised industries. These are now thankfully behind us with most trades unions now acting as responsible members of the community and with the nationalised industries now firmly returned to the competitive world of capitalism. All attempts to turn those clocks back have so far been sensibly resisted, and should continue to be resisted.

However, the Tories failed to follow through on their initial promise to reduce government size and surprisingly made no attempt to apply the principles of capitalism to the business of government. In fact it took New Labour to begin to question the inefficiencies of government operations and expenditures. Unfortunately such efforts remain in their infancy and with the inevitable passing of Tony Blair and a resurgence of Old Labour, the matter looks destined to be taken little further no matter the government in power at Westminster. Needless to say, apart from a few token statements, improving government efficiency is also low on the agenda at Holyrood.

Government inefficiency in Scotland and in Westminster has its roots in the 'state socialism' of the thirties, forties and fifties. That is now seen by most to have been a period during which substantial social progress was made but – such progress having been made – when it continued to be a major factor in government in the sixties and therafter it began a drag on efficiency and a burden on the taxpayer. It also produced no significant new social progress – in fact money that could have been used for that purpose was wasted.

Although such attitudes were driven from the private sector during the 1980s and although the worst types of nationalisation were eradicated, some of the malaise has remained deeply rooted in government and it is particularly tenacious at Holyrood.

The belief that government should not only supply funds for

government services but should also manage and carry out such services (actions for which government is clearly not suited and which being free of competition may be inherently wasteful and inefficient) strongly pervades Scottish public life. Our so-called mixed economy is in effect the application of capitalism to the private sector economy and that of old-fashioned 'state socialism' to the business of government. Not one political party, the Tories included, makes any attempt to address this matter and often all the parties at grassroots and at parliamentary level vie with each other to flaunt their 'statist' credentials. We believe, however, that it is time to have done with this attitude and to openly bring the principles of capitalism to the business of government at every level – including that of the ubiquitous but undemocratic quango.

There is nothing new in such a proposal for most of the Scandinavian countries, long considered the epitome of 'state socialism' because of their relatively large GS, in fact make every effort to ensure that all government expenditures are made in a competitive environment. In fact, unlike Scotland, these countries have growth rates in excess of the OECD average for their particular GS levels, achievements which may also be attributable to lower corporation tax rates and high expenditure on R&D, steps which we will later advocate for Scotland.

The most obvious area where large sums of money are spent and managed by government with no competition is the NHS. Among others are the multitude of quangos which are even further removed from parliamentary scrutiny.

Government inefficiency takes many other forms: redundant programmes which are perpetuated because their purpose is never questioned; universality which has led to the repeated expenditure of large sums of money on causes and people which clearly do not need it; the practice of making large settlements with public sector unions, including those representing doctors and teachers without securing improvements in productivity and changes to restrictive working practices. We could go on almost *ad infinitum* but the point is made, we think. Government inefficiencies abound and they are nearly always associated with this old-fashioned attitude and ethos which permeates every nook and cranny of Scotland's public services.

The challenge is to replace this ethos with one in which the need as well as the method of all expenditure is being constantly questioned and modified to maximise the return for our citizens. A simple credo might well sharpen the mind when deciding on government activity, e.g. 'let government be the customer and let every job and task of government, however lowly or however complex – wherever possible – be carried out in some form of competition by the private sector.' This may seem a tall order given the history of government in Scotland but if Scotland is to progress and meet the challenges of world competition it is a battle which must be started and which must always be kept in mind, even if never completed.

We shall return to the detail of governmental programmes in the next chapter and make some more suggestions for change but it is clear from all the foregoing that, in economic terms, Scotland is presently walking through the doors of the 'Last Chance Saloon'. We can expect at the most a further ten years of substantial, sustainable domestic oil and gas revenues. That is ten years in which to use such revenues to cut our government down to size and to transform our general economy to a highly competitive model fit to thrive in the era of globalisation. If we remain in the UK then the bell is also tolling, for the Barnett largesse will eventually come to an end as the squeeze from population growth divergence and other aspects of the formula begin to bite into our revenues. In addition there remains an ever-present threat of a political revolt against Barnett from south of the border. Of course if Barnett is really damaging the situation that would be no bad thing, except that the damage comes from the way the formula works, not just from the money. To lose the money and yet not have our own resources to fall back on would be hard and would lead to hard times.

> There remains an ever-present threat of a political revolt against Barnett from south of the border.

There is no doubt that we have some huge opportunities as well as some huge potential difficulties. So we would argue that the time has come to play to our strengths and seize those opportunities before they disappear forever. To do that we need to cast aside partisan politics and look to the common good, for the window of opportunity that we presently look through has been there for thirty years, and yet we have not only done nothing to stop merely observing, but we have actually chosen to be passive onlookers as our life chances and life blood has been taken away, and used by others for their benefit.

Now is the time to devise and accept a programme that can change our country and change it utterly and for ever. Ten years is not a long time to do that, so we must get started very promptly. We of course favour a programme which will lead to an independent Scotland. However, a devolved Holyrood with full fiscal control, including our own currency, can implement all of this programme and still ensure that Scotland and her citizens benefit from it.

We might start by holding a new 'Convention' to plan what could be called as we proposed earlier 'Devolution Stage Two' or the 'New Union'. This convention would seek to devise a plan

Now is the time to devise and accept a programme that can change our country utterly and for ever.

which could combine nationalist ambition with the caution shown by those who are not yet convinced but who know that full economic powers for our present Parliament are essential. It would be better if that convention were not dominated by established politicians, and we would want to see Scottish business strongly within it although we are most attracted to the type of 'Citizens Convention' which was used in the Canadian province of British Columbia to recommend a system of proportional voting and which we have already referred to on several occasions. We already envisage a role for such a Convention in democratic terms, and we will come come back to this in our final chapter and expand its remit.

However at present politicians will have to start the ball rolling and we are encouraged that Scottish Labour and their Liberal partners have taken a few faltering steps along the route of fiscal autonomy and the welcoming of a full market economy, even if as yet those steps are few and feeble. We would encourage some firmer sense of direction, given the urgency of the situation. We are however more surprised that the Conservative Party in Scotland has been so lukewarm, for it should be meat and drink to them given their belief in free markets.

The Tories' problem is that their Unionist ideology is overcoming their free market common sense. Of course there is always something wrong when ideology overcomes freedom of thought, despite the evidence presented and that tension continues to hold the Tories back and make their Scottish pronouncements less than convincing.

In this case the evidence is overwhelmingly in favour of economic powers being exercised in Scotland and moreover being exercised in a radical way. Consequently the ultimate test for all our politicians is whether or not they have the courage to stand up and demand from their colleagues in Westminster what is best for Scotland, even if that is not best for Westminster or the narrow interests of their UK parties. A united front that sought and won the powers which we need now in Scotland would restore more faith in Scottish democracy than a hundred gimmicks from showboating politicians keen on winning votes but clueless about winning real economic prosperity for voters.

However, let us assume that we could put our prejudices aside and agree on a progressive constitutional stance – say a move to the 'New Union' proposal as an initial step. Let us now turn our attention as to how over a period of say, four years, we could, by combating the Union factor and Government Inefficiency factor in the manner outlined in this and the preceding chapters and by purposively reducing GS, transform Scotland to a tiger economy in the Irish mould. Our proposals in this regard and the financial consequences are summarised in tabular form in Appendix A using the actual Scottish Executive government and expenditure figures for 2002-03 as our reference point – the latest real and verifiable government figures available at the time of writing.

> We could transform Scotland to a tiger economy in the Irish mould.

Looking at the figures for the 'Old Union' Scotland's real annual tax receipts are about £31.6 billion, excluding our share of North Sea oil revenues. The figure of £31.6 billion, set against the overall Scottish budget of £40.9 billion leaves a massive deficit of £9.3 billion, financed by Westminster (or so Westminster claims) under the Barnett formula and which is of course regularly seized on by Unionist economists and economic Unionists to demonstrate 'what a poor wee country we would be' if we became a normal independent nation.

However, £2.6 billion of this deficit is in fact Scotland's share of the UK's borrowings for this year. Thus the real contribution from Barnett is £6.7 billion. However on the establishment of the 'New Union' arrangements, with the inclusion of oil and gas revenues of £4.55 billion, our borrowings are reduced to £4.75 billion, only £2.15 billion more than would have been the case in the Old Union. Nevertheless, it is too high so let us see how we can reduce this deficit or indeed turn it into a surplus as we transform our economy over the next four years.

Once the powers are in place, we would start with what is essentially a seven-pronged approach to reducing government size and boosting growth rate.

Those seven prongs would be:

- freezing and cutting government expenditures including the freezing of recruitment by government and quangos

- boosting business growth by reducing corporate and personal taxes

- countering the negative Union factor

- improving government efficiency by exposure to the free market economy

- building the number of economically active citizens by facilitating the transfer of civil servants (and potential civil servants) to the private sector as well as by boosting immigration

- increasing investment in R&D and education

- development of our neglected natural resources.

Our programme –
call it a
programme of
national
recovery –
would need to
be carried out
progressively
over a four year
period.

We accept that negotiating such an approach, particularly across parties, would be very difficult. But as we believe that ideas and thinking about our future need to be radical and far-reaching, in order to respond to the great need for change that now exists, we hope that the effort can and will be made at some not too distant future date. To help that we offer our own plan, as a contribution to the debate as well as, perhaps, as an indication of what is possible and could be achieved, with will, effort and optimism.

Our programme – call it a programme of national recovery – would need to be carried out progressively over the four year period. We acknowledge that this would be a period of limited austerity, though perhaps more for those used to the perks of government than for the ordinary voter for as government size declined so growth would accelerate in the private sector.

The targets we would wish to achieve by the end of the four

years would be to reduce government spending by £4.0 billion per annum offset by additional spending of £2.2 billion per annum leading to a balanced budget of £39.1 billion; a GDP of £121 billion; a GS of about 32%; a growth rate of 4% per annum and accelerating and a budget balanced or in excess. Some might throw up their hands in horror when confronted with these figures, and we would expect them also to prophesy doom and gloom if our ideas are followed and government is made smaller and more efficient. However we cannot but point out these targets are little different from what Ireland has already achieved, and achieved without the huge advantage of massive oil and gas reserves. Indeed if we don't have the courage and ambition to set ourselves such targets then we will be doomed to continued decline for our window of opportunity is slowly closing, and the threat to our well-being and prosperity which that implies will affect us all.

> We would be asking all parts of government to increase their economic efficiency by some 12% over four years.

Perhaps those who are most worried should recall again that 'family' of which Adam Smith spoke. They and he would have seen the problems we are experiencing today as inevitable, and they would also have seen as inevitable the remedies we are proposing, particularly the remedy of attempting to live within our means, whilst seeking to expand those means.

Our first and tough decision would also be one which they would have anticipated – the freezing of all government spending across all budgets for a period of four years. By so doing we can spread the difficulty evenly in this transitionary period although we will make recommendations for some exceptional cuts in areas outwith benefit-related and social spending which will bring Scotland's GS down even more rapidly than a budget freeze.

Of course there will be much lamenting and special pleading which will require a strong political nerve if it is to be resisted. In reality we would be asking all parts of government to look to their priorities and increase their economic efficiency by some 12% over a four year period, a not unreasonable request. Substantial savings in low priority areas could be used to maintain budgets in priority areas while adhering to the overall totals. It would be a period of great challenge for the government and its employees but it would be an opportunity for them to shine and become heroes leading the country to new economic heights!

We would note that civil servants will also be recipients of our proposed 25% reduction in income taxes (see later) which reduction would replace most and perhaps all of their losses from frozen salary increases.

The freeze in government spending should logically be accompanied by a freeze in government and quango recruitment. For once demographics will be working in our favour for as the ageing population retire the number of young people entering the workforce and hence available to replace them will be dramatically reduced. Our challenge during this period will be to employ in the private sector those young people desiring a fresh start and those civil servants desiring an invigorating and beneficial change, and ensuring that the new and expanded businesses exist to do just that, mobilised by the extra capital released from our proposed tax cuts.

Government trades unions may understandably be concerned about such changes for they will affect their membership numbers. However we suspect that both under a 'New Union' or devolution stage two, or under full independence, the vast majority of civil service redundancies are likely to occur south of the border as functions of government are transferred from Westminster to Holyrood. Such problems will test the leadership skills of our politicians, for they will have to hold firm to the programme and carry the unions with them in the greater interests of the common good.

We note that reorganising and/or reducing the size of the civil service is sometimes touted as a serious attempt to reduce GS. While we applaud any such moves to reduce government inefficiency unfortunately on their own they are unlikely to have a significant effect on GS unless accompanied by significant reductions in government programmes and taxation.

As an aside we would observe that while the obvious methods of providing for an ageing population are increased immigration and later retirement age, little or no attention has been given to a third and to us equally important solution – the crossover in time of large numbers of public sector employees to the wealth-producing private sector thus boosting the potential tax base available to provide for all government requirements including the ageing population. In other words whether we like it or not our demographics will force us to reduce government size and hence the number of government employees – so the sooner we face this challenge the better. Later we will suggest a pension plan which will also help in this regard.

In fact Scotland's existing expenditure of £40.9 billion is actually ripe for some immediate savings, which could be relatively painless. It would be prescriptive to list every possibility, and decisions on how to adjust spending need to be taken in the light of a full debate on national priorities. But a few things stand out as obvious. A non-nuclear small nation does not need to spend 2.7% of GDP on defence. A reduction in defence spending to the 1% level over the first two years of our period of reference is appropriate. This would save in the order of £1.5 billion and reduce our expenditure to £39.4 billion.

We will propose later the replacement of the current Enterprise Company structure with a Scottish Development Bank, based on models that have worked much better elsewhere and which will have greater long term effect on our economy. This decision is based on our philosophy of enterprise which leads us to reduce the tax and bureaucratic burden on business, but also leads us to reject the ill-targeted and often economically counterproductive handouts to business which has been the stuff of Scottish economic policy for too long. This will save £0.5 billion over the first two years offset by £0.1 billion reinvested in the development bank and the skills and learning portion of the present Enterprise Company activities which are worthwhile.

We will propose the replacement of the current Enterprise Companies with a Scottish Development Bank.

On the same theme we would follow the example of New Zealand and seek to eliminate – over the first four years of our budget – all subsidies to the agricultural, fishing and forestry industries, thus saving £0.7 billion.[4] In this regard we will be in step with the World Trade Organisation aims which seek to reduce subsidies and other barriers to trade, particularly in agriculture, in order to assist the struggling Third World economies. In addition we note that more people are employed in agriculture

---

[4] Whilst aware that there are many who argue for this step including figures in the Scottish farming and fishing industries, Michael Russell acknowledges that such subsidies are vital at this current stage in our economic and social development and supports the SNP policy of retaining and developing them, though a continuing debate is of course essential.

in New Zealand today than were employed during the time of high subsidies, and the growing evidence that subsidies to farmers are actually subsidies which fatten the profits of supermarkets whilst leaving the actual agricultural industry ever weaker and more fragile. We would expect to work with the farming and fishing organisations to achieve this aim, and to be able to maintain individual earnings at the end of it. In keeping with our interest in alternative energy the diversification of some of our agricultural land to the production of ethanol and biofuel crops is worthy of consideration. We are, of course, perfectly aware of how this aim will be presented by those who fear it but in fact many in these sectors stand to gain by such a move, over time, as does Scotland itself.

Scotland would achieve in two years a budget with borowing levels no different from the UK.

We note that even the current Executive's very modest efficiency savings have identified £1.5 billion, later reduced to £1.1 billion, to be taken out of present and planned spending. We have taken a figure of £1.4 billion over the first two years although as stated previously we can do a great deal better by having a clear philosophy underpinning what government should and should not do. Consequently we are already after two years at a reduced budget total of £37.2 billion. Yet none of the actions we are suggesting are so painful that they cannot be contemplated, nor yet so difficult that they cannot be sensitively managed and introduced over the four year term. But by taking these steps Scotland – with or without independence – would achieve in two years that which the UK government contends is impossible, namely a Scottish budget with borrowing levels no different from that of the UK and with oil and gas revenues little changed from those in 2002-03.

But we can do more. During this period of reducing GS and arresting the decline brought about by the Union and Government Inefficiency factors we would expect Scotland's growth rate and hence taxation receipts to start to accelerate from the current 2% (or less) level and ultimately reach a level of at least 4% per annum. This, along with the freeze in government spending, would result in the accumulation of excess tax receipts and we estimate those at around £1.1 billion per annum reaching £4.4 billion per annum by the end of the four years. That, and the accelerating oil and gas revenues in years three and four would give us considerable sums available to reduce taxation – thus returning the taxpayers' money to the taxpayer – and for additional expenditure in areas which would enhance our growth rate.[5]

The two fundamental ingredients of economic growth are people and capital. One of the real challenges in achieving increased economic growth is in converting a significant number of our civil servants into private sector wealth creators. So, in our period of prudence, as we reduce our civil service we must also stimulate the economy to provide them with alternative employment. To this end we will add that other ingredient – capital. We will do so by carrying out a comprehensive reduction of a wide range of taxes which have accumulated in such a way as to retard business growth, and which take revenue out of the consumer economy and reduce our national potential.

Capital and its sources are the lifeblood of an economy and to tax capital makes no sense as it results in an immediate and substantial brake on our economic growth. One means to address this problem is not just to cut corporation tax, as has already been correctly suggested by the SNP, but to go further by eliminating it entirely. This adds £2.1 billion per annum to the private sector economy but the purpose of so doing is not simply to hand over profits to shareholders. If companies chose not to re-invest such monies or to pay them out as dividends then they would be taxed in the usual way and perhaps at an even higher rate. Yet if re-investment took place, as it surely will, it would be money well-spent in terms of future benefit to the prosperity of Scotland and the creation of private sector jobs which are the only long term guarantee of greater prosperity and – as we have seen – of better health, increased happiness and improved life expectancy.

Continuing with the same theme it is logical to look at local government business rates. It is only reasonable and fair that

---

[5] Since this was written a report by Professors David Bell and Sir Donald MacKay, commissioned by the *Sunday Times*, reportedly maintains that £4.5 billion per annum could be cut from Scottish government expenditures without impacting on service delivery. We have been unable to obtain a full copy of this analysis but were it to be proved correct then the programme of government reform which we propose in this chapter could be achieved with a freeze in spending for a single year, and not for the four years as we anticipate.

business pays for what it consumes. However, a significant portion of business taxation is simply punitive and whilst we recognise the politicians aim to use such taxes for redistribution of wealth, in fact this is the worst way to do so. Accordingly we want to go much further than the present Executive and reduce local business taxation in such a way that it equates to use of services. We accept that local authorities will require to be compensated for this so we have set aside £0.8 billion per annum (about 50% of current local tax take) for reductions in this area.

Controversial as these moves will be, particularly to the high tax parties which are in the majority in Scotland, we want once again to go further still. The same principle of reducing taxation in order to increase re-investment and overall national wealth needs to apply to a whole slew of other taxes which have gradually accumulated on the statute book, part of our Union inheritance. Taxes such as the aggregates tax, capital gains tax, inheritance tax, air passenger duty and agricultural levies have a minor take in Scotland (around £0.5 billion per annum) but they are inherently unfair and reduce the ability of business and individuals to contribute to national prosperity. They imperil economic growth by removing from the economy resources, often in trivial amounts (in government terms but not personal terms), which in most cases would most likely have been reinvested thus stimulating economic growth. In addition the elimination of such taxes is also necessary as a step towards an ultimately simpler tax system.

> A whole slew of taxes have accumulated on the statute book, part of our Union inheritance.

Inheritance tax is a tax on monies that have already been taxed. It is a tax aimed at preventing the build-up of wealth in the hands of the people, a build-up that would make them independent, an anathema to the political classes. No longer a means of re-distribution, it is merely a way of raising extra revenue and it hits more and more ordinary people. It should have no place in a country like Scotland, which desperately needs economic freedom for its citizens and the growth of national and individual wealth.

Business tax is not the be-all and end-all of taxation, nor are taxes that hit the minority of the population, albeit a growing minority. Changes in them are an important indication that government is thinking about, and acting on, policies that will bring prosperity to all of society, yet the really central issue for most voters is one tax and one tax alone – income tax.

Income tax affects the backbone of the economy, the individual wage earner and it is that individual wage earner who is ultimately the source of decision making about any policy of fiscal prudence. They determine whether or not it can succeed. We will therefore need to demonstrate to such individuals the benefits of our approach and reward them as it begins to bear fruit. In that regard we would intend, over the four years, to reduce personal taxation by £2.0 billion, a drop in personal rates of 25%.

This would of itself act as a major stimulus to our economy and would also attract people to Scotland – in particular the skilled immigrants we desperately need, including those from south of the border, for economic growth can only be helped by reversing population decline. One way to do that is to have economic policies that attract the ambitious and the able who have no prior connection with Scotland but who see it is a profitable place to work and do business. Another is to have economic policies – low personal taxation and an expanding economy – which help to retain our productive young people, encourage others who have left to return and lay out the welcome mat to the wider Scottish diaspora.

We would intend, over four years, to reduce personal taxation by 25%.

We would want to go further on personal taxation in time. In the meantime our reductions in personal tax would apply as a fixed percentage reduction applicable to every tax rate.

Our final taxation target in this radical, but we think well-founded series of proposals, is fuel duty. Our fuel duty is amongst the highest in the world and taking as it does £1.2 billion per annum it plays a major part in making Scotland a high cost and less competitive economy which presents a major problem when confronted with present and future challenges, particularly from the east.

Fuel duty is tax with little economic justification except governmental need (and sometimes greed). Much is of course claimed with regard to the environmental justification for current levels of fuel duty and we are also, as we shall show, deeply concerned about our environment and particularly the damage to the atmosphere caused by hydrocarbon gases. However, we do not believe that taxation is necessarily the best way to deal with any environmental problems and particularly not in the way that fuel duty is presently being used. Fuel duty at the current level has become a levy which raises substantial sums. The environmental excuses given by successive UK Chancellors are mere window dressing, just as much as his purely cosmetic road tax increases for 'gas guzzlers' were in the 2006 budget. There is no evidence which suggests that these levels of duty have acted as a restraint on use – the sole environmental argument – but plenty of evidence to show the ways in which the duty is damaging business and domestic life particularly in rural Scotland.

The levying of this tax is made even worse by the addition of VAT to the price. In fact we believe that VAT is the correct means of levying a users' tax and we would leave it in place while endeavouring to eliminate fuel duty entirely. However, we have other pressing needs for expenditure such as education so, pragmatically, instead of cutting it out entirely, we would choose to reduce it by £0.6 billion or 50%. In so doing we would venture to predict that this radical change will have no impact whatsoever on fuel consumption. People and businesses will not go rushing out on a driving binge but will simply carry on as normal and a major source of discrimination in the rural areas will have been ameliorated.

With all these changes implemented, our budget still has a surplus. So in the last two years of our programme we want to invest this in the future of the country, and in particular for a future in which this rich nation is no longer a significant oil producer. It is simple prudence to take such a step and we would do so by introducing a range of measures, chief amongst which would be one to sustain and develop our historic ability to be inventors and innovators which we shall call our Intellectual Futures Fund.

Scotland's investment in R&D in 2001 was 0.6% of GDP (excluding the oil and gas component) an unacceptable level of investment when compared to 1.3% for the UK, an OECD average of 1.6%, over 2% for USA and Japan and over 3% for Finland and Sweden. We therefore want to spend an additional £1.0 billion per annum on R&D in our areas of traditional expertise such as medicine, infrastructure and – more recently – information technology. To these we would add environmental sciences and energy, particularly alternative energy production; the only means by which we will be able to move from being oil-dependent to being a post-oil economy. In so doing we could be among the world leaders for every nation will have to make that transformation too.

However we would make much of this expenditure not as simple grants, but as equity investments alongside matching funds from the private sector. We do believe in supporting and sponsoring pure research, but we also believe in making sure that applied research provides a return to be re-invested in future R&D programmes. By so doing we would be able to leverage substantial additional investment in such programmes – up to £2.5 billion or 2.2% of our GDP. We would thus be well-placed to exploit the natural talents of our citizens and compete in the international arena way beyond our size, as we have in the past.

Some people may think that we should take a different approach and place these monies and more in another type of fund – a sort of super savings fund which accumulates a proportion of oil and gas revenues in order to bankroll the time when the wells run dry. Such funds have been established in Alberta, Canada and Norway where they have been popular. However Alberta, it is instructive to note, eventually decided that its Heritage Fund was better utilised in paying down its provincial debt, a decision which ultimately allowed the province to become debt-free and to emerge as the richest part of Canada, and indeed one of the richest parts of the Western world – an outcome which owes much to its careful adherence to the basic capitalist principles originated by the Scot, Adam Smith!

We are of course attracted to such an idea but we believe that on close examination there are several very good reasons why such a fund would not be the best way forward for Scotland, the most important of which is that it is simply too late to do so. Such a fund should have been set up in the 1970s or the 1980s when production was in the ascendancy and not today when it is in decline. If we are to transform Scotland to a competitive independent nation then as our projections have shown we will need every pound of revenue that still comes from the North Sea in order to achieve that task. Frankly we believe that achieving such generational change in Scotland is more important, and more important now.

The second reason is that given our present democratic system our politicians and not the people would control such a fund. We fear that the temptation to use the fund at some point for political reasons would prove irresistible to our politicians and we believe that the existence of a fund available for such purposes would act as a further disincentive for politicians to change the way that democracy fails to work in Scotland.

The third reason is as of 2002-03 Scotland will inherit a debt of £32 billion, part of the legacy to Scotland built up by successive UK governments and Chancellors, Gordon Brown included. This is a sobering thought for every Scot will inherit a debt of £6,400 which increases as each year goes by, the interest on the debt being £1.7 billion per annum or £337 per person.

Despite the fanciful figures bandied around in the political arena, the return we could expect from investing any oil fund, given usual risk prudence, would be less than the interest on this existing debt. So our priority must be to pay down the debt we have, not squirrel away money for a rainy day. The rainy day is, in fact, today. [6]

So much for the bad news. The good news is that a real and effective Heritage Fund is alive and well for it is the billions of pounds that we propose to reinvest in the Scottish economy by means of the programme we are outlining here. It will return far better dividends than any artificial heritage fund.

However, we do believe that it is prudent to have a short term government contingency fund of say £5 billion. Our budget shows that at an oil price of $70 per barrel in our year four we are running with a surplus of £2 to £3 billion per annum part of which we would set aside for such use.

We appreciate that all this is a more detailed programme than usually offered in Scotland when the topic of a future vision of our country is concerned. We outline it largely to show that there is no shortage of possibilities, potentials or prescriptions which could be applied though we also believe it contains the elements which would guarantee twenty first century Scotland success and

---

[6] Michael Russell continues to support the establishment of a legacy fund, as proposed by the SNP, although he believes that informed discussion of the highly successful Alberta model should take place within the party and the country at some future date.

prosperity. We have however one final thought about the matter.

For our last, but certainly not least significant or effective, budget proposal we would, over the last two years of our budget, make a 19% increase in that area of social concern which has been most wrongfully neglected – state pensions. Just as we hope that we can encourage participation from citizens in a programme such as the one we suggest, and that one of the factors in so doing would be a cut in income tax, so we would wish to encourage our pensioners to think about a radically different future for their country by demonstrating the financial reward in so doing. A 19% increase would do that and would also give the lie to the present insistence that most citizens can only look forward to a longer working life, and less support at the end of it. It is possible to envisage, and deliver, something better in a different and better Scotland.

That is, of course, the key point. Most of what we propose could be undertaken in a devolved Scotland, though not in today's devolved Scotland. Full fiscal powers are required for a start, including those over oil and gas, and as we have seen we believe that it is necessary to have control of interest rates and currency. These can be acquired as Scotland progresses and our eyes should remain fixed on the prize of that better Scotland, which can only be obtained by a Scotland that exercises more of the powers of a normal nation from within the nation itself.

But what would the citizen get as a result of such constitutional change? That is a question which must be asked, and which usually gets no particularly tangible reply. However we have a substantial answer. Four years into our New Union – an arrangement still short of full independence, which would be even more beneficial – and we have seen a substantial portion of government revenues returned to our citizens. Our private sector has been freed from the burden of ever-increasing taxation and is better able to compete. Our GDP is at least £121 billion, we have a balanced budget and a smaller government – in fact with a GS of around 32.4% we would have one of the lowest GS levels in the western world. Our growth rate would be at, or above, 4% and we would be well on the way to rivaling Ireland's impressive growth record. The standard of living of all our citizens would be increasing significantly, and the consequent benefit of encouraging wealth creation would be obvious in our poorest areas with concomitant spin-offs in our health statistics, and we would have lost none of our social, health or education entitlements.

Given all this and we will still be running with a budget surplus of £2 to £3 billion per annum at current oil prices of $70 per barrel. However if global oil production has peaked, as we are convinced, then an an oil price of $100 per barrel as predicted by many may be upon us soon. At such a price our budget surplus would be a staggering £11 billion per annum and we would be one of the richest nations in the world with a GDP per capita of £26,300, 47% above that of the UK.

But that we would have to forego if we continue to cling to the Old Union. So is it possible that this Old Union can mean so much to Scots that they are prepared to give up the prosperity which is rightfully theirs and which would transform their lives and those of their children?

We cannot believe so.

Consequently the challenge, particularly for nationalists in Scotland today, is to present the financial case for continuing change, for a possible and temporary 'New Union' and for eventual independence in honest and compelling terms which combat the streams of misinformation which will inevitably flow from unionist politicians south of the border. We hope that all those involved will develop more open minds and the ability to read the runes of necessary change, made essential by today's rapidly developing world.

We would therefore appeal, as strongly as we can, to all the unionist politicians in Holyrood to put the interests of Scotland and Scots to the fore and support the financial empowerment of our country, at the very least, if only because the improvements we must have are not presently – and will not be – on offer from the British state.

Of course we accept that even that future would have its fair share of problems. But our new problems would be those of Ireland – problems such as the inflationary pressures of an expanding economy. However, unlike Ireland an independent Scotland would have the tools to deal with this problem – control of our own currency and the fiscal control that flows from that should we care or need to use it – and with any and all other such problems.

We would also encourage a few innovations which Ireland has not adopted, at least as yet. We would learn the lesson of some American states and Canadian provinces, and enshrine in legislation a requirement for the Scottish government to balance its budget except in the event of a national emergency. Allied with that might be a legislative requirement to ensure that government does not rise above a certain size, except by prior authorisation by the voters.

Of course we would also have begun to revolutionise our democracy, as we have earlier anticipated, and such authorisation of government action by the real rulers – the people – would be an integral part of our new approach. So we would not only be better off, but also better and more responsibly governed.

We would enshrine in law a requirement for the Scottish government to balance its budget.

And just to add to the real progress we would have made we would also have gained the ability and the potential to carry on making a real difference to our nation and everyone who lives in it. By continuing to hold government expenditure and size in check and ensuring that government expansion was kept at less than 2% per annum, we could sustain a growth rate of 4% or more, and by so doing get our GS ratio to 30% or below. Thus in short order we too could become members of the 'five percent plus club' – countries with a growth rate of over 5% per annum. Citizens might well come to insist on such monetary discipline and as, in our new democracy, they would be in full charge, then they would be the perfect guarantors of continuing common sense.

None of our ideas are rigid and this programme can easily be added to, slowed down or even accelerated. It could only benefit from wide debate and discussion but what is vital within it is a determination to decrease government size and return the state to its citizens to allow maximum individual and collective prosperity, well-being and – yes the word is apposite – happiness.

But although we are flexible and want to encourage debate, our programme is strong and – we are proud of the fact – radical. It is not endless tinkering around the edges or that sort of soggy agreement which has damaged Scottish politics since devolution. Nor is it a set of possibilities hedged in by the need to protect special interests and with more than half an eye on ensuring the lowest common denominator of electability. Yet it is not driven by rigid ideology for we see the teachings of Adam Smith as mere common sense. Indeed if it is driven by anything it is three words, which we believe, are part of the Scottish soul – pragmatism, enterprise and compassion.

Above all we do not believe that we are suggesting things that are impossible or even particularly difficult. We would wish to develop the ideas further, bringing other possibilities to the table and looking at issues for concurrent application, like the elimination of quangos as a substantial democratic and economic improvement; the removal of universality and the establishment of a minimum income: a substantial transfer of economic priority in rural areas towards infrastructure development; the introduction of competitive and privately provided healthcare delivery and infrastructure projects and considerably increased competition in public services. We shall have more to say about many of these in the next chapter.

We would be rejoining the world from a position of strength.

All those and many others things could be done from a strong economic base, if our foundation were first put in place. That foundation would also transform Scotland in the eyes of the world, making us a magnet for the headquarter offices (worldwide and regional) of the ever-increasing and expanding international trading companies and, with the incentive of low personal tax rates and an expanding economy, also a magnet for the skilled workers we so desperately need to reverse our population decline and spur on our economic growth. We would be rejoining the world, as Winnie Ewing called on Scotland to do almost forty years ago. But we would be rejoining it from a new position of strength.

But a word of caution. It is important to recognise the magnitude of the problem we face in bringing radical economic change to the bloated corridors of power in Scotland.

The sobering truth is this – at the end of this last four year period (which we could and should have used to transform our nation), year 2006-07 government budgets actually indicate a massive increase in total government spending to about £53 billion, with the GS having risen from 41.3% (by our calculations including oil and gas) to 44.5% as opposed to our suggested, and budgeted reduction to 32.4%.

So whilst new prosperity could have been achieved in that

short period, in fact all that happened was that GS ended up an incredible 12.1% higher than we could have secured. And the growth rate remains stuck below 2% instead of being at 4% and rising. That is a dismal difference and unless action is taken, that dismal difference will continue.

The task of reform is becoming harder every year. It is not impossible, provided we are prepared to throw off the restrictions and impoverishing effect of the Old Union and the Barentt formula, but we must do that, or continue to decline, not least because we are living in a new era of globalisation, which brings its own pressures.

For globalisation is a fact of life. It is here to stay and we can either reject it or find the best way of profiting from it. One of the best ways is not to shun change but to embrace it and perhaps in certain ways (as we did in the past) even lead it. We should invite the world to come here and work with us to do so. But that invitation will only be taken up if there is an independent tiger economy north of the Tweed which embraces, espouses and applies the teachings of Adam Smith. Today's Scotland doesn't. Tomorrow's Scotland must!

2.3 The Citizen and the State

> I have become, and increasingly become, uneasy lest we
> should get our political power without first having, or at
> least simultaneously having, an adequate economy to
> administer. What purport would there be in our getting a
> Scots Parliament in Edinburgh if it has to administer an
> emigration system, a glorified poor law and a graveyard?
>
> **Tom Johnston** (1952)

TOM JOHNSTON was perhaps the greatest Secretary of State for Scotland ever appointed by a UK Government. Holding the office during World War II, he also had more power than any previous, or subsequent, Secretary of State for he had wartime authority backed by emergency wartime legislation.

His support, like the support of all the early Scottish Labour MPs, was for a Scottish Parliament that had the power to make a difference. But, as he indicated in his memoirs, even the most benign and socially concerned Scottish Government would make little progress if it did not have the ability to build and develop a flourishing economy. It would merely be administering 'an emigration system, a glorified poor law, and a graveyard'.

Sometimes that feels like what we now have. And whilst we are by no means opposed to an increased measure of devolution which brings full taxation and fiscal powers back to Scotland, it is the control of currency as we have seen, that is the key element, married to an ability to make macro economic decisions to reduce government size and boost growth. Those are matters, which can only be fully dealt with as an independent state.

But just as achieving independence is not nearly as important as making sure that independence is used to the ultimate benefit of Scots, so achieving the right level of economic powers is of no moment at all unless we know how to use them to produce a more prosperous society and a nation whose wealth flows into all areas of life. So if we are to do more than administer that emigration system, to manage that glorified poor law, and preside over a graveyard full of disappointed citizens, then we have to at least consider how our services should be run.

Those are, of course, matters of party politics yet they are more than that. Consequently we find the inability of most of the members of the Scottish Parliament to think about them outside that straitjacket, and to consider how radical reform can become an impetus that transcends parties, deeply depressing. We are going to lay out some possibilities for change which could be implemented by any or all of the present parties. They are only ideas, but they are ideas ready for action.

We also do so because any Scottish Government – and we aspire to have a Government, not an Executive, a term designed only to downgrade its function and potential – surely has a duty to ensure that the resources it receives from its citizens (and all Government money is citizen's money in origin) are well and wisely utilised. Not only the principles of Adam Smith, but good sense and good judgment demand such an approach. We therefore base our approach to what the state provides not only on the need to reduce government size, nor solely on the need to be certain that Scottish citizens get the best that can be achieved. We base it also on our underpinning philosophy, which asserts that the diversity that arises from a free market approach is the best model and the one which will provide the best results. It should be tempered only by the recognition that there are specific areas in which the free market has to be restrained or resisted for the benefit of all.

Let us start with those circumstances, for they are important and need to be understood clearly. We would assert that in the areas of defence, national security, justice, fiscal control, foreign affairs (political and economic) and to a certain extent national planning, the state must not just guarantee service, but must also be the delivery mechanism. These are, of course, the basic functions of government and they constitute the bulk of the 20% GS, recommended by Scully *et al* as being around the optimum GS in terms of allowing significant and necessary economic growth.

Since the beginning of history the key function of government, from the most primitive to the most sophisticated, has been the defence of its territory. At no time has this been more important than in the age of democracy and even more so if the age of a citizen's democracy dawns at last. The more freedom that the individual has within his society the more he has to lose if the territorial integrity of his country is threatened. We therefore have no hesitation in making defence a core issue which government must deliver itself.

There are many ways that a country like Scotland, acting in concert with others, can effectively defend itself with a modest budget. One of those ways is to rely on proven alliances and for that reason – as well as for pragmatic reasons in terms of policy presentation and the creation of confidence – we have long advocated a reversal of current SNP policy with regard to withdrawal from NATO. (This was a main plank of Michael Russell's SNP leadership campaign in 2004.) We have already indicated that a non-nuclear and appropriate defence policy, much like that devised by the former SNP Defence spokesman Colin Campbell, will incur a lower cost than at present. We have also suggested the possibility that our forces could operate within a joint UK command in certain circumstances and we think that solution has much to commend it, providing it is an arrangement entered into by equals, and for specific and clear objectives. Of course we will also wish to have freedom of action in terms of quasi defence activity such as fisheries protection, policing of territorial limits and contributing to international peace keeping.

> One action that would immediately give the lie to such tartanry (the best wee country in the world) would be the creation of a large scale and ambitious National Development Plan.

The defence of our territory leads us to the defence of the citizen and their property within the territory. Law and order and the justice system join defence as essential functions that should be financed and controlled by government, subject to the justice system being free from political interference. These are areas in which private enterprise should not play a role other than the provision of an efficient marketplace to provide the goods and services that these departments of state will require, at competitive prices. In such a market, value for money should be the order of the day certainly, but the cost of a state monopoly is worth meeting in order to provide the bulwark of liberty and the free enjoyment of full human rights.

Defence, national security and law and order appear unrelated to the overall economy but in fact if the state gets these services right – balancing threats with freedoms, and always ensuring that civil liberties and ordinary freedoms are guaranteed – then by supplying stability and surety the conditions for better government and higher growth, leading to greater individual prosperity, are put, and maintained, in place. The state must guarantee them and deliver them for otherwise there is no state.

Turning to fiscal matters we have already dealt with control of our currency and have made it clear that we believe such control to be an essential power of any Scottish government, be it devolved or independent. Taxation is, of course, also a major lever of fiscal power and with currency the main tool for guiding the course of an economy. Our fallback position on taxation, short of independence, would be for a devolved Scotland which raises all of Scotland's taxes and which makes payment to Westminster for the services provided to Scotland and its citizens by a UK Government.

We find many of the suggestions in the recent Steel Commission report for the Liberals to be encouraging, in that they clearly indicate that the tide is running in favour of more powers being returned to Scotland and that the Liberals are prepared not just to float on that tide, but to actively (and thoughtfully) seek to make it run faster. However the complexity of their taxation proposals, and their suggested splitting of taxation powers would, we believe create a bewildering cat's cradle of responsibilities.

Steel's ideas are a political compromise, and we would contend that in the matter of taxation, such compromises are more likely to worsen the situation than improve it.

The reality is that any system which allows two separate governments to tax the same electorate is fundamentally flawed for it assumes that both governments will have compatible economic policies – a most unlikely occurrence as witnessed frequently in federal systems of government. It is not uncommon in countries such as Canada for taxation reductions by federal government to be met by taxation increases from provincial governments of a different political stripe and *vice versa*. Such practices negate decisive and consistent economic policies and such policies are essential, particularly in Scotland given the challenges we presently face.

It should, in any case, be crystal clear that Scotland requires different economic policies from those imposed by Westminster. Even Labour has failed to square that circle, despite being in power in both countries. This could become even more marked if we had parties of different political views in the two parliaments – a distinct possibility at some time in the near future.

There will be those who will argue that, given the relative insignificance of the existing Holyrood taxation powers and the fact that they have not as yet been used, we effectively have a single government taxation system with Westminster as the taxation government and that this should not be changed.

But there are two very strong reasons for removing taxation powers from Westminster in their entirety and passing them to Holyrood, even in a settlement short of independence.

Firstly, we have already stated the obvious need for different economic policies for economies that are significantly different in size and composition. Secondly, it is only logical that the parliament which is responsible for the greatest portion of total government expenditure in Scotland should be the taxing authority. Given the current fiscal arrangements that government is clearly Holyrood which is responsible for 61% of total government expenditure (excluding accounting adjustments and debt interest) – a percentage which would increase considerably if the devolved powers are expanded as is generally expected. Thus we propose that Holyrood and only Holyrood should tax the Scots with, whilst Devolution is still with us, Holyrood paying the UK parliament for the services which it provides to the Scots.

> The parliament which is responsible for the greatest portion of total government expenditure in Scotland should be the taxing authority.

Our preferred position is of course an independent Scotland, which would be free to make its own sovereign decisions on taxation and pay its own way in the world. We see income tax and user taxes, such as VAT, as the primary source of taxation revenue in an independent Scotland which brings into question the myriad of other taxes still in existence most of which were introduced for political reasons and which defy economic logic.

Our primary targets for elimination, as we have indicated, would be taxes on business and capital, which act as a brake on economic growth. In the initial years of an independent Scotland, as outlined in the previous chapter, we would concentrate on the reduction of government size until we had stability and strong growth.

Fiscal matters lead us to foreign affairs and trade, two functions of government that we believe must be inextricably linked to maximise the benefits to the nation and help national growth as well as personal income. In large countries the department of foreign affairs posture and prance on the world stage forming alliances and enemies *ad infinitum*, with yesterday's enemies becoming today's friends in regular rotation. Scotland should leave them to do so while we concentrate our resources on promoting our country and its products to the world and seeking trade agreements whenever and wherever they benefit the Scottish economy. This means, of course, not only within existing or future Europe, but also further afield, for example with NAFTA countries and the tiger economies of the east.

On virtually every continent one sees advertisements for the Royal Bank of Scotland which was recently voted the second most respected and influential bank in the world. Our government should take a leaf from the Royal Bank of Scotland's book on international advertising and the gaining of international influence for RBS does more in one week to promote Scotland and the nation's ability and talents than the Executive does in a year. We should also look to Ireland, which has had enormous success with overseas promotion. Scotland could do even more, but will never do so when obscured by the shadow of the UK.

Our Ministry of Foreign Affairs and Trade – a ministry of international promotion as well as international diplomacy – would not start off with the daft and self-defeating proposition that we are seeking to be the 'best wee country in the world'. We should not seek that. What we should seek is to be, first of all, ourselves and to let the world see how good that is in terms of our endeavours and our confidence. That diminutive, that self defeating, 'wee' would have no place in our Scotland.

One action that would immediately give the lie to such tartanry would be the creation of a large scale and ambitious National Development Plan. While the compilation of such plans should be a joint exercise between government, the private sector, academia and the trades union movement, its management and coordination should rest squarely with the Ministry of Foreign Affairs and Trade. Our combined Ministry of Foreign Affairs and Trade of course applies to an independent Scotland. In any 'New Union' of the sort we have previously posited, foreign affairs (in a limited and negotiated form) would remain with Westminster in so much as it applies to diplomacy but not to trade and its obvious international components which would be the responsibility of Holyrood.

For hundreds of years Scots have being emigrating to all parts of the world. With few exceptions they have secured a reputation for honesty, fairness, frugality, hard work and economic astuteness. They rapidly established themselves as leaders of their communities and are responsible in no small measure for the creation and development of some of the outstanding democracies of modern times including the USA, Canada, Australia and New Zealand. Their descendants now number over thirty million. They have established for Scotland and its people a latent legacy of goodwill, which if properly developed, can propel Scotland to the forefront of nations with which beneficial trade relations are an imperative. Yet while devolution can lead us some way down this road only independence will allow us to maximise such an asset.

> We have to show our diaspora that we know the proper place for government.

In doing so, however, we have to be clear about what government should do, and shouldn't do, not least because that is a matter much better understood amongst our diaspora than by ourselves. We have to show that diaspora that we know the proper place for government and the way in which government can help rather than hinder national progress.

We can all accept (we hope) that the state has no place in providing services in a range of matters which were however, within living memory, nationalised in the UK and which included such diverse activities as motor manufacture and telecommunications. In almost every one of those cases privatisation – bitterly opposed at the time for understandable reasons by trades unions and individual workers – has improved choice, up-graded services and usually after a period of adjustment offered great job variety and sometimes even an increase in job opportunity. That is what the market can do.

There are exceptions, of course, and the railways are perhaps the most obvious. But there the form of privatisation was at fault; a balkanisation of an integrated system which broke that integration. A different means of introducing private capital and the fresh stimulating air of competition would have produced better results.

But there remain areas of continuing government monopoly or partial monopoly where we believe there is considerable scope to introduce the free market economy and greatly improve efficiency of delivery and cost. These improvements could be carried out concurrently with our four year programme of government downsizing and which would, by improving government efficiency, add further to our goal of increasing our growth rate.

We stress at the outset that such change will not threaten high quality provision – it will enhance it as experience worldwide has shown. Indeed only by such change can better provision be brought about for the state can neither afford, nor has it the means to secure, these things itself. Even Sweden, one of the world's foremost social democracies, insists on competition in its public services, especially in health and education. Far from damaging those services, it has greatly improved them and voters who were initially sceptical are now won over to the benefits that this policy has brought.

Consequently we want to re-think the prevailing Scottish orthodoxy, which continues to hold that health, and education – and some other services – must still be delivered virtually exclusively by the public sector. We believe it is in the interests of every consumer of government services for us to rethink our national approach. It will lead to greater value for money, greater efficiency and better services for all.

In reality Scottish public services remain organised, by and large, in the interests of the service providers, not the consumers. That leads to waste, duplication, empire building and inefficiency. It also inevitably leads to dissatisfaction amongst citizens adding yet another level of criticism to the already widespread dislike of our devolved government. It is undoubtedly contrary to the wisdom of Adam Smith.

Take health first of all. We would encourage the private sector to compete with established NHS hospitals, clinics and other services. We would encourage NHS management and staff to buy out existing NHS facilities and services under favourable financial terms and join the private sector. We would require NHS facilities that remained in government ownership to be run at a profit however modest. Those that failed to maintain profitability over a reasonable time period would be privatised. In each geographic area the government would solicit bids from the area's medical facilities and GPs for the various services it required for its citizens. Fragmentation of services may well see the redundancy of large general hospitals and their replacement with privately run clinics specialising and competing in particular medical procedures and services, at least in the more highly populated areas. [1]

One idea that is worthy of further study is the possibility that some provision might be supported by 'payment vouchers' made available free of charge to citizens in order that patients could receive treatment wherever they wished. Citizens who wished to make their own arrangements with medical service suppliers would be free to do so. Armed with their voucher they could shop for the fastest and best service and if they so wished add to the value of the voucher. To underpin this freedom we would expect in those circumstances that a system would be established (and in our envisioned Scotland that would be a guarantee) in which no citizen would or could be refused provision. Need will result in service, just as in the early days of the national health service. But the provision of service might well be faster, better and more effective.

Need will result in service, just as in the early days of the national health service.

We note that in mid-2006 this imperative drove the new Canadian government to begin to consider broadly similar health reforms to that country's increasingly inefficient health service, in order to secure better public satisfaction, better provision and better use of services. As in Canada, so in Scotland we would hope.

Specialist services catering for need are, indeed, more likely to arise in these circumstances rather than in the current, bureaucratically bloated ones. A good example is the postcode lottery in which those who suffer from Multiple Sclerosis (the incidence of MS being significantly higher in Scotland than south of the border) were refused effective long-term treatment by beta interferon in some places, but could access it in others. It took much effort (and much individual suffering and anguish) to change that situation in Scotland and it still prevails in Wales. However, under a more market-based approach, an individual armed with the power of the consumer and with vouchers, which

---

[1] Michael Russell believes that a clear distinction is required between commissioning and delivery mechanisms and accordingly is happy to assert and argue for the current SNP policy of NHS development and delivery.

will meet the cost of the best treatment, would quickly find the right place to go. As a result soon all places would make themselves the 'right place to go'.

We believe such changes would establish a competitive, efficient and cost-effective health service. We are not suggesting that government should withdraw from the funding of medical costs but only that it should withdraw from the complete control and management of such services. Health care always available at the point of need to all citizens must remain an absolute guarantee and should never be departed from. The debate as to how this is best delivered in a modern society should be a wide-ranging and open one and indeed must be given the proportion of the national wealth that the provision of health services now consumes. In addition to some or the ideas we have looked at, we must also bring into the discussion those systems which rely on compulsory health insurance. It would not be impossible to envisage advantages from such a system, and the public should be provided with enough information to decide if the nation should be setting a long term objective which required those in employment to accept responsibility for their own health costs, always funded by compulsory subscription to competitive national medical insurance schemes with the state acting as 'insurer of last resort' when required. It might be appropriate to introduce such schemes as income tax rates are being reduced and Scotland would be open to learning from places where this is the norm, and take the best examples to improve on them. In the present debate the worst examples of other nations' practice are always used to defend our own system, but our own system may be, in the longer term, unsustainable and we must be open to considering that, and if necessary acting on the fact.

The fact that we were, post war, the innovators in national health care does not mean that our original innovation is still the best model, or the one that can perfectly suit present and future times. To claim that is to take conservatism (real conservatism which fears change and resists improvement) to its ludicrous limit. There is nothing radical, let alone progressive in so doing.

Medicine and health are areas in which Scotland has tradition-ally excelled. We believe that the establishment of a health delivery service as proposed together with the elimination of corporation tax and low income taxes could well result in Scotland becoming once again a centre of medical excellence. Our medical companies, and others attracted to our shores by the opportunities available, would not only be providers of medical services to the Scots but could also become a major force in business providing leading-edge medical services to the international community. It would not be long before the pharmaceutical companies followed. Such a nucleus together with our low-tax regime could also become a magnet for the world's best medical practitioners at all levels. If only we would think big and plan accordingly our health service could be transformed from a major problem to a national asset.

The health crisis is matched by a developing crisis with pension provision. With an ageing population Scotland, like most of the western world, is facing real choices in terms of retirement age and the provision of support for those who no longer work.

In Scotland's case this is particularly aggravated by its declining population and its low growth economy. Both of these lead to a reduction in numbers at work, and a greater burden on each person in work because of the declining ratio of economically active citizens to those who are no longer economically active. This aspect of the problem can be reversed over time by the adoption of the economic philosophy and policies already covered. We also note the beneficial effect of immigration on that situation, for the economically ambitious who come here from, for example, the new European Union Member States (and we would encourage a wider group of states from which to source such immigration) help to raise economic performance and the potential of our economy. It is therefore essential that Scotland should have its own immigration programme (or in the interim have a fully shared responsibility with the UK, such as that prevails between Canada and Quebec) so that we can balance immigration to the particular needs of our economy. Neither the EU 'open door' or the UK's inherently racist 'closed door' help Scotland in that regard.

However in our current situation within the UK the requirements imposed by the state pension as it presently exists will soon overtake the ability of the state to meet all the necessary costs. The funds, which our citizens thought they were contributing for their protection in retirement, have been consumed by an insatiable government exchequer. In reality of course the state has no discreet pension fund at all, but only a promise: a promise that is turning out to be unrealisable. In a sense the state has been as reckless as those companies who have plundered their pension funds and then fallen into liquidation and as heartless as those insurance companies which cut retirement benefits to their policy holders whilst vastly over-rewarding the management which was responsible. The record speaks for itself – neither government nor some of the private sector can be trusted with a matter as important as our pensions.

Does this create a difficulty for our preferred democratic and economic model? No, because rising above both private and public sector is the requirements of the people, and if the people are put in charge in an appropriate way, then the inherent common sense of the people will prevail, not least because the people are the ultimate beneficiaries, and they know that.

Accordingly we propose a people's solution. For an independent or even a more fully devolved Scotland we propose the formation of a National Pension Fund to which it would be compulsory for all adults of pre-retirement age to subscribe a portion of their earnings. The return would be a substantial and secure pension on retirement at a nationally agreed retirement age which would be somewhere between 65 and 70. There would also be provision for early retirement for health reasons and death in service benefits. Non-working partners would have the same benefits as their working cohabitees.

In keeping with the desire to create a participatory democracy and involve citizens in decision making – particularly on an issue as crucial as this – a National Pension Board would be elected by a national citizens' vote. A prerequisite for election (and an essential qualification for inclusion in the ballot) would be experience and expertise in pension matters. The role of the board would be the setting of rules and regulations and the control of the management syndicate which would consist of a group of our best money management companies, rotated and replaced at predetermined intervals by open competition. They would be as free to invest in any venture as private pension companies are now, but they would be required to meet minimum levels of return. Thus we would harness the skills in money management for which Scotland is renowned for the benefit of all of our citizens. Further, as mentioned later we could use the investment power of our National Pension Fund to give all of our citizens an effective stake in our major national infrastructure and development projects.

This is clearly a long-term programme with a substantial overlap period in which the National Pension Fund would gradually replace the state pension. Citizens would also be at liberty to take out additional private pensions or contribute to company pension schemes should they so wish but the National Pension Fund would, we would anticipate, provide a substantially greater pension than the present state provision and would be guaranteed to be independent and not subject to the vagaries of governmental policy change. This would also mean that, far from being a weakness in the overall independence offering, the issue of pensions and their future after the break-up of the UK would become a positive strength.

The economic and moral health of the nation is secured by our education system.

This combination of private sector expertise, guided and controlled by the people for the benefit of all citizens, is a good one. The exact balance to be struck is of course always a key issue, but the assumption that the state will always, and must always, provide is as false as that which says that the private sector will always, and must always, prevail. Our balance is strongly towards the private sector, but sense and judgment should always determine the final outcome in such circumstances. Today blind dogma has a tendency to overcome such sense and judgment and in Scotland that blind dogma – in favour of the state – is getting in the way of ensuring that all our citizens enjoy the best possible life and have the best possible opportunities.

Providing opportunity is central to the education system, at all levels. To this end we have provided an increase of £0.6 billion per annum in our budget programme and we would argue for providing more in time. The economic and moral health of the nation is secured by an education system which guides and helps all young people, and can assist and improve the chances of those who are older. Once again Adam Smith is a wise guide in this matter. In both *The Wealth of Nations* and the *Theory of Moral Sentiments* he makes it clear that the education of our citizens to the full extent of their ability and at the expense of the state is a prerequisite to both the economic and moral welfare of the people. We concur.

Improvements in education – modeled originally on Scottish

provision – have been cited as one of the main causes of the Irish economic revival. That is little surprise because education is a field in which we have traditionally excelled but which in recent years, with the removal of a competitive environment and a weakening of a national as well as individual striving for excellence we have slipped down the ranks.

We are no longer great fans of a wide application of the principle of universality, as we shall indicate. But we do remain firmly wedded to the idea in education. The state can only benefit if there is an absolute right for every child and young person to have their studies financed by government from nursery school through to university and on to postgraduate education if they are able to take up that opportunity.

Nonetheless some competition is essential to get the best out of our young people and to get the best out of our tax revenues. Many commentators have noted the success in Sweden of education vouchers and a debate about their utility in Scotland would be useful and instructive, particularly if shorn of ideological prejudice. These would provide the full cost of education on an annual basis for all those who eligible, at every educational level. The consumer – the child along with his or her parents, the student seeking to go to college or university and the mature student, seeking to improve his or her qualifications – would be able to choose the best facilities for their particular needs, and be able to force new provision onto the market by means of their purchasing power, provided by the state.

> The state benefits if every child and young person has their studies financed by government.

These vouchers would be issued to all, indeed to do so is only fair. Parents who wish to continue to use their own resources to fund private schooling might also have them, and will therefore no longer be paying for the cost of education twice – simply paying for that portion which is unmet by national costs. Other parents in those circumstances may find the choice of private education easier to afford. Scotland will not benefit if any good school closes, and that principle applies right across the sector. Choice and diversity are the hallmarks of a mature and confident society and this system will encourage the emergence of new types of private provision, which are not seen as exclusive or class-ridden. That can only add to our maturity of outlook.

But we are confident that the introduction of vouchers would be of most benefit in the state sector. Good schools would flourish and schools that are failing would have an incentive to improve. Of course in many rural areas choice is presently impossible – with vouchers that need not be the case. Smaller and different types of education will become sustainable and the pattern of provision over time may change. We are keen to see a development of e-learning and new models of access in rural and other locations. Vouchers and a diverse market would assist this process.

We must also be less rigid in terms of educational philosophy. The 'one size fits all' approach does not work and has often held back our ablest children. Yet it is self-evident that holding back those who can achieve with less difficulty does not help those who have more difficulty or who require different stimuli to achieve. Perhaps we need a system which may use setting, or a properly tailored and thought-through Scottish equivalent of city academies, in order to stretch young people who can move faster and go further, in terms of learning, than some of their compatriots. Equally we need a system flexible enough to support and encourage those who have greater difficulty. Good teachers and good schools have always recognised such issues and responded to them. It is time the state did, and freed good schools and good teachers to get on with that job, whilst encouraging the not so good to up their performance.

Of course education is about more than schools or even universities. We all have a need for development both in terms of our personal lives and growth and also because the ever-increasing acceleration of the information age is resulting in a corresponding acceleration in the redundancy of skills and the need to acquire new ones.

In that regard constant re-education and training on a scale never before envisaged is essential if we are to meet the challenges of an ever-changing world economy and keep our citizens gainfully employed. We have to embark on an unprecedented expansion of technical education with an emphasis on theoretical and practical re-education to meet the demands of the new age, and the ages to come. This movement should be guided by the National Development Plan, which would seek to forecast future areas of education and training need to meet international and internal competition.

Constant re-education and training is essential if we are to meet the challenges of an ever-changing world economy

162

Colleges for such education have been closing or converting to multi-purpose universities in recent years. We need to re-establish the absolute worth and validity of such technical and vocational education and make sure that new colleges are established which provide these services and which are open to all regardless of previous education, experience or age. Their purpose should be to equip all of their students for work in the prevailing and anticipated future economy. Indeed all who are unemployed should be guided to study and train through these colleges as a first option.

Since the dawn of the industrial age to recent times Scotland has led the world in inventions per capita. It is a national resource which seems to be rooted in our natural curiosity and which we should endeavour to develop and exploit to its fullest extent. Therefore, as outlined in the previous chapter we would significantly increase the research and development budget of our universities and our private sector with the objective of increasing our national R&D investment by a factor of four.

We need to re-establish the absolute worth and validity of technical and vocational education.

The intellectual property rights from such research should be shared equally between the government, the universities, the corporations and the researchers. In this way the government would get a return on its investments, the universities an income stream to be applied to further research, the researchers a just reward for their talent and the corporations discoveries to be exploited. While we have led the world in inventiveness we have been tardy in exploiting such assets to our national benefit, as often as not allowing foreign companies to reap the financial benefits. It is therefore imperative that such programmes should form part of the National Development Plan and should be regularly reported upon to all levels of the Scottish private sector to encourage their participation in the ensuing development and exploitation.

As we have observed the belief that government must provide all – and particularly must provide all services – is one of the most sacred of the many sacred beasts presently grazing contentedly on the threadbare pastures of current Scottish politics.

That beast is nurtured by the principle of universality, the provision of government services to all heedless of need or regardless of the ability to pay. The origins of such a belief, like so many worthy things which are now not beneficial but actively harmful in our country, are easily understandable and basically creditable. The first significant moves by the Liberal Government of 1906 for social reform, and the later more comprehensive postwar actions of the Attlee Government were necessary within a society in which poverty was endemic and in which general investment applicable to all was more efficient in administration, and more effective in producing change than any attempt at targeting. It was easier and cheaper to provide for everyone than to make distinctions.

It is no longer so. In fact the development of such blanket provision had an inevitable consequence when a rising population (in UK terms certainly) needed to be serviced whilst costs were rising and standards increasing. Put bluntly universality – one size not only fits all, but will be given to all – now drags down both the quality of service that can be provided to those most in need, and the ability of government to provide such services. However our political parties do not have the courage to address the issue for fear of losing votes.

Universality now drags down both the quality of service and the ability of government to provide such a service.

That is tragic, because their actions are in effect going against every principle they claim to defend. Universality as presently practised robs the poor of resources which would be best in their hands. It takes away from those who most need help and who most deserve support and rewards those who need neither. It is unjust and indefensible.

The difficulty in effecting change is very often the product of fear and uncertainty. We need to remove that fear and uncertainty about the basic provision which should be available to all – the safety net below which no citizen will be allowed to fall. Our solution to moving forward in public services is to continue to extend an absolute guarantee of provision for all those who require it and, moreover, to make that guarantee legally binding. But it is then to encourage a range of provision so that real need can be met with the best and highest standard of response – in other words to greatly improve services for all those who access them.

An innovation in this area would be to discard the myriad schemes that reinforce disadvantage by making it more and more difficult to rise above it. It is truly shocking that the clusters of deprivation in Scotland are not reducing and that, for example, a quarter of our young people in those areas are cast on the scrap heap as a result of poverty. No modern society can move forward if poverty is allowed to blight life chances. No modern society can flourish if drug addiction and crime are fueled by lack of opportunity and despair. And no modern society can be proud if the prospect of social, economic and educational advancement has actually decreased in recent years – as it has in parts of Scotland.

A growth in employment opportunity – which would be an absolute concomitant of faster national economic growth – is the first tool to use in these circumstances. But on the way, and to assist those in most need when we get there, each citizen must be guaranteed a minimum national income, set at a level which would allow choices to be made and to ensure an ability to contribute to a National Pension Fund. Present state benefits, split between many schemes and entitlements and hopelessly bureaucratic in their delivery, are both too low and too complex and they create a dependency culture which is no fault of those who come to depend on them.

A simple National Guaranteed Income, set at a realistic rate, is essential and the provision of vouchers for health care as part of that minimum national income – and for education provision as well – would place every citizen on an equal footing and allow them to choose not only how to live their lives but also where they received health services and where there children were educated: a choice presently available only to the affluent.

Care must, of course, be taken to ensure that the system is not abused. Able bodied persons who are out of work would be required to make every endeavour to obtain employment and if unsuccessful would be required to undertake re-education or re-training or to accept employment identified by the government. But lest it be thought that we are about to propose further regressive actions such as means testing – something that is growing in the UK and in Scotland – we should say clearly that we want means testing as at present operated to be abolished.

We should instead move to a situation where benefits of any nature – including the payment of the National Guaranteed Income – are triggered by an individual, and annual, tax return. A flat tax of course would help in this matter, but in an era of growing computerisation, automatic payment in such circumstances is not complex and in a small country can be done efficiently. Should circumstances change during the year then individuals could quickly submit a change in forecast or actual income that would trigger a change in their entitlements.

Such systems also avoid rigidity. A sudden cut-off of eligibility would be unfair to those whose income is just above the benefit threshold. In such circumstances a graduated system of eligibility based on income level could easily be applied. It should be well within the ability of any efficient taxation department to implement and manage such a system. It would also replace a multitude of government programmes and eliminate a large number of bureaucracies. Thus not only will the services and payments to the needy be vastly improved but also the cost of implementation will be greatly reduced. In essence we are replacing the myriad of social provision – much of it ill understood and badly administered – with a simple system in which debit taxation becomes credit taxation at a predetermined income level.

Services and payment s to the needy can be vastly improved.

We should not leave this overview of government roles and responsibilities without considering infrastructure. Our previous addiction in the UK to public ownership, followed by mostly successful privatisations has helped improve matters, but some Scottish infrastructure still lags behind the standards required for a cutting edge modern nation. Transport and telecommunic-ations are two such areas, but so are the renewal of educational and health facilities, and these have been further hampered by clumsy attempts at involving private finance.

Second/third world countries such as South Africa could teach Scotland a number of lessons in this regard. It, for example, has a superb road system which would put Scotland to shame. In a number of instances infrastructure has been placed in the hands of the best provider which is nearly always the private sector. It is a pleasure to pay tolls just to drive on low traffic density high speed highways.

However South Africa has made a mistake by then abdicating the real role of government in terms of infrastructure which is the long-term identification and planning of an integrated pattern of provision based on long-term economic projections. By long term we mean five, ten and fifteen year plans covering everything from internet, telecommunications, ports, airports, roads, sea transport, railways and water. Such plans would be an integral part of our National Development Plans. The government should consult with the best brains in the country (and overseas) particularly from academia and the relevant industries. Government should actively promote and co-fund studies and research by our universities, corporations and inventors to find the solutions to the problems and opportunities of tomorrow – just as we have earlier proposed for other sectors. For such funding the government should retain a pro-rata ownership in subsequent discoveries and benefits.

When it comes to investment in infrastructure we would wish to see a much increased role for pension funds and other such investment vehicles, and particularly our proposed National Pension Fund. By such means our citizens would have access to long-term stable investments, indeed they would be a large part of the 'Private' in what would be in essence PPP projects, but with a much wider economic base and a much wider sharing of the profits. In every area of infrastructure throughout the world there are numerous examples of the successful application of this approach.

> Transport services and projects would come on stream earlier and provision would be of a higher standard.

There are of course other possibilities. In respect of existing government controlled areas such as water and transport there should, at the very least, be a new, detailed consideration of, and wide-ranging debate about, the way in which private resources for maintenance, operation and construction of the services can be introduced and sustained. This should include an examination of the benefits that such policies have brought in other countries. In Canada, for example, toll roads, using sensors and remote billing, have greatly improved both commercial and private life. Not all roads need to be built this way, but when new roads are built there needs to be at least a consideration of other models that work well elsewhere. Only when a link is the sole one – as for example with the Skye Bridge – should there be an automatic assumption that usage would be free, paid for by the state. The government spends £1.2 billion per year on transport, a sum which could be greatly reduced by the gradual privatisation of existing services and future projects. In addition such services and projects would come on stream earlier by utilising models from elsewhere, and the provision would be of a higher standard. The identification and planning of future infrastructure projects would be an essential component of the national development plan.

The same principles could be applied to infrastructure that is the responsibility of local government. However, infrastructure is an essential prerequisite for the development and improvement of some remote areas, and it is there that the public sector may be required to start the ball rolling with investment that has no quick or direct return. This would indeed be a better use of tax-payers' money than the schemes presently run by Enterprise Companies particularly those in the Highlands, which involve direct investment in small, medium or large business.

New thinking is necessary in all part s of our public life.

In addition, innovative ideas such as Land Value Capture (not to be confused with Land Value Taxation) and Local Amenity Companies as suggested by Adam Bruce are worthy of consideration in terms of infrastructure projects large and small.

New thinking is necessary in all parts of our national life, and amongst the areas which most need refreshed are those which have gradually fallen away from the control of the citizen and even from the control of politicians and which are often a complete affront to democracy, even in the limited version that we presently are able to experience. That means a major review of quangos, those quasi-government organisations, which spend our taxes outwith the direct scrutiny of the citizens and their representatives.

The most ubiquitous of such bodies, which interferes with the enjoyment and use of our land (our greatest natural asset) and which does so with only an occasional nod to accountability is Scottish National Heritage. SNH is seen in most of the Highlands, and by many rural dwellers as an organisation which may consult *ad infinitum*, but which never changes its mind once it has expressed a diktat.

SNH and its predecessors have enmeshed many places in Scotland in a bewildering array of overlapping designations which are strangling our ability to carry out even the simplest of economic or domestic developments. These desperately need reviewed and many of them need discarded, as they are a positive brake on rural development, without performing any concomitant function in terms of our overall ecology or environment. They are just bureaucratic devices.

Organisations such as SNH – and there are many, many of

them – should have no place in a citizen's democracy. We would advocate a review of their functions followed by their dissolution with the jobs they presently do – if those are necessary – absorbed into either national or local government. It would take too long to show how that should happen, there being such a wide range covering so much of our national life. However a few words on Scottish Enterprise and Highlands and Islands Enterprise will illustrate our thinking in this regard as well as illustrate some other important issues in economic and rural development.

Government funds the Enterprise Companies to the tune of about £525 million pounds per annum. A further £120 million comes from other sources such as the EU, special grants and miscellaneous investment returns. These companies, or their predecessors have been spending broadly similar sums for some four decades, and spending them on a welter of governmental priorities which have changed regularly, though the overall aim has always been claimed as being to provide assistance to Scottish business.

We do not doubt that there have been some individual successes, but in general the use of the word enterprise to describe this activity is a cruel joke for this structure has shown little enterprise in the management of significant amounts of government (and therefore taxpayers') money. Their difficulties during the early part of 2006 are a matter of recent record, but in the longer term it is worth noting that the enterprise companies have a mere £320 million in net assets to show for the tens of billions of government largesse they have showered on the business community over time. More importantly and as we have seen, by every economic criterion they have failed to improve Scotland's economic standing *vis a vis* its largest trading partner and greatest competitor, England.

The policy does not come cheap. A staggering 27% of the monies provided is consumed in the administration of the companies alone. A further 28% of their funds is spent on 'skills and learning', an area of specific expertise which would be better managed by schools, universities and (particularly) vocational colleges. A high proportion of expenditure goes on 'consultants' whose inputs and outputs are poorly quantified.

The remaining 45% of direct expenditure on business appears

to be used within two broad strands: 'growing businesses' and 'global connections'. In both of these areas decisions are taken by civil servants with little or no business experience. The appointment of business people to enterprise company boards provides little comfort for they appear merely to rubber stamp the management proposals. Neither side of this equation seems to understand that the process they are engaged in is not just uneconomical but actually harmful.

By interfering in the market place, usually to assist the inefficient, they are in reality putting productive and competitive businesses at risk. Whilst we believe in removing the burden of excessive and misplaced taxation, in all of its many guises, from the backs of the business community we equally believe that they should not be the recipients of taxpayer's cash in the form of government grants and other handouts. That helps no one in the long term.

We therefore propose that the Enterprise Companies be wound-up with those 'skills and learning' functions deemed necessary being absorbed into the education sector. The wind-up process should involve the staff being found suitable employment in the private sector although some of them may find a place within a new organisation that we do think would make a difference to start-ups and high risk businesses, particularly those which fall outwith the restrictive lending criteria and innate conservatism of our commercial banks. This organisation would be called the Scottish Development Bank (SDB).

The SDB would be a lender of last resort, lending to established and start-up businesses that are unable to obtain financing from commercial sources. It would be run as a commercial banking operation, charging interest commensurate with loan risks. We would set its primary capital at £500 million (equivalent to about one years budget for SEC and HIE) which would be provided by government. Government would be the primary shareholder in the bank. Secondary capital of up to £6 billion would be raised on the money market as required by loan demand, normally by issuing financial instruments such as interest bearing preferred shares with government guarantees if necessary. The bank would be required to operate at a profit with a policy of paying a dividend to its primary shareholder, the government, whenever possible.

We envisage that the SDB would operate closely with commercial banks and other sources of loan capital with the objective of filling voids in the lending spectrum whilst avoiding competition with commercial lenders. In addition it would act as a broker, charging commercial fees, where it obtained alternative sources of loans and equity for its clients. It would also provide feasibility study and other such consulting services to its clients at commercial rates. An exception would be small start-up businesses that would pay for such services only if the business was eventually financed and established to profitability.

Professional bankers would manage the bank and its board of directors would have a majority with financial sector experience. While its lending criteria would always be driven by commercial returns it would be guided by the National Development Plans with regard to favouring particular business sectors and geographic areas. The transition from the enterprise companies to the SDB would probably take from two to three years after which the government would save between £400 and £500 million per annum of the monies it currently spends on those companies' annual budgets. The SDB would have appropriately sized branches throughout the country – it might even use a small amount of the vast Enterprise Company estate – and would take over existing loans and holdings from the Enterprise companies.

Our analysis of what could be done in Scotland is by no means total and completely comprehensive – it is more a survey of some issues on which action could be, and needs to be taken. There are other things which are of importance too, and some of them could be undertaken to the great benefit of the nation at zero cost. Chief amongst these would be the passing of a modern Minerals Act.

Virtually every nation in the world regardless of size has taken such a step bar a handful and that handful includes Scotland. Certainly there is Scottish legislation that governs some aspects of mining and the extraction of natural assets but these are largely archaic acts from the Middle Ages governing precious metals and some base metals, acts from the industrial age concerning coal and acts from recent times with regard to oil and gas. There is, however, no modern framework of legislation which ties these together and opens up new and very lucrative opportunities for the nation.

Oil and gas are of course controlled by Westminster but all other minerals fall under the jurisdiction of Holyrood. That same Holyrood rushed to pass a land reform act but bizarrely failed to include in it any updating of the major opportunities presented by the control and development of mineral rights. A resolution was passed at an SNP conference in the late 1990s advocating the establishment of a modern minerals act for Scotland, the first time such a need was recognised by any political party in Scotland. There was some opposition to it at the time from the green lobby within and outwith the SNP despite the fact that the resolution was clear that any such act would have to be subject to every one of the environmental regulations pertaining in the country, as all such acts usually guarantee. Unfortunately this internal opposition in the SNP was not persuaded by this commitment and succeeded in ensuring that the mater was not raised by the party during the passage of the Land Reform Bill at Holyrood.

We see no conflict in proposing new mining legislation whilst also proposing major initiatives to 'green' our country.

We would not propose a major increase in minerals activity in Scotland if we thought that it would damage Scotland's environment or ecology. We shall deal with those topics – with Scotland's third great challenge – in our next section, but we see no conflict in proposing new mining legislation and activity whilst also proposing, as we shall indicate, major initiatives that 'green' our country.

Why should minerals be important to Scotland? Firstly, they are a major component of the resources of a country – a major element in national wealth – and to ignore them is akin to competing in the global economy with one hand tied behind your back. Secondly, it is one area in which we can compete with the commodity-hungry tiger economies of the east, not just on level terms but on superior terms, given our technical knowledge and efficiency. Indeed we can become an exporter of minerals, reversing the usual flow of commodities and capital.

As our oil and gas reserves decline, a thriving minerals industry would also take up some of the experienced workforce which will be surplus to requirements. But before then we need to do significant exploration, for little or no investigation of the required detail has been conducted in Scotland by major mining companies for the simple reason that meaningful exploration requires the investigation of relatively large areas of land. In a long inhabited place like Scotland this means having to reach agreement with a multitude of both land and minerals rights owners who are seldom the same people.

A modern Minerals Act overcomes such problems by vesting the control of exploration and development of minerals in the hands of the government. The government issues licences to mining companies for exploration and development at a fee, which covers the cost of administration. These licences lay down minimum exploration expenditures, environmental compliance requirements, compensation payments to landowners, royalties payable to mineral rights owners and local authorities and numerous other controls and regulations. They give the mining company surety of ultimate development provided they comply with the clearly stated government requirements.

We have some of the most exciting geology in the world.

Scottish licences for exploration and exploitation would need to be on a par (in terms and conditions) with those of other nations so that we can be players in this highly competitive field. Perhaps in Scotland's case they would need to be more competitive for whilst we have some of the most exciting geology in the world, it is largely unexplored and large sums of money will have to be spent on initial exploration by companies within the local economies. However if, as is likely, discoveries are made then much larger sums and many more jobs will accrue.

Local democratic control would be important in this matter too. Individual local authorities, acting on the wish of local people, should be entitled to participate in or withdraw from the minerals act. Those that participate would be rewarded with a royalty on all minerals produced from their area.

This proposal is no fantasy. In the 1940s the Republic of Ireland passed a minerals act, which galvanised exploration from the 1950s onward. By the 1970s the Stormont government in Northern Ireland, envying the successes south of the border, passed their own minerals act. Today, realising that they share the same geology, both governments frequently jointly promote their exploration potential at the leading mining trade shows around the world. Since the 1960s thirty mineral deposits have been discovered and eleven mines brought to production through-out the island of Ireland producing such diverse minerals as zinc, copper, lead, silver, and gold. In the Republic of Ireland more zinc has been discovered per square kilometre than in any other country in the world – a total of 14 million tonnes valued at $22 billion. Even so Ireland is just at the beginning of its exploration potential.

In Scotland there are occasional tantalising glimpses of what is possible. The accidental discovery of sapphires in Lewis, an event which would have produced an immediate staking rush (today a rush for licences) of Klondyke proportions elsewhere in the world, was greeted in Scotland by something known as a SSSI which promptly froze the environment and all possibility of the sapphires being used for the benefit of the people of that island. No local person was allowed a say in the matter.

The inhabitants of Harris were treated in a similar fashion with regard to the Lingerbay quarry project – a major attempt to supply aggregate to the burgeoning European market. Despite clear indications that the local community wished the quarry to go ahead, years of government inquiry resulted in an independent judicial process which recommended that the project should proceed. All came to came to an end with a governmental rejection which had been preceded by much mis- and dis-information.

We cannot but help compare the draconian suppression of enterprise and local opportunity in Harris with the enthusiastic embrace by all levels of Canadian government with a similar project on Vancouver Island which will supply aggregate to the Californian market. A project, incidentally, in which the relevant local native Canadian population have taken a 12% interest and from which they will reap considerable profit.

It seems never to have occurred to those responsible for both those decisions – the civil servants in Edinburgh operating their Ministers like glove puppets – that the pristine landscape of the north and west which they want to preserve (and whose people they are actively impoverishing as a result) is only still beautiful because the people who inhabit it care for it. If they cannot stay there, then it will cease to have any meaning at all and those who take their places will lack the skills and the passion to keep it beautiful. There are no better custodians for the future of the Highlands than those who live in the Highlands, just as there are no better custodians of Scotland's future than the Scots themselves. Means must be found of allowing both groups to go on living in their own environment and they must be allowed to make their own decisions about that environment. Do civil servants not know that even quarries have fleeting lives, that such places now will always have their landscape re-instated, and that changes to the local eco systems can produce benefits, if sensitively and imaginatively managed?

For example one of the wonders of the modern world, the Butchart Gardens on Vancouver Island, were built in a huge disused limestone quarry by the Butchart family who originated from Forfar. Their grandson Ian Ross, a Scot on two sides of his family, is credited with the development of the modern gardens for which he was honoured with the Order of Canada.

Scotland has much to offer in the world of minerals, even with the limited exploration to date: sapphires in Lewis; diamonds in Sutherland; platinum and nickel in the Shetlands and Aberdeenshire; gold all over; lead-zinc in the Central Highlands and the South; copper in Argyll and the South; copper-zinc in the Shetlands, Ross-shire and the Central Highlands; lead-zinc-gold in the South; barites in Perth, marble in Skye and coal – the fuel of the future – in the centre and off-shore.

In addition the unique physical qualities of Scotland's rock, particularly down the west coast, make them ideal for the production of aggregate. Scotland could, given the abundance and ease of access of this resource, quickly become the major source of aggregate for most of Europe yet such a position would, environmentally and aesthetically barely scratch or dent our land and landscape. We could have a significant new industry to bring wealth and opportunity to our poorest and remotest parts, if only our politicians thought clearly and assessed facts, rather than bent to every pressure brought by lobbyists.

Moreover it would be an industry unthreatened by the competition from the east – the type of industry we desperately need if we are to prosper in the challenges ahead. Yet the Lingerbay decision by Holyrood followed by a green driven aggregates tax imposed by Westminster killed, to all intents and purposes, an industry which would have been uniquely Scottish and uniquely good for Scotland. And which, it is important to say, would have been operated within all – and that means all – current environmental regulations.

Finally coal is worthy of a special mention. Scotland has vast reserves of offshore coal in places up to thirty metres thick. These occur in the Forth and Moray firths, the central North Sea and east and west of the Shetlands. There are also substantial reserves onshore in the Central Lowlands

These resources were uneconomic until the recent explosion in energy prices but now, almost overnight, coal is becoming one of the fuels of the future. It is now viable to spend large sums on the recovery of coal energy and the purification of its by-products in order to establish zero emission power stations. Underground coal gasification is particularly suited for Scotland's offshore deposits where redundant oil and gas facilities could be converted to drilling and igniting underground coal and piping the gas to shore for electricity generation and hydrogen production. Gaseous wastes such as carbon dioxide could be pumped back into our redundant oil and gas reservoirs and burnt-out coal fields. As our oil and gas production declines some of it could be used as the ignition fuel for the gasification of our coal.

With such careful, and integrated, planning it should be possible to maintain and extend Scotland's energy production for generations to come. However, there is one significant problem. Just as in the case of our oil and gas assets, our coal assets are controlled by Westminster for energy is a reserved matter.

The situation is further complicated by the fact that there are also large reserves of coal off the North East coast of England and that all of the research on the aforementioned uses of coal are being conducted in England. So who is going to be looking after Scotland's interests as we contemplate a second energy bonanza? Presently it looks as if it will be Westminster, once again.

It is therefore likely that this second boom will enrich England and not Scotland. But a minerals act that brought coal back into the purview of a Scottish Parliament – even without independence – would avoid that which is another good reason for the devolved administration treating this matter as one of urgency.

We have one concluding thought about the matter of competition and our economy, and it is one that has to do with that traditional mainstay of the Scottish economy, now much in decline – manufacturing.

We simply cannot compete with the low cost eastern economies in the field of manufacturing, including our much vaunted electronics industry. But we can and should compete in the supply of high quality luxury goods and services and this market has huge potential for us.

The tastes and desires of the growingly rich middle classes in the Eastern, and new European, economies are little different from the tastes and desires of such classes everywhere. Scotland, to such consumers, already has a reputation for quality – quality clothing, quality foods, quality drinks and quality personal and household goods. Some of our old established brands have in recent years been given the necessary new lease of life to allow them to take advantage of these new opportunities. We need to do more of that, and to expand our horizons.

But we can not only make the best high quality woollens, we can also give the best high quality investment advice in the world, and provide a service to manage new-found wealth and a safe place to store it. At the same time we can offer the chance to experience our culture, history and magnificent scenery, play golf in the land of its birth and having illness treated in the country that gave the world anaesthetics and penicillin.

The selling of Scotland and its many strengths should be pushed forward by a large scale integrated advertising campaign, co-ordinated and led by the government and financed primarily by business. Never a day should go by when the world does not read, see or hear the word Scotland linked to the quality which it implies. But we must ensure that such quality is maintained and improved, and in the modern world that means beating back the degradation of our environment and the debasing of our culture.

So having considered democracy and economics, we now need to turn our attention to the environment and to the widest understanding of that term, in order to consider how we overcome the third big challenge to the Scotland we live in.

Once we have done that we should be in a position to finally demonstrate how the people of Scotland can choose to move forward into a much more secure, and much more prosperous, world. One in which our government has something much more profitable and much more advantageous to administer than, in those opening words of Tom Johnston, 'an emigration system, a glorified poor law and a graveyard.'

3. The Challenge of the Environment

Aile a gheallas Earrach
ged a tha e fuar fhathast
tha spiorad uaine san aire
aig talamh is daoin'.

> Myles Campbell *Latha Faoiltich,*
> from *Balitean* 1987

A promise of Spring in the air
although it is still cold
people and earth
Are aware of a green spirit.

3.1 Making the future

America is addicted to oil (but) by applying the talent and technology of America, this country can dramatically improve our environment, move beyond a petroleum-based economy, and make our dependence on Middle Eastern oil a thing of the past.

President George Bush
State of the Union Message, 31st January 2006

IT IS difficult for any politician to wipe the slate clean and reach out to those who are hostile to him. Many of George Bush's critics derided his appeal to America to change its attitude to oil, particularly as his administration had rejected the Kyoto Protocol and pursued policies which most environmentalists have claimed to be at best useless and at worst highly damaging to the planet.

Yet even if that were the case the fact that he is now prepared to talk about 'moving beyond a petroleum-based' economy and to link that, at least in part, to the need to 'improve our environment' should be a sign of hope. If the leader of the world's largest economy recognises that it is time to move into a new and cleaner age then every human being should be pleased, for we all share this small and fragile globe as our home.

George Bush may also have understood something that some other politicians have missed. The fact is that the environmental crisis – and we have no hesitation in calling it a crisis – has until now failed to grip the public consciousness or at least grip the public consciousness in a way that leads to large scale individual action, perhaps because of the complexity of the issues involved. Now – at last – it is beginning to do so. Most people are realising that only by setting clear goals which challenge, encourage and inspire individuals can nations make any progress with this worldwide problem.

In discussing this issue we want to take a similar tack. That is, we wish to cut through the multiplicity of claims and the confusion created by competing scientists to focus on solutions rather than merely describe problems. Our approach to this issue is similar to our approach to both the democratic and governmental crises we have already discussed – we want to involve people in finding a way forward, not delay change by the usual political means of blame shifting and name calling.

We would concentrate our efforts to reduce carbon dioxide emissions in three specific areas, namely in the conservation of energy usage by people and business, in the generation of electricity by pollution-free power generation (but only using nuclear power as a last ditch and temporary stop gap if absolutely necessary) and in the replacement of carbon dioxide emitting fuels with hydrogen, using ethanol and bio-fuels as *pro tem* stop-gaps if required.

It would be imagined that the future of our planet would concern every citizen and that in each part of the planet there would be a huge interest in, and passion for those things which could help secure it. But in fact environmental issues have appeared, to most voters, to be too complex and far too wide-ranging to allow, let alone encourage, clear and consistent engagement. Put bluntly it is hard to see what can each of us can do when faced with such a morass of conflicting information and evidence about issues which are hard to understand. We have responded in the same way as the Inuit of Greenland, who when confronted with the failure of the sea to freeze firmly enough for hunting in two successive recent winters merely observed, 'this isn't an issue because it's not in our power. As hunters we follow the tracks that are there, not what might be. There is only ever the bird in the hand.'

That point is borne out in past studies of Scotland's attitude to environmental issues. Public concern about global warming has actually fallen in recent years with 42% of respondents being 'very worried' in 1991 but only 25% in 2002. The biggest concern was not the planet *per se*, nor the impact of pollution, the lack of a strategy for environmentally sound economic growth or the pressures of population. The biggest concern was the discharge of raw sewage and the possible impact of nuclear waste, though once again concern was falling, not rising.

For most people the task of solving worldwide problems has seemed something not in their power. In addition, for most Scots such problems lack a purely Scottish dimension and accordingly it can seem daft to discuss solutions to them in a Scottish context.

Whilst, in 2002, 77% of Scots agreed that changes to lifestyles will be needed so that future generations can enjoy a good quality of life and environment, less than half (some 46%) thought that they themselves needed to change their own way of life. What concern there was, was focused on the mote in someone else's eye rather than the beam in our own.

However there is some evidence that individual concern has grown since that 2002 survey, and George Bush's response indicates that politicians in many countries are aware of such a change.

Politicians have, of course, been taking some action even before now. Scotland has made some tangible recent progress in key environmental areas. The quality of Scottish water has risen, our rivers and shores are cleaner, our GHG emissions are falling (albeit too slowly) and after a faltering start, Scotland is beginning to take recycling seriously with the best Scottish Local Authority (Angus) dealing with a quarter of its waste that way, even if the worst (Dumfries and Galloway) is only scratching the surface with a miserable 3.8%. Others elsewhere do much, much better, however. For example the city of San Francisco already diverts 63% of its waste away from landfill, and aims to have no new landfill at all by 2020. Its latest innovation is to use the tons of dog waste deposited in public parks to produce methane which will be used as a natural gas.

But even with such achievements still far ahead of us, we believe that the modest Scottish successes to date indicate that ways are being found of engaging Scottish citizens in actions which will make a difference. As is entirely in keeping with our views on democracy, governance and public services, we also think that much more needs to be done to deepen and broaden such engagement for only if we can involve each and every citizen in deciding on solutions will we be able to find the best way forward.

Take global warming – one of several environmental issues that should concern all of us. It is easy enough to accept that the present average global temperature – around 15^0 Centigrade – is steadily rising. In Scotland annual land temperature has gone up more than a degree in the last one hundred years.

Then the complications start. That temperature may be worrying, but it has been much higher and much lower in the history of our planet and our country. However those variations were natural (a similar temperature spike made Greenland a haven for Norse settlers at the end of the first millennium, and then as it disappeared, it led to their extinction) whilst the present one appears (almost certainly) to be the result of man's intervention, and in particular the build-up of 'greenhouse gases' in the atmosphere.

How this will affect the world is, however, far from clear. Some argue that the increasingly rapid melting of the ice caps will produce a catastrophic rise in sea levels. Others think that this process will interfere with currents such as the Gulf Stream, changing temperature patterns worldwide. It may also increase periods of drought in some places, whilst resulting in increased rainfall in others.

Narrowing down the predictions to work out what it could mean for the individual citizen in Scotland is essential.

These uncertainties are well illustrated in a report for the English Department of Rural Affairs in January 2006 which suggested that the full consequences of the melting of the Greenland ice cap might not be experienced for a thousand years. However it then went on to say that it may be impossible to achieve planned-for reductions in carbon dioxide levels which were designed to prevent such melting. Digging further into the report, the reason why Europe in particular may fail is not technological, but governmental and, put starkly, because no one, even in government, is entirely convinced by what the scientists are telling them.

Trying to make sense of all this information is difficult enough, and it is a task made no easier by sensationalised fictions (such as *The Day After Tomorrow*). Nor is it made any easier by expanding the problems to take in, in no particular order, soil erosion in developed and developing countries, narrowing of biodiversity and a fear about the eruption of a super volcano. All these are issues which have attracted journalistic and even fictional attention but the sheer multiplicity of problems as our modern media presents them actually adds to the difficulty of persuading individuals to try and solve any of them. In order to devise local solutions, we must be able to focus locally.

Narrowing down the predictions to work out what it could

all mean for each of us as individual citizens in Scotland is therefore essential. Some predict that by 2100 Scottish temperatures will be approximately $3.5C^0$ higher during the summer and $2.5C^0$ during the winter. Others however assert that Scotland will in fact cool down because the temperate waters of the Gulf Stream presently give us a climate warmer than that on the continent. The melting of the Arctic ice-cap may alter the density of the sea in the North Atlantic, thus switching off the gulf stream. Not so much warming, for us, as dramatic cooling!

So will our country become a more pleasant place to live and possibly even a drier one? Or will rainfall increase – something it is hard to countenance in an average West of Scotland winter – in the way that other scientists expect, with up to 30% more in winter? Or could we even be heading for a mini ice age?

Will our country become a drier place or could we be heading for a mini ice age?

Any of those things are possible and the likely consequences of change are equally diverse. Would they be catastrophic – much of Glasgow, for example, would be underwater if sea levels rose by anything like some of the predictions – or merely cosmetic, with warmer summers and colder winters actually helping our tourist trade and increasing the variety of what can be grown here?

Accepting that some change is coming about, and that it is as a result of greenhouse gas emission, how is Scotland – and each one of us – doing in terms of restricting our output so as to contribute to some sort of solution? The UK is committed under the Kyoto Protocol to reduce emission of a basket of six GHGs to 12.5% below baselines by 2008-2012. Scottish emissions need therefore to fall by at least that amount in that timescale. In fact a 3% fall had taken place by 2001, but that is nowhere near enough.

Anyway, what can individuals do particularly considering that global warming is only one of many serious environmental issue that demand our attention? Population growth is causing a shortage of key resources such as water, particularly in the poorest parts of our planet. Inequalities in health and life expectancy, already stark, are worsening as a result of environmental changes. At the same time industrial and social development in the under-developed countries is causing new pressures and leading to increasing pollution.

The slow (and sometimes not so slow) poisoning of our

environment by nations which are trying to improve the lot of their own citizens and emulate the advantages already experienced by existing wealthy countries adds a further element of difficulty to the entire issue. Pollution is an inevitable by-product of over-population and an inevitable side effect of prosperity, and thus the increasing industrialisation of China and India is adding to global warming, although it is helping the poorest in those countries. At the same time in other places over-population and shortage of key resources is dragging others down.

The cacophony of problems grows every louder, so we are forced to repeat the key question – what can individuals and governments do to help? Can solutions be found collectively or individually?

Green lobby groups and parties throughout the world – and in Scotland – argue that taken together these issues add up to the most pressing matter facing humanity and that a total change in our approach to government and the economy is the only way to solve it. A huge reduction in personal freedom in developed countries including the freedom to travel, may be one result. But asking individuals to endorse such things is, frankly, not going to be successful, or not at least until individuals fully realise the problem and are fully committed to assisting in its solution. Voters already see politicians as being unduly keen to intervene in ordinary lives and over inclined to tell others what to do, whilst doing none of it themselves. Politicians, therefore, are in no position to impose solutions. Instead they are going to have to negotiate them, and (for once) to lead by example.

Nor does it help that at one time in the very recent past that the green position was diametrically opposed by the arguments of business and mainstream politics who were neither convinced by the science nor prepared to accept that there were limits to growth and who accordingly equated environmental concerns with Luddism and extremism, a message that has partially got through.

Fortunately there has been some more helpful meeting of minds in recent years. For example in February 2006 the Scottish Green MSP Mark Ballard and the leading business commentator in the *Scotsman* newspaper Bill Jamieson found themselves in agreement about the need to find 'sustainable' business models which would help the environment, and united in their criticism of the use of that word by the Scottish First Minister, who seems to think that 'sustainable' means freezing what is done now and refusing to innovate. George Bush's awakening to the perils of relying on oil is another example of the, partial at least, conversion of an environmental sceptic into one who realises that business, industry and government need to engage with the issues presented by the environmental crisis and change ideas, minds and public attitudes in order to ensure that the public follows.

For our part we believe that these various crises are of vital importance for Scotland for two clear reasons.

The first is that we cannot be immune to the eventual effects of a damaged planet and a world seething with injustice and resentment. If we are to have a secure and prosperous future we must plan for that, taking into account the context in which we live, and that context is a global one. So as world citizens we have an obligation to do as much as we can to secure the future of the world.

The second reasons is more self interested. We will not be left alone by these problems, and if we tackle them promptly and earlier than others do, we may be able to profit by our experience and our new-found skills. We anticipate that Scotland could carve out a new place of influence and respect in the world were it to move ahead of the game and start to develop solutions for problems that others have not yet fully noticed.

But there is a third and more complex reason for our concern. We also recognise in Scotland a crisis in confidence – a crisis which weakens our ability to grow in the way that we must grow in order to survive and flourish in the world. We are not secure in who we are, and we are not passing on to the next generation the skills needed to improve upon our own efforts.

The issue of where we live, and confidence in where we live, is part of those issues. The complete *patrimonie* of Scotland is her people, her culture and her land. These three are inextricably linked and if any of them is weak, the others suffer.

So our land – our environment – must be protected and preserved for the future, alongside our culture and our confidence as individuals and as a nation. And we must find a way to reconnect our people to our land, in order to build a new appreciation of who we are, and what Scotland is.

We shall look at those issues in the next two chapters, but in this one we wish to make some positive suggestions about the way in which Scotland – a Scotland with an increasingly democratic means of government and a smaller public sector which is more responsive to its citizens – can be greened, and by so doing become not only safer and more prosperous, but also a better participant in the necessary global move towards a greener planet.

How then can each of us contribute?

On a global level we must support global action. Ordinary citizens can make their voices heard by agitating for, and showing approval of, steps which make nations co-operate on setting environmental targets, sharing environmental information and working across borders to ensure progress on environmental issues. They can also express their disapproval for actions which damage the prospects for the planet, and ensure that their government does not aid and abet such things even when those things are popular.

On this level encouraging wide public knowledge of the issues and ensuring that children and adults are educated about the overall problem are necessary to assist in providing solutions is very important. NGOs and independent nationally funded environmental agencies need to be supported to do that work.

Such bodies can also channel finance – and practical assistance – to where it is needed and can influence aid and trade which is environmentally sustainable.

It is presently hard for Scotland to play a significant and helpful role in any such activities. It is, in this as in all things, spoken for on the international stage and as the record of the UK in these matters is poor, it follows that we are not either being influenced, or exerting influence, in the way we should. Consequently our ability to innovate is limited.

In the North Sea for example, our existing oil industry has the potential to play a role in battling global warming and in providing new forms of energy. Some of the oil reservoirs in the

North Sea could be used as 'sinks' for CO_2, and the Norwegians are already investigating the commercial potential of such sinks. We have to follow a slower path, as the UK government is merely 'considering' such things, and when the UK government considers, it takes a long time to move from there to action.

There is also, as we have seen in the previous chapter, the possibility of using *in situ* gasification of coal deep under the North Sea to generate electricity and to produce hydrogen for use as vehicle fuel. But once more, as such innovation lies outwith the present powers of Holyrood, that idea is more likely to be utilised and brought to commercial benefit elsewhere.

This is yet another example of how independence – the ability to work on a world stage and to choose the way in which we do so and the priorities we set – would benefit not just ourselves, but those around us. We could contribute greatly to the debate on, and action to improve, our worldwide environment but to do so to most effect we need to be able to contribute directly on a governmental basis, rather than at one remove.

If this is the 'top level' of action and activity – the level of international co-operation – then the next level comes with governmental policy setting within national boundaries followed by implementation within national borders.

Once more our position as a devolved nation as opposed to an independent one limits what we can do. Certainly the devolved settlement gives the Scottish Executive and the Scottish Parliament responsibility for environmental policy. But energy policy is reserved to Westminster and an inability to use legislation to encourage or punish activity and the inability to prioritise action in terms of *all* national revenues inevitably restricts what can be done.

For example whilst, in an earlier chapter, we have indicated that we would wish to remove fuel duty we might also wish to use legislation to discourage 'gas guzzling' cars (in a manner rather more effective than that used by Gordon Brown in his deeply disappointing budget of March 2006). The present Scottish Parliament could not do either and that exposes a weakness in our ability to produce a total package for governmental action.

Nonetheless there are things government in Scotland could and should do. It should devise a real plan of action, delineating the necessary reductions in the production of greenhouse gases, the essential elimination of polluting activities in our environment and the means by which individual citizens can contribute to national and international targets. This should be an essential part of the National Development Plan which we outlined in a previous chapter.

It can also educate and inform on such targets and provide encouragement and directed activity to ensure they are met. It can ensure that its economic – and indeed all its policies – are environmentally sound and it can encourage business to see environmental progress as being a route to secure profitability rather than an inconvenient add-on.

Government must convince the Scottish people that the overall balance of supply will keep the lights on.

It can spur new developments by, for example, offering financial incentives as it presently does to those wishing to install alternative energy sources in new-build, though that scheme is currently under very short-sighted threat. It can mandate considerable improvements in building standards (and steps in that direction are being taken). It can earmark revenues (though ideally those should be oil revenues accruing to an independent Scotland) for 'post-oil' research and development.

But it must also act as the guarantor of continuity. By this we mean that government must satisfy itself that, taken together, all its actions are able to underpin a growing and economically successful society which is also environmentally sustainable and which is contributing to global and local environmental targets.

In that regard the state has a place in terms of influencing the debate on, for example, nuclear power versus renewable energy. In those matters it must have real control and must not be left on the sidelines, as it will be by the present constitutional settlement. It must convince itself, and then convince the Scottish people, that the overall balance of supply will, to put in bluntly, keep the lights on in any and all circumstances.

Presently about a third of our electricity generation comes from nuclear sources, a little less than a third from coal, a quarter from gas and oil and about ten percent from renewable, which includes hydro. The renewable element is being encouraged to rise to 40% by 2020.

We do not intend to take a definitive position here on the

issue of nuclear power, which is the most contentious of the possible sources of future generation though we do note the opinion of the UK Government's own Sustainable Development Commission which after a year's investigation has come down firmly against new nuclear facilities. It is also instructive that the only reason that the Scottish public would support such new builds would be if it led to less reliance on imported power, according to a poll undertaken for the BBC in early 2006. It would be ironic indeed if America moved away from oil consumption in order to avoid dependence on the Middle East, whilst we took a retrograde step and increased nuclear risks for very similar reasons.

We therefore believe that if the nation can be provided with power from means other than the traditional GHG emitters, that would be preferable for nuclear has the unfortunate disadvantage of leaving a residue which will take not years, but centuries to render safe. It is also potentially more hazardous than any alternative other than those that contribute to GHG emissions.

Our preference is for a non-nuclear mix, except if no other alternatives exist and can be shown, categorically, not to exist. In those circumstances a continued reliance on nuclear power for a limited period whilst alternatives develop might be tolerable, although the more reliance is placed on nuclear, the less incentive there is to ensure that the alternatives, and especially decentralised alternatives are developed in ways that make them more cost-effective and more viable.

As in all our plans, we wish to make sure that we base our actual decisions on clear principles and underpin them with clear objectives. In this case our primary objective should be the generation of electricity from processes with zero emission of pollutants and the replacement of fossil fuel usage with other alternatives – such as hydrogen for vehicle propulsion.

Of course as electricity is the primary generator of hydrogen from electrolysis of water, the development of cheap electricity could revolutionise all our energy needs. Hydrogen can also act as an energy store, with the energy available to be used to generate further electricity at times of high demand.

That whole prospect might seem like something out of science fiction – the discovery of a cheap means of producing electricity

> Our primary objective should be the generation of electricity from processes with zero emission of pollutants.

191

which can then be used to double, triple and more the power available to society. But in fact in the Scottish Highlands it is a real prospect.

In the last half century is in the Highlands that most experimentation with renewable energy has been undertaken. In the 1950s they were at the forefront of developments of mass production by means of hydro power – the generation of electricity using water. The technology fell out of fashion, but is being revived today. In the 1990s Inverness was where Wavegen was born, which today leads the world in the development of electricity generation from wave power. The Pure project in the Shetlands is now pioneering the production and use of hydrogen as a fuel and as a store of power from erratic electricity sources such as wind power. In Orkney, Oref is pioneering renewable energy and in the Western Isles the concept of mega wind farm projects is being tested, particularly in terms of public acceptance.

Taken together all these innovations indicate that the answer to the cheap, natural, production of electricity is likely to be a reality within the Highlands within the next decade. Moreover the visual pollution of wind farms may be eliminated by offshore construction, as in the outer Moray Firth, a project which involves the Canadian company Talisman.

Yet all these may be dwarfed by another Highland project, driven by the new University of the Highlands and Islands (UHI). This will harness the energy generated continuously by the fierce tidal races which rush through the Pentland Firth and between the numerous islands off the Scottish north and west coasts. In fact so great is their potential that it has been estimated that an initial five tidal projects in this area would generate an incredible 30,000mw of power which is equal to half of entire UK consumption. This is power without the unreliability of wind and wave and without the pollution of nuclear and hydrocarbon power stations.

Herein may lie the potential to find and exploit that endless source of cheap electricity and hence cheap hydrogen from the electrolysis of water which could free Scotland from dependence on hydrocarbons and atomic power for electricity generation and fuel and make us not just self-sufficient, but the exporter of vast quantities of power. What is needed to get to that stage is the will to believe it can be done and the investment of the type of

R&D funds which we have already indicated we wish to apply from a revitalised Scottish economy.

A project such as this (and perhaps also another devoted to the gasification of offshore coal) requires a 'Manhattan Project' approach with the rapid mobilisation of all the financial, engineering and scientific resources required to bring it to rapid fruition. Regardless of Westminster's claims to energy control Holyrood should seize the initiative now and make it Scotland's priority, as it surely would if we were an independent nation. The starting point could well be initial installations at the Churchill Barriers in Orkney and the Stroma-Caithness channel in the Pentland Firth.

Once supported in that way, this tidal power project would, in its size, its potential and its boundless bounty reduce our present North Sea oil and gas bonanza to a footnote in history. It should be a priority for every politician.

This tidal power project would reduce the North Sea oil and gas bonanza to a footnote in history.

In fact such projects need to be approached by all politicians in a way quite different from that used for other energy issues. The objective of securing cheap, pollution-free electricity and hydrogen should be the core objective of energy policy across all political parties. Such programmes could also result in an unexpected and potentially massive financial windfall from the sale of carbon dioxide emissions credits to major polluting countries. UHI have shown a most important lead in this matter by striving to create a centre of engineering excellence to replace the run-down of the Dounreay nuclear establishment with a minimum of government assistance. Ironic as it is, the prospect of a new era of Scottish success in the field of power generation is arising directly from the failure of a previous dream – the dream of nuclear generation from a fast reactor. Final success may well come not from what man put into the dome on the shore, but from what was sweeping past it, twenty four hours a day, and had been since the dawn of time!

This project alone shows that full university status for UHI is long overdue. In fact it is something of an insult to the Highlands that such status has been constantly deferred. UHI should also become the national centre of excellence for renewable energy, with the national R&D funds for such developments administered from there.

The debate on our future energy sources, is one that Scotland should have openly and fully. It is to be regretted that it is presently turning into yet another sterile party political issue with much heat generated, so to speak, but very little light.

The citizen, as ever, should be at the heart of it. Supra national and national activity is all very well, but we believe in the primacy of the citizen. So consequently the citizen will have to make a very substantial individual contribution to all types of environmental change.

Consequently we propose a citizens' action plan which will enroll every Scot in the task of conserving energy and improving our country and creating a sustainable Scotland which can contribute to achieving a more sustainable world.

That plan will have at its heart each individual and the responsibility of the individual will be its driving force. For example the fact that switching off TVs, DVDs and computers each night rather than leaving them on standby would, in Scotland alone, mean that we would need one fewer power station. This needs to be illustrated to every individual, for about £75 million worth of power in Scotland is wasted in this way each year.

The solution in our action plan? Firstly an information campaign. Secondly an initiative to persuade manufacturers to drop the standby mode on all electrical equipment that does not need it (set-top boxes for digital television are about the only ones that do). Thirdly, perhaps, a more expensive domestic electricity tariff overnight, discouraging such usage.

Work with manufacturers to increase low usage electrical equipment would also be important, as would development of more energy saving devices. Individuals need to be shown – in simple terms – what are the lowest usage appliances, and they should have a price differential that makes them more attractive.

Better home insulation and better home design can also lead to substantial reductions in power requirements. Home surveys to assist in identifying ways of saving on power usage should be offered free of charge and those willing to invest in the domestic generation and consumption of alternative energy should be encouraged by tax incentive as well as by grant aid. More resources are needed for this, not less, and we would willingly allocate them from an independent Scottish budget. A systematic approach is now urgently needed, balancing support, incentives and assistance with clear governmental action and a concomitant commitment from the private sector.

This is also needed, to return to our quotation from George Bush, in order to set an objective for the nation – one that ordinary people can understand and sign on to.

So let us set that objective. In Scotland we should aim, within ten years, to be in the forefront of environmentally responsible nations, contributing positively to the improvement of our country and, by so doing, to the world. We should aim to be not just self-sufficient in energy but to be a net exporter of pollution-free energy, and to be recycling as much of our waste as the world leaders (for example emulating and then quickly surpassing the 600,000 tonnes of glass recycled per year in England which now saves the same amount of power as is annually consumed by all England's primary schools).

By those means we can become a leading nation in terms of the conservation of energy and we should accordingly state that we want to not just meet, but exceed, all internationally agreed environmental targets. Moreover those aims should be agreed across the parties at Holyrood and the powers necessary to allow us to succeed in meeting them should be an essential part of any future package of constitutional change.

The aims should be underpinned by a Citizens Action Plan, which shows how each individual can contribute to achieving them and governmental policy should be developed to include incentives and other means of encouraging individual action.

That action plan might, for example:

- Provide a easily understandable summary of present scientific information on the environmental crisis and outline how individual action can help provide solutions.

- Contextualise this information with a summary account of Scotland's history, natural history and culture, stressing the importance of pride in our surroundings and our individual role as guardians of our country for future generations.

- Present our macro objectives and plans to generate cheap

and pollution-free electricity and replace fossil fuels with alternatives such as hydrogen and – in the medium term – bio-diesel.

- Give comprehensive guidance on means to save power in the home and reduce domestic power consumption. Incentives, perhaps including tax concessions, might be provided for those who can prove that they are reducing their power and water consumption year on year by their own actions and investment.

- Give information on recycling and offer advice and support for participation in local authority recycling schemes, whilst ensuring that such schemes were comprehensive and nationwide.

- Encourage the development of cheaper and better public transport, developed to ensure better contribution to cutting GHGs, and encourage a diminished use of individual vehicles. Where individual vehicles were still essential, ensure that hybrid vehicles were advantaged in terms of taxation (such as the waiving of VAT on them) as were vehicles that run in whole or in part on environmentally more friendly fuels and operate in a cleaner fashion. We must also ensure less use of air transport, first of all by explaining its harmful consequences.

- Integrate into such information lifestyle advice, including healthy eating, smoking reduction and sensible drinking. Encourage a more positive self-image, associated with a cleaner and more attractive country. Stress individual responsibility in these areas too.

No doubt other information, positive assistance and offers of incentives could be included. The action plan and its distribution would also require to be backed up by consistent and continuous national publicity and MSPs and others – working through their information channels enhanced as we anticipated in the first section – would also be key communicators.

As with the National Development Plan, private sector involvement in ensuring governmental aims and objectives were being met would be crucial. Accordingly the private sector should be encouraged through the National Plan and the promotion of the Citizens Action Plan to implement, market and provide environmentally aware products and services. A national 'green mark' might be awarded to these and information on them, as they develop, included in the national publicity effort.

We have leant very heavily on individual action in this chapter because we are concerned that whilst the macro issues are debated and discussed by politicians, and covered by journalists, the micro issues – the issues which, if they are acted on by individuals, will go a great distance to help resolve the macro problems – are not being promoted energetically enough to ordinary citizens. There is not only a major threat to our collective well-being, there is also a major opportunity; an opportunity to democratise, involve and energise public participation in national policy priorities which should be taken.

In the area of macro power there are two projects above all which we believe will address all of our global warming concerns and which require the undivided support of not just the people but also all of our political parties – the harnessing of tidal power and the pollution-free *in situ* gasification of offshore coal reserves.

Seen in that way – as part of the move towards a participatory society – our national response to this global crisis has the potential to make a positive out of a negative. But we can and should go further for we need not only to create a new approach to the environment and to international and national issues, we also need to nurture and develop – as part of it – a new attitude to our history and our culture so that our whole national well-being is improved and our national confidence restored. The next two chapters suggest how that might be done.

3.2 Creative Scotland

> At a recent cabinet discussion every single Minister was not
> only enthusiastic about our cultural development but
> thoughtful and helpful about how it could be applied to
> their own area of responsibility. And each made the
> commitment to use the power and creativity of culture and
> the arts to help them in their work. To entrench cultural
> development in their portfolio – because for our country's
> future it can be neither peripheral nor an add-on.
>
> **Jack McConnell**, First Minister, 30th November 2003

BEFORE we tackle the issue of our history and heritage, let us look more widely at the issues of culture and creativity – the issues that are often called those of the arts, though they go more widely. As we have indicated, we believe that these issues are so much part of the overall question of who we are, and how we live in this land, that they need to be considered as part of our national debate on our environment and how we relate to it. Each citizen's individual relationship to our country must be a relationship that embraces creativity and is fuelled by culture. A national responsibility for our culture rests on each of us, and is the overall responsibility of our government.

This is, of course, understood worldwide because throughout the world government involvement in the arts is a given. Only in the darkest political backwoods is the possibility of no formal governmental responsibility or input to culture debated as a serious notion. Consequently in Scotland instead of endless doubt about the principle, we should actually be considering only the details. We are happy to say that we fully accept the Culture Commission's view that at least 1% of GDP should be spent in formal cultural policy, and we would expect any independent Scottish government to meet and indeed exceed that target. It is an area where expenditure does not equate to national control, still less exclusive national delivery and although there are many parts of national polity that are wasteful in terms of public resources, culture is not one of them. It is a rare example of where more spending is needed, and it must be found. So too must new means of introducing money into culture, including endowment funding, state supported sponsorship schemes and, as we indicate later, new means of state support for individual artists.

Yet in this context the key question and the key variable is not just the level of government involvement, nor only the means by which that is exercised. The expectations of government, and the relationship it establishes with artists, are vital parts of the mix too.

Models vary from place to place. In the United States the tax system is used to encourage private, corporate or institutional donation with a comparatively low level of government expenditure and directed demands. In France and many other European countries, however, the state takes a much larger role, setting firm directions and underpinning those with substantial resources. The UK has tended towards the latter model, but with elements of the American reluctance to impose too greatly on the sector and with a concomitant lower level of spending.

Another difference lies in the methods used to promote artistic activity and access to culture. Direct funding of artists has always been a strong element in the Scandinavian system, as Peter Duelund's monumental study of Nordic Cultural Policy showed in 2003. Allied to such support is a high level of public expenditure on the arts, the use of stringent copyright laws (a matter hardly discussed in this country) and a strong encouragement of public participation.

The principles underlying such practice are well enunciated by a colleague of Duelund's, Marit Bakke, in a study of specifically Norwegian policy. These are identified as enlightenment (culture that helps the individual find him or herself), liberty (economic, political or other forms of pressure should not be applied to the arts), egalitarianism (equal opportunities for all) and social welfare (culture as an integrated part of social policies). These are bound together with a national aim – the protection and promotion of the national cultural heritage.

In the type of dynamic and entrepreneurial Scotland which we wish to see take the place of the pallid and dependent Scotland we have today, there should be little difficulty in all sections of society signing up to these principles and particularly to the protection and promotion of the national cultural heritage. Even if one was only interested in making sure that such a heritage was still available as a tourist draw that aim would be of importance as the International Charter on Cultural Tourism makes clear. But in fact most people in Scotland are enthusiastic about protecting and promoting what it means to be Scottish and how we look at the world. Yet comparatively little progress has been made in converting them into the key elements of a national cultural policy and then making that policy a mainstay of our drive for economic and social renewal as a nation.

Devolution repatriated responsibility for the arts and culture but governmental response has been slow and very patchy: the clearest inference one can draw so far from the series of Commissions and studies is that no-one in government in Scotland has any clear idea about what priority cultural spending should be given, which model would best suit this small country, and how that model should be implemented. Scottish artists, always used to traveling hopefully rather than arriving, are now increasingly drawn to that maxim from the Book of Proverbs: 'Hope deferred maketh the heart grow sick'.

Devolution repatriated responsibility for culture but governmental response has been slow and very patchy.

It took more than four years for the issue of culture to be made the subject of a major speech by Scotland's First Minister. His contribution was made on St Andrews Day 2003 in Glasgow and in it he laid out the principles on which his government would base its approach to the arts. Re-read after several years, as the quote opening this chapter indicates, the speech itself is somewhat dull and very driven by process.

Yet this St Andrew's Day vision quickly assumed iconic status in the mind of the arts minister (the last one that is) and in the public pronouncements of our legion of cultural administrators. Apparently seeking nothing less than the establishment of culture within the mainstream of government delivery it presaged the establishment of the Cultural Commission whose deliberations were supposed to form the basis of Executive cultural policy for a generation (McConnell's words, not ours).

That of course has not happened. His own government, presumably with his agreement, later rejected most of the recommendations from that commission and belittled its chairman and members. The Executive therefore remains stuck at the stage of trying to formulate some coherent cultural policies whilst pretending that the matter is done and dusted. Of course, as we have noted before, such a gap between rhetoric and reality is very typical of McConnell and his administration. Nonetheless it does not diminish both the grave problem that faces Scottish culture, shorn as it is of any intellectually coherent framework of governmental support.

Another former Finance Minister turned head of government had greater success in taking good intentions to full fruition. Thirty years earlier the late Irish politician Charles Haughey, addressing the Harvard Summer School Institute in July 1972, considered the topic of 'Art and the Majority'. In political exile after the celebrated arms trial, he was already known as a keen patron of the arts. In his finance role in government he had freed creative artists from tax liability on their work. Ten years later as *Taoiseach* he was to introduce the Aosdana Scheme, guaranteeing a minimum income to 150 artists.

Haughey's reputation ended in tatters. Harried by the Irish Revenue, he was hemmed in by a plethora of potential court cases. He accepted back-handers, peddled influence, bullied friend and foe alike and lived an extravagant lifestyle supported by others. Yet his influence on Irish cultural life cannot be underestimated. He did not just talk about bringing the arts into the mainstream of national life – he did it.

The difference between what is, and what might be, is graphic. In the 1950s and 60s Irish artists felt marginalised and neglected but Ireland during the 1980s and 1990s was, a cultural power-house. Working artists moved to Ireland and young Irish artists had the opportunity to develop. Whilst no cultural scene is ever without its problems, the overall health of Irish culture could not be denied and is still robust. It is valued by the state and by the people and its principal priority is to nurture and develop the artist, from which all the rest flows. Haughey's intention to ensure that in Ireland 'the relationship of the artist to the community might be less distant than elsewhere' has been achieved.

We believe that this cultural dynamism is not unconnected to the economic dynamism that the Irish state has also shown. While we have already outlined the way in which Irish economic growth has been directly stimulated by a reduction in the size of government in Ireland, the enthusiasm and commitment of the

Irish people with regard to making their country grow and flourish is, in great part, a product of their national self-confidence. That has been greatly stimulated by their growing cultural self-confidence.

Scotland needs to build that same cultural self-confidence but one cannot be sanguine about success given the crucial differences between Haughey's expression of what a cultural policy should be, and that enunciated by our First Minister.

For a start Haughey's speech hardly mentioned his own country whilst McConnell's hardly mentioned anywhere else. There is a chippy insularity about our First Minister's approach to culture as well as a nervous self-justification of the very idea that a country, let alone a country's leader, might take art and artists seriously. Even if one did not know it, one would quickly realise that Haughey's speech was drafted in part by an artist (the writer Anthony Cronin) whereas McConnell's was written largely by arts administrators.

Haughey concluded with a magnificent peroration:

> If the real purposes of human living are to be served, and the instinct we all share to work towards something we can glimpse beyond ourselves is to be fulfilled in the happiest and most creative way, then we must certainly recognise that government has both a role and a duty where the artist is concerned.

This belief in this humanistic 'real purpose' of life for all citizens and the role of artists in achieving it, in part supported by the state, remains the prime motivator for most governments in terms of cultural spending particularly those which have a successful arts policy and a flourishing arts scene.

But this is clearly not the approach of our First Minister. To him a vibrant Scottish cultural life is necessary for very different reasons. First of all he believes that the purpose of cultural activity is to allow the world to see 'how successful a contemporary country and culture we are'. This is art as politician's *machismo* and has little to do with individual artists let alone individual Scots. It is a long way from the personal impact of Haughey's view of art as a means to glimpse 'beyond ourselves. . . in the happiest and most creative of ways'.

Confidence is not about arrogance or self-publicity. It is about self-fulfillment, and it appears that Haughey understood that, whilst our First Minister does not.

Yet McConnell insists on going even further down what is a blind alley. He went on to assert in his St Andrews Day speech that cultural diversity is to be encouraged because it will 'attract more and more talented people to come and experience Scotland.' Furthermore cultural spending is to be judged by its 'use' in terms of boosting educational achievement, achieving healthy bodies and minds, and delivering social justice. The right use of such cultural spending, he claims, will even instill a sense of community pride in open spaces and reduce vandalism.

These are big claims to make for the effects of the arts. They are even bigger claims to make if the purpose in so doing is to justify cultural expenditure for if they are not achieved, then presumably such spending can no longer be considered as a legitimate priority for government. In contrast Haughey's assertions were not only more modest but because they were directed towards individuals, they appeared to be more likely to produce results. They were also regarded by Haughey as worthy in themselves, not worthy only because of the need to achieve stated non-artistic outcomes.

This question of a measurable degree of return on arts spending is a difficult one. Professor John Carey, in his somewhat dispiriting recent book *What good are the arts?* comes to the conclusion that the benefit of culture is impossible to quantify whether in personal or community terms. Whilst that is an extreme position with which we disagree, whether the arts make a society or an individual 'better' is a key issue. We think there is evidence which shows that community confidence and national self-confidence can be improved by a stimulating artistic and cultural environment but even with that belief we would never tie such a situation down to the narrow set of parameters that the First Minister seems to have chosen. The degree of certainty about specific community and national outcomes which McConnell not only predicts, but requires, is a large leap of faith, as well as of rhetoric.

Perhaps the implementation of the Cultural Commission recommendations would have given us a chance to find out if that stance was correct. But as the recommendations have by and large been abandoned and, as a result, the Executive's new proposals appear to have no systematic thinking or clear philosophical justification behind them, it will (as ever) be difficult to judge if McConnell is right or wrong.

However we can look at other societies and work out if their approach to national cultural policy, and its expression in a policy framework has succeeded. McConnell was indeed correct to say in his St Andrew's Day lecture that mere discussion of structures for administering the arts is the wrong way to proceed. Structures are the means by which policy is delivered, so it is important to devise the policy first. To do that we must decide on what our priorities are and how they can contribute to our overall aims.

> Mere discussion of the structures is the wrong way to proceed.

To see how that works, we could do worse than to look at Ireland once more. When we do so we can see that although in later years Haughey increasingly imposed his own prejudices on national artistic policy, the basics of his approach were broadly correct. As a leader of government he extended the emphasis on individual artists and institutionalised the primary arts objective of supporting individual artists and individual creativity. He believed that when such creativity is supported over the long term, national cultural renewal and new cultural confidence would result and he proved that this vision worked.

Surely, therefore, our own overall aim in Scotland should be to invest in individual creativity in order to establish and maintain cultural creativity as an underpinning factor of our national life? Moreover we should do this not just because others do it, nor just because there are financial benefits from it. We should do it because it is, in itself, a useful activity. It nurtures the talents and outlook of individual citizens and therefore nurtures the whole nation. It develops ways of seeing, tells our national story to ourselves and lets our national story be influenced, changed and developed by interaction with other national stories and with wider views. Health spending may help our bodies and education spending our potential but cultural spending underpins and creates the holistic and confident self, both as an individual and as part of the community.

Government, in this definition which should ideally apply across the whole spectrum of public service delivery, is essentially the guarantor of diversity, freedom and continuity. It does things that others cannot or will not do, though it should always seek to work with others and particularly the private sector, in partnership.

How should this be done?

The first priority is to take actions that recognise the primacy of artists in the process. Just as hospitals cannot run without doctors, nor schools without teachers, the arts cannot exist without artists. The centrepiece of the policy must therefore be to encourage and sustain artists themselves. From their work grows the possibility (in certain art forms) of performance whilst in others publication or dissemination will create the opportunity for access. The state certainly has an interest in supporting performance and dissemination not least in order to attract and inspire others and showcase ourselves but putting performance before creativity is putting the artistic cart before the horse.

> The first priority is to recognise the primacy of artists.

Without original work there will either be no such opportunities or opportunities that can only be met by those from outwith our country. That is no bad thing, as part of the diet, but the level to which it can provide the whole meal is limited: taken too far it means that our national story will go untold, our deeper reactions to our changing world will be ignored and the process of national construction will be skewed. If art is, as Haughey maintained, a 'unique reflection of our state as human beings' (and he quoted André Malraux in his support) then part of that unique reflection lies in our own experiences on this particular part of the planet and contains the narrative of what that means to us.

Presently national support for artists is *ad hoc*: we tend to support art works rather than those who make them. Funding is project specific and the gaps between creations remain unfinanced.

The establishment of a Scottish Academy of Artists, with Scotland's foremost artists from all the genres as members, drawing a state subvention, would be the initial step. However it would be mere elitism, of the most tokenist kind to boot, if this was limited to a handful of the chosen. It would also not be enough to limit tax incentives to a very small number. Scotland could and should sustain an academy of diversity and excellence and that Academy would, in members, run into the hundreds.

It would also not be static, or any type of sterile Pantheon. A system whereby new, or candidate, members were admitted and in which there was a dynamic in membership would be required and we can learn from the Irish experience of their more modest Aosdana scheme. Allied with a tax exempt status for artists below a predetermined minimum income level – a wide-ranging exemption with an inclusive definition of the arts – we would begin to create an infrastructure for creativity.

The so called 'creative industries' should not be separate from this. One of the arguments for a more determinist and economically-led model is the rising prominence of these industries and the threat of globalisation but to change one's whole view of the relationship of the arts to society on that basis is a knee-jerk reaction. It is better to enroll these disciplines and the pressures of internationalism and learn from that process. Consequently film makers, rock musicians, television directors and critics would be an important part of such an institution, as would be those who teach. Funded by government but largely self regulating – the structural arrangements should keep it as far distant from government control or influence as it is possible to get – it would provide a developing powerhouse for the nation's cultural life. It should have premises and a physical incarnation as well as a strong voice and a central involvement in the wider funding and policy process. It should also have the mechanisms to attract and use private sponsorship for both individuals and art works.

In tandem with it should be a basic structure for arts performance and for the encouragement of art forms. Our national companies form the basic foundation for such a development, but they would need to be added to or the functions of existing bodies expanded. We need a national hub for the traditional arts and one for literature to supplement a national opera company, a national theatre and national orchestras. The National Library and the National Museum require to play a more proactive role in encouraging creativity, rather than just recording it.

These bodies or hubs are a declaration of the core areas which government supports and will go on supporting. They provide the core opportunities for high quality provision and high quality, easy access. They are the government's means of ensuring participation as well as consistency in quality and continuity in operation and the prime responsibility for supporting them should lie with government, though once more there needs to be a creative approach to private sector sponsorship and investment. It may be that the best way to fund certain of the national companies is by the long term development of endowments and the involvement of the private sector in that would be crucial.

The third part of this structure might be concerned with stimulating partnerships with local authorities and commercial bodies, with the funding and encouragement of community activity and with the nurturing of new ideas and new talent. Its radical task would be to let a thousand blooms flourish and a thousand ideas contend. Some artists might start their careers with assistance from this body, and move on into the Academy, or into the national companies. Others might choose to remain working on an *ad hoc* basis and they should have not only the right, but the opportunity, to do so. Long established companies and organisations, of crucial importance to their sector and their locality would fit happily into this wide-ranging and outward-looking funding pattern, as would small events and individual creators.

All these bodies – the Academy, the national companies, and a new and re-focused Arts Council – would interface with education (and education through the arts and about the arts must become a vital part of the Scottish educational experience), with health, with social work, with justice and with community development. But their purpose would not be to serve those other worthy ends, but to produce more than the sum of the parts.

One of the most important differences between this model – which is in essence an updated and revised Haughey model leaning on much other practice and achievement elsewhere and particularly in Scandinavia – and the first Minister's supposed work in progress lies in the very relationship of the arts to government.

The First Minister seems to believe that the arts – and the artists – have a duty to Scotland: a duty that requires them to subsume themselves in other policy objectives and to earn their keep by so doing. But the alternative view is surely closer to the mark – in order to 'glimpse beyond ourselves in the happiest and most creative way' and to contribute that sense of national self-confidence which we urgently need we have to ask not what the arts can do for Scotland, but what Scotland can do for the arts.

That was Haughey's generous approach in Ireland and the paradox is that the return that Ireland has gained has been far greater than if it had begrudged every penny and bean-counted every subsidy. We should lay on our Government and our country a duty to support artists and artistic activity for only by so doing can it reap the full and unfettered benefits of both creativity and access to creativity.

That might be called the real 'arms length' approach. Determinism implies control: it is a bargain made between the government and artists which requires a price for support to be set, and agreed product and outcomes delivered. The recognition and acceptance of a duty of government to the artist does no such thing. It pays in good faith for what it knows will be valuable and bases the relationship on shared trust and shared belief in a better future.

That idea was put well by another Government leader – the present Irish *Taoiseach* Bertie Ahern who told the Irish Arts Council on a visit in April 2005:

> I believe there is only one persuasive case for supporting the arts. . . that is art itself. Art challenges not only what we think: it changes the way we think. Real inspiration cannot be planned for.

Alas we live in a country which is led by those who believe that everything can be planned for, measured, and its worth assessed. Determinism, managerialism and overstated objectives have been a hallmark of the first seven years of devolution. Our Executive truly knows the price of everything but the value of nothing.

There is however, an emerging thirst for something else across the whole political, social and cultural spectrum. Government should be providing it not least (but not only) because in this area government investment will pay huge dividends in terms of national improvement and national progress.

Government should also be creating the context not just for creativity, but also for a better understanding of who we are and where we have come from. So we must add to this rich mix of environmental concern and cultural renewal – the mix that will make us what we need to be – a new assessment of our past and how it relates to our present and future.

3.3 We are who we are

> In a further insult to his Scottish crews, Nelson had one of
> his ships at the Battle of the Nile named HMS *Culloden*.
> England expects us Scots to be the Uriah the Hittite of
> England's wars but do not ask us to celebrate its heroes. The
> first memorial to this enemy of Scotland was erected by
> English foundry workers at my neighboring village of
> Taynuilt. I intend to piss on it on Trafalgar Day.
>
> **Iain Hamilton QC**
> in a Letter to the *Herald*, April 28th 2005

AFICIONADOS of the great and unjustly neglected Scottish novelist, Robin Jenkins, are split on what was his finest novel but *Fergus Lamont* must be a possible choice. The book is vast in scope, and deals with a whole range of themes – memory, ambition, politics, war and friendship – as well as touching upon the issue of what Scottish children should be taught about their nation.

Set in a town on the West coast – probably Greenock – and opening at the start of the twentieth century it is the book's fictional headmaster, Mr Maybole, who discovers a teacher telling his class about the Highland Clearances and warns him:

> You are filling these children's minds with poison. You are
> undermining their confidence in legally constituted
> authority. It is a mistake to study the history of one's own
> country. It divides us instead of uniting us. . . Why bother
> with stuff so out of date?

But the response comes from one of the children in the class, who lives in the squalor of the local slums. 'It isn't out of date,' she says. 'People are still put out of their houses.'

There could be no better justification for being taught, and for learning, our own history. Only then will we be able to take the steps that stop 'people being put out of their houses'.

For anyone living in Scotland, it is hard to feel a sense of immediacy and relevance when studying, say, the Wars of the Roses or the fate of any of Henry VIII's wives. But such

211

immediacy and relevance is to be found in the story of our own past, of things closer to home and those sensations usually prove a considerable spur to any young person living in Scotland who comes to the study of Scottish history for the first time.

Quickly such children discover that they can understand a great deal more about contemporary Scotland by acquiring even a basic knowledge of the forces which have shaped it. Such an understanding also equips them to make more informed and more constructive contributions to their society and their nation.

Yet it is, as history teachers often point out, possible for a child going through the Scottish educational system to be immersed in the world of ancient Egypt, the Romans or the Vikings several times (these being popular 'topics' for cross curricular teaching) but never once be confronted with the ideas of Adam Smith or David Hume, still less Tom Johnston or John Knox. Worse still, if history is to be – as it is in some primary schools – merely a matter of interrogating one's grandparents about their lives, then collective historical memory is not now stretching back much beyond the age of skiffle, and perhaps not even as far as that. Such an approach lacks any rigour or coherence.

Extraordinary as it is, there still remains no legal requirement for schools to teach anything at all about Scotland's past and history itself need only be offered in the first two years of secondary education. The average time devoted to that is less than an hour a week and in early 2006 two schools in Glasgow were reported to be planning to abolish history teaching altogether in the early secondary years. Some pupils would therefore never learn anything about Scottish history in the whole of their Scottish schooling.

Quite the reverse is required, for there needs to be a major expansion in the teaching of our own history. Although opposition to that move is usually couched in pseudo internationalist language which deplores 'parochial' thinking in reality making the study of Scottish history much more widespread is a positive and outward-looking ambition.

If we base our study of our own past on where we are and who we are we will soon draw in lessons from elsewhere and build an accurate view of the past, present and future potential of a small nation on the edge of Europe yet fully engaged with the world: a small nation with every reason to feel confident, but no reason at all to feel arrogant.

We need that type of perspective – and we need it to inform not just the ignorant, but also the prejudiced.

2005 being the two hundredth anniversary of Nelson's victory at Trafalgar, it is perhaps not surprising that the features pages of the quality newspapers should have carried the occasional piece celebrating the event, or reflecting on aspects of it. The media, after all, is obsessed with marking time.

There are, of course, several grounds on which to object to such celebrations – those of warmongering and over-interest with the imperial past spring to mind. But an objection on the grounds of offence to Scotland seems harder to understand. Nelson's fleet was full of Scottish sailors of all ranks. No doubt some were press-ganged, but the historical evidence does not indicate that such forced service was any more prevalent amongst Scots than amongst those from other parts of the UK. Some of Nelson's most effective officers and petty officers were Scots and distinguished themselves in battle. All of those did credit to their country as they knew it, even if that country was not an independent Scotland.

> Nelson's fleet was full of Scottish sailors of all ranks.

For Nelson, whilst an English Admiral, was serving a British state in which Scotland was an integral part. One can regret the Act of Union and indeed oppose any and all of its consequences, but surely such energy might be better expended on looking to the future. One cannot change the past nor undo its unkindness and the most useless activity of all is to rage against those unkindnesses in a way which eventually goes looking for the slight to Scotland in every incident in the past.

Ireland has learnt such lessons, admittedly painfully, as a letter to the *Irish Times* in July 2005 illustrated. A William Gibson, writing from Co Kildare about the same topic noted:

> In this period of more mature relationships with Britain
> it is important to understand the part played by Irishmen
> and Irishwomen in the wars of the eighteenth and
> nineteenth century.

Such a rational approach, however, is still the exception rather than the rule amongst certain Scottish Nationalists such as Iain

Hamilton QC, a quote from whose letter on the subject prefaces this chapter.

Mr Hamilton, whose primary claim to fame is his role in the repatriation of the Stone of Destiny in 1952 lives in semi-retirement in Argyll. He is an icon to many nationalists because of his dogged and long-lasting resistance to the Union. He has been a powerful and respected, if somewhat quixotic, voice of the independence movement throughout his life and it is to be regretted that he did not make it into the first Scottish Parliament in 1999 where he would have been a trenchant and experienced voice.

This type of historical and political myopia cripples us in terms of developing positive ambitions.

But his letter to the *Herald* about Trafalgar shows another side of him. It is an example of 'grievance politics' *par excellence*. In fact it is 'grievance politics' which has become 'grievance history'. It demonstrates exactly why Scotland, needs a new approach to its own past, present and future.

This type of historical, cultural and political myopia prevents us from standing straight on to the world and cripples us in terms of developing positive ambitions and then fulfilling those ambitions. It skews our identity, makes us take up indefensible stances and misrepresents our country. But it is, alas, not uncommon.

In April 2006 Scotland's First Minister addressed Harvard University as part of the Tartan Day celebrations. In the peroration of his speech, widely covered at home as being one which confidently assured Scots that a 'new Enlightenment' was dawning, led by the First Minister's own Executive, he said that Scotland was using,

> . . . education to liberate individuals with the power of knowledge, rediscovering our enterprising and entrepreneurial spirit through increased opportunity and choice and (using) the power of culture and the arts in the pursuit of human happiness.

And he went on to claim that

> Our work has only just started. Seven years is only a short time compared to our historical achievements. But we Scots are starting to lift our heads again, looking beyond our borders with unity and ambition. And if those of us in

positions of leadership within Scotland stay true to
Hutcheson's principle of bringing 'the greatest good to the
greatest number of people' then we might just help to create
the conditions in which a new stream of modern thought
and invention could flourish.

This book has indicated – as all impartial scrutiny of today's
Scotland must indicate – that these assertions are simply not true.
In fact our 'enterprising and entrepreneurial spirit' is being stifled
by overweening government, education is under constant threat,
and the bureaucratic policy applied to our arts and culture is far
distant from the artist-centred and creatively liberating approach
which is required. The nation is not showing unity, not least
because it has a bitterly partisan government presiding over an
equally partisan Parliament and our national ambition (as the
First Minister himself admits on other occasions) is weak and
fragmented. That alone makes it clear that those in 'positions of
leadership' are manifestly failing, particularly if their aim is truly
to bring the 'greatest good to the greatest number'.

So how could a 'new stream of modern thought and invention
flourish'? How could an 'enlightenment' be based on these
unpromising foundations?

Of course it could not. The sentiment may be vaguely laudable
but the actuality is starkly clear – what is being said is pretension,
bordering on deceit.

But of course misuse is the purpose. There is no plan here to
spread the lessons of the enlightenment, or to deepen the understanding, at home and abroad, of our shared past so that we can
profit by it. Equally there is no intention to find ways on which
we might use the lessons of the enlightenment to develop a new
society. All the words are designed to do is to reflect some glory
on the speaker, to assert that he is a leader who is changing things
and achieving things. Like Mr Hamilton, Mr McConnell talks of
the past in terms that seek to help him achieve his present
ambitions.

Yet it is vitally important that Scots come to grips with the
reality of the Enlightenment, that they do learn about its
achievements and that they do understand the ideas that flowed
from it. We have quoted Adam Smith ourselves in this book, and
attention to his views would help Scotland understand its present

difficulties and assist the country to find new opportunities. But rather than simply recreate past glories, we should be seeking to achieve fresh heights. Only those who fail to understand the past, to paraphrase Seneca, seek constantly to repeat it.

There are many other examples that we could point to, which would further illustrate the way in which prominent Scots – who should be showing an example – flaunt their misreading, and sometimes deliberate misreading, of Scotland's history and by so doing prolong our alienation from the healing and strengthening power of our own culture.

Tory Secretary of State for Scotland Iain Laing was guilty of just that when calling on Robert Burns to justify a lack of democracy and a lack of constitutional progress in Scotland during the Major government. As part of a reply to a question in the Commons, he quoted these lines from 'Does Haughty Gaul Invasion Threat'

> Be Britain still to Britain true,
> Amang ourselves united;
> For never but by British hands
> Maun British wrangs be righted!

But of course he totally ignored the circumstances in which the lines were written, just as his interrogators ignored other important aspects of the poet's life and circumstances when swopping equally partisan quotes. All might have benefitted from a reading of Conor Cruise O'Brian's magnificent essay on Yeats, in which he lays bare any supposed connection between day-to-day politics and the real poetic impulse.

So it goes on. The Braveheart myth becomes more real than the facts about the wars of independence and the battle of the Clearances becomes a tussle between a Tory historian and a Labour former Minister, with accusations of 'Clearance denial' being thrown about. Meanwhile our ability to relate to, know and be enriched by our actual past – in order that we can make a reasonable job of living as Scots in this actual present – remains fatally undermined.

The cynical politics of bread and circuses play their part in that too, of course. In May 2006, when confronted with an imminent football World Cup competition in which Scotland would not be playing, two of the most senior Labour politicians in the UK vied with each other in an attempt to cash in – for their own political benefit – on what they imagined must be the prevailing sentiment.

South of the border Gordon Brown, desperate to be Prime Minister of the UK and therefore desperate to ingratiate himself with middle England (where the battle for Westminster is always won or lost) sought an opportunity to put on record not only his support for the England football team in the World Cup, but also his long-standing (so he claimed) admiration for the team, and in particular for several of its performances against Scotland.

No one who had ever seen Gordon Brown speak to a Scottish audience could have believed these statements. To Scottish audiences he would, it seems certain, have made it clear that he backed the Scotland football team to the hilt, and indeed he has, over the years, made much of supporting his own 'local' team in Fife, Raith Rovers.

No one who had ever seen Gordon Brown speak to a Scottish audience could have believed these statements.

So his position is one that lacks any credibility. It is not a conversion, or the showing of a moderate and modern example. He shows himself not as a man keen to change Scottish attitudes or help Scotland out of its tribalism, but as someone who just wants power and will say anything to get it. The old phrase 'toom tabard' springs to mind.

But the First Minister erred in just the same way, though by moving in the opposite direction. If he had taken a more moderate stance, made it clear that supporting a team was a minor matter, and had wished England good luck but reserved his own position, that might have been enough to have shown a modicum of leadership. But he did not.

Instead, perceiving a possible outflanking by the nationalists, and keen to distance himself from Labour south of the Border, he opined to any journalist who would listen that he intended to support Trinidad and Tobago, or Angola, or any other 'underdog' who fielded players who had a connection with Scotland. It sounded – and it was – small-minded and petty. It sounded – and it was – calculated and the antithesis of true sporting enthusiasm.

Both positions were cynical, self-conscious attempts to use football enthusiasms for political gain. Both were calculated and deliberate and both debased politics and leadership.

But did the press see it that way, and provide the leadership that was lacking. Mostly no, it has to be said, with the vast bulk of the media seeking to take sides, and to encourage others to do so.

It might be argued that these are all small matters, but a nation which finds it difficult to be honest about small matters will have even greater problems when confronted by life or death issues. If we misrepresent who we are and what we are, and if we fail to find the way to be at ease with ourselves, then we will find it (as we have found it) hard to govern ourselves, for we do not know who we are governing.

A nation which finds it difficult to be honest about small matters will have even greater problems when confronted by life or death issues.

Fortunately there are signs that new thinking is beginning to take hold in key places. Steps being taken to ensure a more systematic and sympathetic approach to teaching Scottish history in schools for example, inspired by that influential and highly significant Scottish historian Professor Tom Devine, who has proposed to the Scottish Executive a 'spine' of study which consists of nine modules to be taught to all pupils at some stage during their education and which cover topics such as the Wars of Independence and the Disruption. He admits to being less than confident that the Executive will take the suggestion up, but his involvement does indicate that change in this important area has at least started. That might, eventually, ensure that Scotland's young people have accurate information on which to base their knowledge of their own nation, and a firm foundation on which they can then begin to understand the rest of the world.

Political parties have also brought forward a few individuals prepared to think the unthinkable. The most radical and original voice in this regard was Andrew Wilson, the leading younger SNP MSP until he was brutally and foolishly demoted down his regional list in 2002 to a position in which he was bound to lose his seat in 2003 (which he did). His victimisation was, at least in part, undertaken for challenging the party to be much more open in its views and much less prejudiced. When he talked about the need to be open-minded about England as a football team, he was telling he truth as he saw it, not – like Brown and McConnell – trying to selfishly play on an audience though he paid the price for it amongst certain of his own colleagues. He is no longer active in politics and therefore there is no one of his ability and charisma continuing to force the pace in that way and arguing for an altogether new and positive style, based on a new and positive assessment of our history.

We think that these ideas need to be taken further. We are keen to introduce into the debate something we will call 'post-grievance Scottish identity'.

For us Scottish identity should be a positive force, outward-looking, generous, confident, and brim full of ideas and good intentions. It must be informed by a sense of history, but that sense of history must not control it, and especially not burden it with negativity. It neither can nor should make any attempt to redress the wrongs done at Flodden and the savagery inflicted at Culloden, nor should it seek reparations for the Clearances. It must acknowledge that it can do nothing except regret the unequal carnage visited on Scottish soldiers used as cannon fodder in so many wars even up to the present day.

Scottish identity should be a positive force.

It is not that this more contemporary type of Scottishness does not care about such things – it cares deeply. However it knows that to secure its cause (Scotland's cause being, as John Steinbeck described it to Jackie Kennedy, 'not lost' but 'still unwon') it must fare forward, rather than always be dragged back by ghosts from history. Scotland cannot change the past, but it can make a better future. Indeed only by so doing can it ensure that the past is not endlessly repeated. A real knowledge of our history, and a real appreciation of who we are, would be a prerequisite for remaking ourselves in a way that secured a better future for the whole nation.

Immediately we say that, however, we know that we will be dismissed by some for being 'narrow nationalists' by those who regard any concern for what lies around us as being parochial and limiting. Yet paradoxically others will attack us, simultaneously we are sure, for compromising on what they could call 'real nationalism', always fueled, in the view of such critics, by a necessary feeling of injustice and an essential level of resentment.

We would reject such accusations. We say again that we not only wish Scotland to be an independent country but also that we think that such a change of status is needed more than ever as we move into the second decade of the twenty first century. But that change will not come about unless the whole nation is confident enough to choose it and such confidence cannot come from false understandings of who we are, still less from false prospectuses of who we might become.

A curious aspect of post-devolution Scotland is that some of the oddest and least sensible statements about our nation and what it is have come from Labour ministers. Chief amongst those has been the First Minister, who was even to be seen standing in front of his favoured 'narrow nationalist' slogan when greeting international statesmen arriving for the G8 summit in July 2005.

That slogan is 'The best small country in the world' which actually sounds like something from *The Hitchhiker's Guide to the Galaxy*. 'The best small planet in the solar system' would be the next entry, and then the 'best small star cluster in the nebula'. It has an air of insecurity and irrelevance, much like the 'best small clothes shop in Comrie' or the 'best small teashop in Troon'. It is in reality the sign of a struggle to find some way of distinguishing ourselves from the crowd not because the crowd can't do it, but because we can't. Independence is the opposite of that dilemma – for independence allows us to differentiate ourselves.

The words also bring to mind some of the worst aspects of Scotland and the Scots. It is a sort of modernised version of 'Here's tae us, wha's like us', and one can imagine it being intoned drunkenly by a swaying, kilted, Scotsman reeling down Edinburgh's Royal Mile on Hogmanay. It manages to be both aggressive and self-deluding, which is always a combination to be avoided.

The slogan is also risible because it is not true. If our sole ambition as a nation were really as narrow as to be 'the best small country in the world' – and there are lots of other better ambitions, such as eliminating poverty, contributing to international aid, resourcing and valuing our culture, improving our public services and positively enabling each and every one of our citizens – then even a casual glance around the present small country would indicate that we have a long way to go.

This is not to diminish what we have, or what we might achieve. Certainly our hills and glens are magnificent, our natural talent great and our resources plentiful. But whereas other small countries like Ireland do so much with so little, our tragedy is that we do so little with so much.

This type of slogan – and once again it should be emphasised that it comes not from a nationalist but from a very anti-nationalist Labour Scottish government – is equivalent to looking at Scotland through the wrong end of a telescope. It is not open, generous and shot through with the required degree of hubris. It is the swagger of small men who seem to proudly parrot (as if pleased to have stolen them) only the silliest things from some version of nationalism that should no longer exist, such as that sense of Scottish inferiority which leads to grandiose, truculent, claims. It signifies nothing about the real Scotland let alone the one that we should wish to create. Independence of course, does just the opposite.

Perhaps this appropriation of perverted nationalism gives the reason why the core political cause of independence has not yet prevailed. It may be that many voters, on the receiving end of such nonsensical assertions from Labour find it difficult to separate national truth from national fiction. But some of the difficulty also lies in the failure of the SNP to accurately address Scotland's past and to move itself out of the twilight zone of grievance history and grievance politics.

We think that the real argument for independence is not what others have done or what has past in our country: it is the potential for what we can do in the future. That potential is based upon and can and must draw nourishment from our past, but it can only do so if our relationship with our past is informed and positive.

The core argument for independence now is that which looks accurately not just at Scotland, but also at what is happening today across our planet. Scotland is a small, not terribly efficient society operating on the margins. We need to know how it is has come to that position and then we need to work out how to move beyond that position.

Scotland has failed to distinguish itself from its southern neighbour (in fact its government still takes far too much cognisance of what that southern neighbour thinks and feels, and plays to it in a way that is good for neither) and it is not fulfilling anything like its full role. It must find a way to do so – and, to add to the difficulty, to do so in a world which is rapidly changing.

In twenty years China will be the largest economy on the planet with an enormous global reach. America will be defending its position and trying to find a way to maintain relevance and financial punch. The European Union, if it still exists in its present form, will be deeply divided between the fast growing and the falling behind. And we could be – at present are likely to be – amongst those who are falling behind – our people growing poorer and our public services growing worse whilst our environment degrades and our culture and sense of self continues to wither.

The only way to change that future is to re-define ourselves and take control of our own resources and assets and then sweat those resources and assets in a way that will give us a unique opportunity to survive and prosper. Environmental (and cultural) considerations, in twenty years time, will not be peripheral or contentious: they will be central to economic and social success. Scotland is a country with a fine environment and the space to grow: we have the key assets of the twenty first century – land, water and the ability to generate power – in abundance and we have the ingenuity to use them. We can therefore survive and prosper. But only if we choose to do so.

In order to choose to do so we need to free the potential of our people – not just to be part of yet another society dominated by politicians, but as a genuine democracy, in which everyone plays a part and has a stake. And to do that we have to apply our genius for ideas and invention, and first of all apply them to our country. We have to learn the process of self-government, make it work, and then make it work even better. Only then can we hope to be what we can be and need to be.

That will not be achieved by bickering about monuments to Trafalgar. It will not be done by re-fighting past battles, recalling past glories or trying to settle again past scores. It will not be achieved by name calling or by retreating into the lagar of our insecurity and sense of grievance. It will be achieved if we can develop a confidence in who we are, based on a knowledge of how we got here, who we were, and what we can become. Then we can join together in creating the conditions for success.

Nationalism in the twentieth century certainly had a bad press. One might observe the same thing about Socialism, if the connection is drawn between brutal dictators and the philosophy they claim to espouse. But Fascism was seen as primarily a nationalist movement, and the huge damage and unparalleled suffering it wrought consequently brought nationalism into justifiable disrepute. The savagery of the later Balkan wars did not help.

That has created difficulties for Scotland and for the SNP. The former SNP Chairman, Billy Wolfe, has often remarked that the name of the party is one of its biggest difficulties and indeed he came very close to persuading the party to change its name during the early 1970s. Others have speculated since then that dropping the word 'national' might help to distance the party from the unfortunate connotations of the added three letters and inject a dynamic new force into Scottish politics which was not handicapped by unfair criticism arising from an injudicious tag. Most importantly of all, because Scotland has a 'party of nationalism' this has at times seemed to obviate the need for the other parties to put Scotland first and to encourage citizens of Scotland to focus on their national concerns and the correct national solutions to their problems.

> Grievance nationalism is a luxury that Scotland cannot afford.

But this problem may be one that cannot be overcome simply by a re-branding for grievance nationalism has one other major disadvantage; it is a luxury that Scotland cannot afford. As a small country we need all the unity we can get and all the positivity and confidence we can command. Grievance nationalism and grievance history contribute to grievance politics, and together they sap the soul and weaken the intellect. They are also deeply unattractive and until a positive nationalism is the norm in Scotland then the cause of independence will suffer, for it will appear much less attractive than it is and should be.

It would be greatly in the interests of the SNP – and of Scotland – to find a way to offer such positive, post-grievance nationalism and politics, and in so doing give an example to the country and to every other political party. Such an approach would truly be one which brought to the fore that type of 'new politics' which Scots have thirsted after since it failed to appear in 1999. If it took on board our own views about democracy and the limitation of the power of parties it would be even more popular, we are sure.

However it is possible that such a positive new type of

nationalism might arise from elsewhere. Some believe that the obvious trajectory for Labour would be towards such a policy, though its deep ties to the south and its ambitions for UK government (which draw its Scottish talent inexorably southwards) are always likely to militate against that. However we accept that there are some Labour members (and a few at senior levels) who see independence as a natural progression from devolution, despite the party's spin. If they were ever to exert their influence and, at the same time, to break free of the statist old-fashioned (and profoundly anti-people) policies which are presently destroying opportunity in Scotland, then they could generate a major change not just in their party but in the country as a whole.

> There are some Labour members who see independence as a natural progression from devolution.

We are also aware that parties come and go and that our proposals on democracy might, in time give rise to new formulations and groupings. Given the current political climate and its likely development the obvious niche for many of them is that of independence.

Smaller parties have started to arise in Scotland already. We have much hope for a positive contribution to the national debate from the Greens who, whilst they lack practical political experience, bring a passion for the planet which is much needed. Once they have found a way to work with others without compromising their ideals, then they will be natural partners in several possible forms of government and in the process of moving to independence.

We have far less confidence in any positive contribution coming from the Scottish Socialist Party. Their appeal is not forward-looking – as the Greens' is – but is narrow and focussed entirely on exploiting real or imagined grievance. Any party that can address an open letter to the Venezuelan President, on his vist to the UK, which asserts:

> like Venezuela, Scotland has lived with the consequences of a close relationship with a powerful neighbour. In our case this has involved us in the economic and military structures of the imperialist British State, a situation we are striving to end. In particular this relationship has, in a parallel to Venezuela's experience, seen our large oil reserves plundered by multinational companies. . .

is clearly living in a cloud cuckoo land in which any and all experiences are grist to a mill of conspiracy and resentment. In any case the splintering of the party around the egos of its senior members is now well underway, their policy proscriptions – daft as they are – are muted as a result and the prospects for the party are dim.

The Tory question is harder to answer. Given the difficulties that the Tories have in formulating specific Scottish policies, the palpable weakness of their Scottish leadership, and the way in which their declining and ageing membership still manages to control the party's message and make it appear out of step with contemporary Scotland, then the challenge of independence is something that may be beyond them. But it does have appeal in certain more progressive and radical Tory quarters.

Yet the idea of a fiscally responsible, socially liberal, prosperous and dynamic Scotland is one that should attract moderate Conservative support and the SNP needs to recognise that and give up its outmoded prejudice against talking with Tories (a prejudice which is rooted in another political age). Presenting a more constructive and more open face to the whole Scottish electorate can only help the country, bring in those who are not yet convinced about the need for Scottish democratic solutions but who know that in post-devolution Scotland Labour is achieving little except shoring up a very old-fashioned *status quo*.

The Liberals and their supporters might find the conversion easier. Even though some of the Liberal vote in Scotland comes from traditional one-nation Tories who are horrified by the descent into chaos of their former party, much of the rest of it comes from rural areas and is based upon finding a single alternative to the Tory party. It is, as the statistics show, often interchangeable with an SNP vote for the same reason (the SNP has taken this vote in Banff and Buchan for example, whereas in North East Fife it has gone to the Liberals, largely because of the effective nature of local campaigns by both parties over many years). As the Liberals are now re-defining federalism (a task taken further forward by the intriguing and positive recommendations of the Steel Commission in March 2006) the party might be sympathetic to a new constitutional settlement. At the very least they could take part in the journey, bringing their skills and fair-mindedness to bear on the problems and possibilities of Scotland even if they required still to be persuaded that the ultimate destination was valid.

Of course Tories, Liberals and everyone else will not buy a pig in a poke. They have to be convinced that the arguments for change are sound, and that the plan is sure-footed. We still hope that they will be lead to that conclusion by a political and democratic process – by a period of democratic, economic, environmental and culture debate perhaps – which reaches out and engages all sections of Scottish society. That process needs to be more accurate in its understanding of our past, more positive in learning the lessons presented by our shared history, and more radical and ambitious when building on those foundations.

So we wish now to draw all these strands together and to suggest how progress might be made, progress that would lead to a more democratic, a more entrepreneurial, a less governed and a more confident Scotland. And how that might happen within a reasonable period of time and in a way that brought in the widest level of support.

Those matters will form the last chapter of this book.

What can be done now?

'The real duty (of a politician) is to analyse discontent, to find the causes of discontent, to express discontent and then to establish a world order that is more in keeping with the intelligence and the ethics of the men and women who live in the great age in which we are living.'

James Maxton MP

What can be done now?

Political nationalism is not going to be enough to express the
nation of Scotland and retain an identity which alone is the
raison d'etre of independence. . . if we launch. . . into a form
of government that echoes the English party outlook, we
shall only be regional minded even under our own
government. Wendy Wood *Yours Sincerely for Scotland* (1970)

In this final chapter we want to address the widest possible
cross section of the Scottish population. Indeed we want to
encourage every citizen of Scotland to grasp the thistle of change
for we believe that the ideas in this book are of universal application and need wide discussion and debate.

Let us start here at home. People are thirsty for something
new, and looking at the experience of devolution so far, we are
mindful of that very prescient remark by the veteran nationalist
Wendy Wood in her 1970 autobiography which we quote above
for at this stage in the process of independence we do find
ourselves ruled by a 'form of government' that merely 'echoes
the English party outlook' .

That problem has existed from the outset of devolution.
Despite much debate about establishing a new system of governance, and some effort in the early days of the Parliament to
enshrine positive differences in the Scotland Act – such as more
consultation on legislation, more accessibility for the public, less
formality in proceedings and a more consensual approach to
ordering Parliamentary business – the political parties changed
very little as devolution dawned. In fact parochial partiality and
irrelevant game-playing has at times seemed more entrenched
than ever, and has blighted the very roots of change.

Take the example set by George Robertson, former Defence Minister, former Secretary General of NATO and now Lord Robertson of Port Ellen. Robertson has a particular visceral dislike of nationalists in Scotland, perhaps borne out of the fact that he himself was once a member of the SNP. His youthful flirting with the benefits of independence – and unilateral nuclear disarmament – arose from his upbringing in Dunoon, at a time when the American nuclear depot ship was based in the Holy Loch. However by the time he reached maturity, as some would see it, he was firmly thirled to the Labour party and keen to establish himself as a 'hammer of the Nats'.

It was as the Labour candidate in the 1978 Hamilton by-election that he coined the term 'separatist' in order to strip the SNP of what he saw as warmer and more positive connotations and since then the word has created endless difficulties for the party. Then, as Shadow Scottish Secretary in the run-up to the 1997 General Election he indulged in regular attacks upon the SNP in terms which on occasion maliciously hinted at possible nationalist links with, or sympathy for, extremism and political violence. It was also on his watch that the most unprincipled election campaign ever seen in Scotland – the one headlined by Labour with the slogan 'divorce is an expensive business' – took place.

But it is his prediction that 'devolution will kill the nationalists stone dead', which he made when Shadow Secretary of State for Scotland in early 1997, that is presently most quoted by those who comment on Scottish politics. Some, on the nationalist side, when faced with reverses occasionally fret that he may be proved correct. Others, of a unionist persuasion, are happy when such temporary events appear to confirm his view, though of course it is a daft statement, with no roots in long term, objective reality.

What the remark really reveals is how shallow and opportunistic Robertson's belief in constitutional change always was and how hypocritical his form of New Labourism actually is. For many like Robertson devolution was a mere tactic, a means to reinforce the hegemony of Labour in Scotland and see off the threat of another party. If it had any purpose in terms of improving governance, then that was a secondary matter. It is little wonder that with such people still in charge of Labour north and south of the border the benefits of devolution are sometimes hard to find, and the role of government in guiding change can appear confused.

We do, of course, accept, that there are some in Labour for whom home rule was an objective grounded in the founding principles of the Labour party and one which was central to their vision of a better society. However their past reluctance to vigorously pursue the issue within their own party for most of its existence, and their present reluctance to demand a greater level of powers able to be exercised in Scotland (let alone to demand a deepening of democracy itself) means that Labour's half-hearted commitment to Scottish self-government remains, because of Labour's administrative hegemony in Scotland, a sheet anchor on the prospects for Scottish democratic self improvement. We are stuck, at present, with that 'form of government' which – because of these factors – does only 'echo the English party outlook'.

However we believe that some politicians in Scotland are capable of realising the hugely beneficial quantum shift in democracy which constitutional change – properly completed – might bring about. Moreover we are certain some of those self-same politicians in Scotland know that such a shift is now essential.

Later in this chapter we shall look at the prospects for parties taking up democratic reform, embracing models of smaller and more efficient government and revolutionising Scottish attitudes towards culture, heritage and the environment. But to kick start the process of change, we have an initial and unifying radical recommendation.

We have already mentioned the success of the Citizens' Commission set up in British Colombia to consider electoral reform. This was selected at random by means of a complex but very fair system that resulted in those serving who had a genuine interest in the subject and were prepared to devote time and effort to it. Its report, recommending the introduction of a Single Transferable Vote system was well received and whilst it very narrowly failed to get the necessary endorsement in a referendum held at the same time as the Provincial election of 2005, its efforts are likely to be carried into law at a later date.

The whole process was an experiment that deserves to be studied carefully. It has had wide-reaching implications throughout Canada, which is a nation (particularly at Federal level) that has had difficulty in handling democratic change. However in May 2006 the new Conservative Federal Prime Minister announced the introduction of fixed term Federal Parliaments and has confirmed that his Cabinet is studying other changes to the Canadian system including the possible use of another Citizens' Commission. Thus the Citizens' Commission, by its very existence seems to have broken a long term constitutional logjam and not only in its core areas of consideration.

Scotland's Constitutional Convention which drew up the blueprint for the Scottish Parliament was largely self-appointed yet it was also a positive and successful exercise in seeking consensus and it also had a wider effect. As we now believe that the time is right for a further step forward we are drawn to the establishment of another Convention or Commission and we are enthused by the example of the BC Citizens' Commission. Consequently we want to see a Scottish Citizens' Convention established that would consider the further democratisation of politics in our country (though in keeping with Scottish usage we have replaced the word Commission with Convention).

We are mindful that a new Independence Convention was established in 2005 which brought together the political parties which espouse independence (the SNP, the Greens and the SSP) as well as many individuals who support that option. We have been impressed by the way in which the Independence Convention has persuaded the political parties to loosen their grip and has encouraged involvement from a wider grouping. We think that the potential for this new body under its recently appointed Convener, the former Political Editor of the *Herald*, Murray Ritchie, is very great and we expect it to play a significant role in focussing on the issue of independence and explaining its benefits, particularly as the 300th anniversary of the Act of Union looms.

Nonetheless this Convention does not have the force of official establishment nor any statutory duty and we would want to see a body with both which could bring forward to the Scottish Parliament a set of new recommendations on how Scottish democracy could be revitalised. In fact even if our ideas were –

surprisingly – to be taken on board in full by any, or most, of Scotland's political parties, or at least taken on board to the extent of being seriously debated within them, we would still be keen to seek the establishment of a new Citizens' Convention for Scotland.

This would be initially launched and led by a 'mentor', a respected and independent national figure, and would be set up by first of all randomly selecting from the voters roll two thousand names which, taken together, would form an accurate demographic sample of Scotland in terms of age, social class and location.

Regional meetings of those invited to attend would be held, chaired by the mentor and those who did attend would be paid for so doing. These meetings would outline the task of the convention, seek commitment from those present to take part, and assess those present by a variety of means agreed by the participants.

Following the conclusion of those meetings a final convention of around 200 members would be appointed, seeking to ensure that the final choice provided as complete and accurate a demographic sample as possible.

The Convention would at that point elect its own Convener (who would replace the mentor in convening and directing meetings and acting as the public face of the Convention). It would be serviced by a civil service team who would report to it and to no one else, and whilst the political parties in the Parliament would be entitled to send one observer each to be present at all plenary meetings these observers would have no other role.

The Convention would be given an initial clear remit, requiring it to consult, research, consider, debate and then make recommendations regarding:

• The establishment of a participatory democracy based on the needs of the individual and the community, not the needs of political parties.

But we would go further. The other two key issues – of government size and efficiency and the pressing needs of the environment – require radical action as well. So the Commission would be asked also to consider and recommend in due course:

- The setting of limits to macro economic matters such as the size of government; the prevention of deficit financing of government and the establishment of a Scottish currency;

- The setting of principles and limits required to ensure and maintain environmental sustainability.

In addition it would be entitled during is initial two years of existence to consider any other related matters.

Its recommendations to the Scottish Parliament would not be binding, but if they were rejected by the Parliament, the Convention should be entitled to seek (by majority vote within the Convention) a referendum on them, and if approved by a referendum they would become binding and would require to be implemented.

The Scottish people may find growingly attractive this means of bringing new ideas and new methods into our decision making structures, so much so that consideration could be given to a Standing Citizens' Convention, whose membership alters every couple of years or so, but which is given or initiates particular issues to examine and on which to make recommendations to Parliament and to the people if necessary. Such a Standing Citizens' Convention would in essence be a citizens' watchdog protecting the sovereignty of the people and putting the political process under constant scrutiny. We therefore have no hesitation in recommending the establishment of a Standing Citizens' Convention as a Fourth Chamber to our recommendations in chapter 1.3.

The Citizens' Convention might also well be able to force the pace on reducing the powers of political parties and insisting that citizens be consulted before the law criminalises anything which is presently legal. The Citizens' Convention should be able to require government to behave more responsibly and to combine the means of securing high quality public services with appropriate sensible restraint on public spending. The Citizens' Convention ought to be able to see through the spin and bluster of government and expose stealth taxation and massaged targets.

Setting up a Citizens' Convention is also one of the few ways in which a dynamic for democratic change could be nurtured and developed despite the disapproval of conventional politicians and for that reason alone its establishment will probably be resisted by some of those politicians. But it may be an idea whose time is coming. Should it fail to garner sufficient formal political support then given the communication and knowledge skills of today's citizens it is quite possible that an internet-driven citizens' movement could spring up and form a citizens' convention outwith the political establishment which subsequently demanded statutory recognition and support. That would be the start of a process in which the people would begin to seize back power.

In the course of writing this book, the two authors have often talked about the difficulty of bringing forward new and original thinking about politics and democracy. Yet in the more than twenty months that it has taken them to draft, re-draft, re-organise and edit this material many hopeful signs have been glimpsed.

The Power Commission which reported in early 2006 has suggested that democracy needs to be extended further and has drawn attention to the deep dissatisfaction hat most citizens feel. The Steel Commission made important observations and recommendations from the Liberal perspective and both the Scottish Liberals and the Scottish Tories have started to talk about 'localism' and about making sure that decisions are taken closer to individuals. The idea of more modern, more accountable and more effective political structures was the theme of both the Tory and Liberal leadership contests, and within the SNP there have been ever wider stirrings about the need for strategic and organisational change such as the *crie de couer* from the former party leader Gordon Wilson published in the *Scots Independent* in March 2006.

The issue of the size of government has become a repeated discussion point in the Scottish press, with both the *Scotsman* and *Herald* publishing figures which indicate a burgeoning public sector pressing on a failing private sector. Environmental fears have accelerated, particularly since CO_2 readings from 2005, which were released in the Spring of 2006 showed the highest levels of atmospheric CO_2 for millennia, a phenomenon accompanied by the ever-accelerating disintegration of the Arctic and Antarctic ice caps. And Scottish culture remains under-appreciated and underfunded by government, which has almost completely rejected the recommendations of its own Cultural Commission.

What we wanted to say has, therefore, been echoed in part elsewhere whilst we have been writing this book. But no-one else, we believe, has placed these issues together within a context of urgency and outlined some possible means by which they can be comprehensively tackled.

We are, of course, aware, that really radical new thinking about Scotland and its politics is uncommon, hard to embark on and dangerous to bring to fruition, at least as far as reputation is concerned. The frontispiece of this book contains a quotation from *Gullivers Travels* that makes the same point about Jonathan Swift's own society. Little has changed in all those centuries, in terms of how some politicians behave and how ordinary citizens long for a different type of public life. Nor has it become any easier to persuade those in power of the need to change.

Perhaps such tensions can never be redressed. But that does not mean those who care should cease trying. We care deeply about Scotland, about our fellow citizens and about our planet. We want our nation, our neighbours and our environment to flourish.

That is why we want our ideas to have wide circulation and that is also why we need to consider who can best take these ideas forward.

A Citizens' Convention certainly would, arising from public demand or created by politicians. But we also hope that one or more of the existing political parties will begin to take the necessary steps to bring a revolution in thinking to Scottish governance. We hope one will start to seek an integrated approach such as that we have proposed, bringing together the creation of a participatory democracy with individual action to achieve environmental and cultural progress, whilst underpinning the whole with a more sensible approach to public spending and government itself. Of course such a shift in perception and policy would and will take time, though we believe there are some signs that the seeds are already sprouting.

But suppose no party will move forward in this way? Then we would expect not just pressure from citizens but also the emergence of new groupings, including new parties which would be focused on the need to create a much more enterprising and successful Scotland. Scotland has already shown the inherent flexibility of its devolved structures in terms of permitting and indeed enabling democratic diversity – a welcome bonus in a set of arrangements that have many downsides – and the election of 2003 demonstrated how such flexibility could work. We expect that to ebb and flow over the next few years, but new parties could and should emerge if the old ones cannot respond to the obvious and increasing need for change.

Nonetheless there are many elements contained within our ideas that should motivate each and every existing party. One of us, as an active SNP candidate, is visibly and actively placing his belief in the fact that the SNP is the vehicle which will attract (as it is presently seeking to attract) the widest cross section of Scottish support. We both know that the SNP, at its best, is always more than just a party and if it can continue to be, in essence, a national movement then it is bound to be enormously influential in terms of encouraging a growing together of Scotland – in fact a growing up of Scotland to political and democratic maturity, the end point of which is independence.

The SNP, at its best, is always more than just a party.

It is vitally important that this road to independence is clearly and simply signposted so that the people of Scotland can find it and follow it. We believe that Scotland will move to independence when the majority of Scots have the confidence to choose that option, realise that it is a more beneficial financial option for them, their families and their country, have confidence in the leaders who propose this option and are re-assured that they will be able to control their destinies by taking part in a truly participatory democracy. In other words when Scotland has sloughed off its dependency culture, re-embraced a radical, enterprising and compassionate governance and has been inspired by a vision of a better future – a vision of independence.

The starting point is that vision. Once inspired the route becomes simple – a route through a referendum, but which will require first the gaining of further powers, the more intelligent use of existing powers, the introduction of new democratic structures, the complete reform of our public finances and a conversion to sustainability and green growth. In other words Scotland must not only gain independence, it must gain it having *prepared* to gain it. Consequently preparing Scotland for independence is the most important political task on the national agenda. That task includes helping Scots to understand what independence is and what it should mean individually and collectively. That is a task which is central to the SNP.

The SNP is set to do well in the 2007 Scottish Parliament elections, particularly because of the increasingly poor and increasingly corrupt performance of New Labour. As it builds towards that moment it must develop the skills, ideas and dynamism that will be necessary not just for government, but for withstanding the onslaught when the soggy centrist *status quo* in Scotland is finally and fully challenged by the pressures of the times and the reality of globalisation. Discussing, examining and debating the ideas in this book would be one (no doubt of many) helpful way to do so and we hope that that process will take place up and down the land and through the website associated with this book www.graspingthethistle.com. We also hope that those not within the party will be encouraged to take part in such activities too.

One of us has argued regularly over the past few years that the SNP should look out for what might be called its Clause 4 moment – a moment in which it can demonstrate graphically to the Scottish voting public that it has changed and goes on changing. We hope it will continue to do so, taking on board new ideas, being open to new thinking, always critically examining the style and substance of its actions, embracing post-grievance nationalism, welcoming the trend towards smaller government, accepting that the world is a different place than when the party was last close to power and addressing those differences with confidence and intelligence.

Of course we would like every citizen to do that as well. In today's competitive world smaller and more efficient government must be Scotland's watchword, married to a passion for wealth creation and the benefits this brings. We must look not just to Sweden and Denmark, Iceland and Ireland for models of policy innovation, but elsewhere as well – to the new countries of Europe whose flat taxes have transformed growth, to some of the Canadian Provinces which have legislated to ensure balanced budgets, and to the work of scholars and others worldwide who have shown the essential link between restraints on governmental spending and economic and social growth.

Independence will not be a sufficient condition for a complete transformation of Scotland but it is a necessary one. Without it such a process cannot even start. The union and those who operate it have made even our new Parliament and Executive inefficient and often incompetent, our financial base precarious and our democracy immature. As we have indicated, because of that experience there may be circumstances in which Scotland will wish to be, and may have to be, reassured as it moves forward, perhaps by the establishment of a stage two for devolution, that 'new union' which we outlined in Chapter 2.2. It would undoubtedly be better to embrace the need for such re-assurance than to risk losing any chance of progress.

The SNP should not baulk at such a possibility – in fact by welcoming it enthusiastically it can prove how pragmatic and ready for change it is (a true Clause 4 moment indeed) for it is a good antidote to the Robertson tag of 'separatists', it will persuade some presently reluctant Scots to support change and it will be useful in finding common ground with, for example the Liberals, with whom common ground should regularly be sought, given the electoral arithmetic of the Scottish Parliament.

Scotland can be made ready for independence by a period of nationalist led government and nationalism can be made ready for the responsibilities of steering the country to independence by that process too. A nationalist government should therefore honestly say that it will hold a referendum on independence when it believes – and the people believe – our nation is ready to make that step. At that time, and no other.

Of course we know that political parties are like oil tankers – slow to change course. However, occasionally a leader comes along who has the high level skills to take their party and country on a new and inspiring course. Both of us have long believed that Alex Salmond is such a politician and as he is in an unassailable position of power within the SNP we are sure that he will demonstrate that grasp of the new and desirable which will allow him to lead Scotland away from the narrow conventional track of party dogma and take the country on the road to a new democracy, a more robust economy and a sustainable environment.

But we do not ask Alex Salmond, or any other Scottish politician, to treat this book as gospel or regard our ideas as being so set in stone that they are either fully accepted or completely rejected. Instead we ask everyone in Scotland, leader or follower, to debate and discuss our democracy, our economy and our environment and to make up their own mind having brought their own ideas, experiences and intellect to bear on the obvious problems in our country today. We have no fear in saying that there are, no doubt, things in this book which may be impractical, or which cannot and will not sit happily within our nation as it is now or might become. These are ideas and examples of thinking, not step-by-step prescriptions. They must be read as such.

A spirit of openness to change is always vitally important, and at this moment in Scotland that spirit is more important than ever. The threats to our well-being are not static, but active. The challenges we have described throughout this book are not possibilities, but facts. Every party should become one which seeks less politics and more participation. Every business and organisation should be finding ways to champion smaller and more efficient government, faster economic growth and greater wealth for the nation. Every citizen should become an agent for environmental and cultural renaissance.

For the SNP to lead that process would be to place it in a commanding position of national leadership. In doing so it would be promoting a Scotland more than capable of making its way in the world and enriching every one of its citizens. That would be a huge fillip to the argument for independence, would enable Scotland to move into the post-oil era, brimming with cultural and collective self-confidence and would finally justify the high hopes and noble ideals which led to the foundation of the party eighty years ago. Scotland would be able to move forward into a better future, secure on the foundations of her past.

And such an ambition should be a unifying one, with relevance for the whole of Scotland and for every Scottish party.

At home we have long seen the Liberals as being possible partners in developing Scotland in a way that fits the nation for independence. Most Liberals are fair-minded, open to persuasion and keen to explore new ways of empowering the people and therefore they should be ideal collaborators in any enterprise that is devoted to making Scotland a better place.

If the Scottish Liberal Democrats are to build upon the radical suggestions from their recent Commission, chaired by David

Steel, they should find much of interest and utility in this book. Their natural belief in the primacy of the individual should make them interested in the proposals to establish a more participatory democracy. Their belief in economic justice and the need for radical solutions to eliminate poverty should make them consider anew ideas that would reduce the size of government and increase the potential for wealth creation. Their current increasing concern for the environment could be expanded by placing those concerns within the wider context of renewal of our entire *patrimonie*. As for their present hostility to independence – that in time might change if the arguments were better understood and their benefits were made more obvious. Just as in the campaign for the 1997 Referendum, however, Liberal scepticism about the final destination should not stop them joining in actions which make Scotland a better place. They will – as all Scots will – have the chance to influence the final steps and as they will be enabled to make their judgment from a more prosperous, more confident base no one who is already persuaded about the need for independence should have any fear of entering into constructive partnerships based on that type of understanding.

Even those who have, up until now, been most enamoured of the Union could move forward on that basis. Indeed if the Scottish Conservatives were to cease their obsession with events south of the border, abandon their narrow and backward-looking concerns about the constitution and embrace the potential for real Scottish progress, they too might find things to agree with and act on in our proposals. They would need to find a leader capable of doing so, and that would mean re-considering their concept of Scottish leadership. But they might manage that in time.

And if the more forward-looking and thoughtful members of Scottish Labour – distinguished almost entirely by the fact that they do not form part of the leadership or governing clique at present – can put aside their dislike of nationalism as currently expressed then they might also be able to take on board a radical renewal for Scotland. Their contribution would be most welcome, for there are many talented people within the ranks of Scottish Labour who see the need for change and who know that such change must lead to further powers being gained by not just the Scottish Parliament but the Scottish people.

There is a common platform for radical Scottish progress within much of what we have argued. The present soggy consensus is based on the easy answers and accepted wisdom and therefore has no strength to inspire. A different type of unity could however be enormously powerful and develop into an unstoppable momentum for independence. That – in the end – is what we would seek.

We accept, and in fact welcome, the fact that our ideas need development, refinement, more research and considerably more distillation. There is much work to be done on the details of, for example, democratic change and input to that from every part of the political spectrum would be useful.

There is a common platform for radical Scottish progress.

Our view on the environment, to take another example, would benefit from further work undertaken by those from the Green party who know more about the subject but who are also beginning to realise that working with others is the only way to make improvements and to bring about radical restructuring of how we operate as a society. Constructive Greens, participating in Scottish governance on that basis, and helping to change it for the better, would be a vitally useful part of a new, positive, Scottish politics.

Will such a politics emerge in the coming years? We have to say that we do not know. We remain hopeful that intelligent politicians recognising public dissatisfaction and allied with a citizenry which is hungry for real participation could provide the impetus for radical change. So could a catastrophic further decline in voting numbers combined with continuing corruption and scandal in public life.

On the other hand we do not think it impossible that demagoguery could take a grip in those circumstances though the cultural roots for it to be fed are thin in our society. We hope however that our contribution to this debate, and other contributions, will create a dynamic for a much more positive and productive set of changes and we hope to contribute to that, for example by our website (http://www.graspingthethistle.com), by promoting this book and by seeking every opportunity to have it read and discussed.

Yet whilst our ideas are rooted in the soil of Scotland, they have been nourished by experience of other places and knowledge of wider issues. That is why we believe that this book and what is contained in it has a wider application. Consequently we also want to see a wider debate, in which Scotland takes a lead and contributes to the UK, Europe, North America and elsewhere those concepts of democratic participation, more responsive, smaller and more efficient government and an integrated approach to culture and the environment which we have outlined and which are already emerging in many other places. An independent Scotland would be ideally placed to do so.

Democracies in the developed world are almost all too focused on political parties and not focused enough on participation by the people. The Bush Presidency has sought to 'export' democracy but in so doing it is also exporting some of the evils of present democracies – the special pleading of interest groups such as big business or trades unions, which is secured by donations that should be called corruption, the over-reliance on a professional caste of politicians who skew power to serve them and their interests and the alienation of ordinary citizens from the task of decision making.

Democracy is not yet at its full flowering.

We believe that democracy is the best system of government, but democracy is not yet at its full flowering. Democracy that is exported needs to be participatory democracy, an engine for involvement and an enabler of positive individual and national growth. If Scotland could establish such a democracy here then – as with our anticipated Scottish investment in alternative energy – it could also seek to help others to take our experience on board and profit by it.

We have pointed out the ways in which our actions on the environment could have implications in the wider world, but we also think that seeking smaller and more efficient government and better defining the role of government are tasks which will inspire emulation, not least south of the border.

But there is also one final sense in which what we wish to bring into the public domain may have other implications and that is in the realm of the Scottish psyche, the Scottish character and Scottish behaviour.

Carol Craig's ground-breaking book *The Scots Crisis of Confidence* has spawned a virtual industry of Scottish confidence building and much of what she comments on, and makes suggestions about is helpful and productive. But it has been no secret that for generations Scots in Scotland have lacked confidence and have failed to assert themselves in the modern world. Many explanations have been put forward for that situation, including that of the 'Scottish cringe', a condition dunned into Scots by three centuries of being at a distance removed from the world, and always being reminded that their neighbours are of more consequence then they are themselves. Perhaps this also explains why Scots often perform better when living and working away from their country, and are sometimes a by-word for intelligence, creativity, hard work and positive foresight in those circumstances.

Whatever the reasons – and certainly the Union has been a substantial factor though not, we are sure, the only one – it has led to the absence of a 'can do' culture in Scotland, and one in which obstruction and excuse for inaction is more common than enablement and determination to act.

In the commercial sphere our low business birthrate is often attributed to this problem, and certainly our fear of failure, and the consequences of failure, are important in that regard. But not only low business birthrate is a problem. So is a determined hanging onto enterprises that fail to succeed (and sometimes their wasteful resuscitation with public money) and – the corollary in the public sector – the common refusal to accept that public sector bodies should not last for ever.

In the Scottish media our national lack of confidence is shown in an excessively critical stance toward new thinking and new ideas, a position exemplified by the media's incessant criticism of the new Parliament and its members which, whilst at times justified, has never been followed up by the promotion of positive ideas for improvement and change.

The Scottish media, Scottish academia, Scottish education, Scottish culture and the whole panoply of Scottish public life needs to be engaged in a process in which constructive criticism of our governance is accompanied by a willing acceptance of not only personal responsibility to bring about change, but also personal responsibility for a change in the Scottish mindset and the development of a 'can do' culture which then pervades every part of our national life. In fact there needs to be a new crusading zeal for such changes, disseminated by radio, television and the press, acted on by our schools, used by our artists to inspire the Scottish people and taken on board by individuals in every part of the country.

Scotland has much to be proud of but the question to be answered is not about who is the best, but about who is doing most to make this nation one worth living in. We should aspire not to be chauvinistically proud of our achievements, but instead to be content that we have established and are sustaining a place of intelligence, ambition, and ability. A place which, blessed as it is with a wealth of natural resources, is always enabling its citizens to make the most of themselves and to live in harmony with their neighbours and their planet. And a place, because we have plenty of space, to which we can welcome others from elsewhere.

At the start of this final chapter we quoted James Maxton. He was right to talk of the 'great age' in which he was living and the way in which politicians have a duty to devise forms of government suited to the intelligence and ethos of the people. We live in an even greater age, and because we know more as a result of mass communications, we have an even larger responsibility to ensure that the intelligence and ethos of all our fellow citizens is employed in the task of mutual support and improvement, at home and abroad.

We must however get rid of the chips on our shoulders that prevent us from seeing Scotland and the world as places for positive action. We must regain a productive, objective and, frankly, normal view of our nation and the world and our place in them both which is neither over- or under-confident. So whilst taking on board the need to change our democratic structures, our governance and the way we think about and treat our surroundings, we must also take on board the need to become more balanced in our view, more aspirational in our thinking and more secure in who we actually are.

Those are big tasks, but this book has been about big things – about the things which we urgently need to consider in order to, as we have put it in our very title, 'respond to the key challenges of the twenty first century'.

For no one owes Scotland a living. We will succeed or fail by our own efforts, and once we realise that fact then our dependency on others will wither and we will, mentally and physically, be better prepared for the future and better able to succeed in that future.

That has been our objective – to tell our fellow Scots that it is up to them, and to suggest what they may need to do in order to be free, in every sense. And whilst we are, by nature and by conviction, confident in the good sense of our fellow Scots and therefore confident that they will take those actions that must be taken, we can now only hope that our thoughts about how to secure a better future for everyone who lives here will be read, shared, discussed and – where deemed to be relevant – acted on. As soon as possible.

Appendix

Projected Scottish Government Total Income Budget (£ billion)

Revenue Source	2002-03 Year 0 Old [1] Union	New [2] Union	03/04 Year 1	04/05 Year 2	05/06 Year 3	06/07 Year 4
Income Tax [3]	7.88	7.88	7.54	7.23	6.97	6.75
Corp Tax [4]	2.14	2.14	1.66	1.18	0.69	–
VAT [5]	5.18	5.18	5.28	5.42	5.60	5.82
Soc Security [5]	5.24	5.24	5.34	5.48	5.66	5.89
Local Authority [6]	3.18	3.18	3.04	2.92	2.82	2.73
Other Revenue [7]	8.00	8.00	7.89	7.81	7.80	7.83
Oil/Gas Revenue [8]	–	4.55	3.87	4.68	8.64	12.20
Borrowings	9.30 [9]	4.75	4.00	2.50	-0.34	-2.16
Total Revenue	40.92	40.92	38.62	37.22	37.84	39.06
Expenditure [10]	40.92	40.92	38.62	37.22	37.84	39.06
GDP [11]	82.0 [12]	99.1	100.4	103.8	110.6	120.6
GS %	49.9 [12]	41.3	38.5	35.9	34.2	32.4

Notes to Appendix

(1) Actual Scottish Executive numbers for 2002-03 using Barnett and debt to finance the borrowings.

(2) As for (1) using 90% of UK 2002-03 oil and gas revenue plus debt to finance the borrowings.

(3) Reduced by £2.0 billion over 4 years and escalated by 2% in year 1, 2.6% in year 2, 3.3% in year 3 and 4.0% in year 4.

(4) Eliminated over 4 years and escalated as for (3).

(5) Escalated as for (3).

(6) Reduced by £0.8 billion (business taxes) over 4 years and escalated as for (3).

(7) Reduced by £1.1 billion – fuel duty by £0.6 billion and elimination of aggregate tax (£0.03 billion), capital gains tax (£0.13), inheritance tax (£0.14), air passenger duty (£0.07) and customs duties and agriculture levies (£0.15) – and escalated as for (3).

(8) 90% of UK oil and gas revenues. Revenue for 2006-07 estimated using an oil price of \$70 per barrel.

(9) A mysterious figure which must include Scotland's share of UK borrowings at about £2.6 billion with only £6.7 billion attributable to Barnett formula adjustments.

(10) All expenditures have been frozen for 4 years apart from the following cuts and increases (figures in £billion):

	YEAR1	YEAR2	YEAR 3	YEAR 4
Defence	−1.0	−0.5		
Enterprise	−0.2	−0.2		
Agriculture *et al*	−0.18	−0.18	−0.18	−0.18
Gov. Efficiency	−0.9	−0.5		
R&D			+0.30	+0.70
State Pensions			+0.30	+0.30
Education			+0.20	+0.40
	−2.3	−1.4	+0.62	+1.22

(11) 'Old Union' GDP for Scotland escalated as for (3) plus 71% of UK oil and gas income in year it occurs.

(12) Excluding oil and gas income.

Index